HT 384 L1

Understanding the Chinese City

Theory, Culture & Society

Theory, Culture & Society caters for the resurgence of interest in culture within contemporary social science and the humanities. Building on the heritage of classical social theory, the book series examines ways in which this tradition has been reshaped by a new generation of theorists. It also publishes theoretically informed analyses of everyday life, popular culture, and new social and intellectual movements.

EDITOR: Mike Featherstone, *Goldsmiths College, University of London*

SERIES EDITORIAL BOARD
Roy Boyne, *University of Durham*
Nicholas Gane, *University of Warwick*
Scott Lash, *Goldsmiths College, University of London*
Couze Venn, *Goldsmiths College, University of London*

The *Theory, Culture & Society* book series, the journals *Theory, Culture & Society* and *Body & Society*, and related conference, seminar and postgraduate programmes now operate from the Department of Sociology at Goldsmiths College, University of London. For further details of the TCS Centre's activities please contact:

Theory, Culture & Society
Department of Sociology
Goldsmiths, University of London
Floors 8–11 Warmington Tower
New Cross, London SE14 6NW, UK
e-mail: tcs@sagepub.co.uk
web: www.theoryculturesociety.org

Recent volumes include:

Cosmopolitanism
Zlatko Skrbis and Ian Woodward

The Body and Social Theory (3rd edn)
Chris Shilling

Immaterial Bodies
Lisa Blackman

French Post-War Social Theory
Derek Robbins

The Domestic Economy of The Soul
John O'Neill

Li Shiqiao

Understanding the Chinese City

$SAGE

Los Angeles | London | New Delhi
Singapore | Washington DC

SAGE

Los Angeles | London | New Delhi
Singapore | Washington DC

SAGE Publications Ltd
1 Oliver's Yard
55 City Road
London EC1Y 1SP

SAGE Publications Inc.
2455 Teller Road
Thousand Oaks, California 91320

SAGE Publications India Pvt Ltd
B 1/I 1 Mohan Cooperative Industrial Area
Mathura Road
New Delhi 110 044

SAGE Publications Asia-Pacific Pte Ltd
3 Church Street
#10-04 Samsung Hub
Singapore 049483

Editor: Mila Steele
Editorial assistant: James Piper
Production editor: Imogen Roome
Copyeditor: Elaine Leek
Proofreader: Leigh Timmins
Marketing manager: Michael Ainsley
Cover design: Wendy Scott
Cover image: *Urban Landscape* (2006) by Zhan Wang (courtesy of artist)
Typeset by: C&M Digitals (P) Ltd, Chennai, India
Printed in India at Replika Press Pvt Ltd

© Li Shiqiao, 2014

First published 2014

Apart from any fair dealing for the purposes of research or private study, or criticism or review, as permitted under the Copyright, Designs and Patents Act, 1988, this publication may be reproduced, stored or transmitted in any form, or by any means, only with the prior permission in writing of the publishers, or in the case of reprographic reproduction, in accordance with the terms of licences issued by the Copyright Licensing Agency. Enquiries concerning reproduction outside those terms should be sent to the publishers.

Library of Congress Control Number: 2013950177

British Library Cataloguing in Publication data

A catalogue record for this book is available from the British Library

ISBN 978-1-4462-0882-3
ISBN 978-1-4462-0883-0 (pbk)

Contents

List of Figures	vi
Acknowledgements	ix
Introduction	xiv
PART 1 Abundance	3
1 Quantity Control	5
2 The City of Maximum Quantities	28
3 The City of Labour	55
PART 2 Prudence	77
4 The Body in Safety and Danger	79
5 Degrees of Care	98
6 Antisepsis	117
PART 3 Figuration	137
7 The Empire of Figures	139
8 Memory without Location	162
9 Colonies of Beauty and Violence	180
Conclusion	207
Bibliography	213
Index	222

List of Figures

1.1	Terrace of Mental Distance, the Humble Administrator's Garden (Zhuozheng Yuan), by Wen Zhengming, 1531	10
1.2	Peasant painting from Yangliuqing, Tianjin	10
1.3	The Forbidden City, Beijing	13
1.4	Olympic Village, Beijing	15
1.5	Shenzhen city centre, Shenzhen	16
2.1	Kowloon Walled City before demolition (photo by Ian Lambot)	33
2.2	Tin Shui Wai, Hong Kong	34
2.3	The site plan of The Palazzo, Jubilee Gardens, and Royal Ascot, Shatin, Hong Kong	36
2.4	An advertised image of The Palazzo	37
2.5	Section of The Palazzo, Jubilee Gardens, and Royal Ascot	37
2.6	The view of The Palazzo, Jubilee Gardens, and Royal Ascot	38
2.7	Kowloon Station, Hong Kong	40
2.8	Sales graphics, Kowloon Station, Hong Kong (photo by Esther Lorenz)	40
2.9	Model of Songjiang, Shanghai	48
2.10	Full-size replica of the Qin dynasty capital, Hengdian, Zhejiang Province	51
2.11	Shops at Yiwu, Zhejiang Province	52
3.1	Cosplay at the Campus of the Chinese University of Hong Kong (photo by Esther Lorenz)	63
3.2	Thames Town, Songjiang, Shanghai	65
3.3	The Grand Lisboa, Macau	68
4.1	Leaning Jade Pavilion, the Humble Administrator's Garden (Zhuozheng Yuan), by Wen Zhengming, 1531	82
4.2	A page from *Manual of the Mustard Seed Garden* (1679)	84

List of Figures

5.1	Handrail, Hong Kong	102
5.2	The Lu House, Dongyang, Zhejiang Province	104
5.3	Balconies behind metal cages, Changsha, Hunan Province	106
6.1	Sai Yeung Choi Street, Mongkok, Hong Kong	120
6.2	Entrance door handle, foyer, Hong Kong Arts Centre (photo by Esther Lorenz)	120
6.3	New Town Plaza, Shatin, Hong Kong	125
6.4	Zhan Wang, *Urban Landscape*, 2006 (courtesy of the artist)	129
6.5	Self-help disinfection station at New Town Plaza, Shatin, Hong Kong	132
7.1	Hall of Supreme Harmony, The Forbidden City, Beijing, 1407–1421	147
7.2	Illustration 2, *Qingshi yingzao zeli* (The construction principles of the Qing dynasty)	147
7.3	Xu Bing, title block, *Book from the Sky*, 1987 (courtesy of Xu Bing Studio)	149
7.4	The Warrior's Leave-Taking, *c*.510–500 BCE	151
7.5	Robert Hooke, Scheme 1, in *Micrographia*, London, 1665	153
7.6	Qiu Anxiong, *New Book of Mountains and Seas*, 2004–2008: *maikenuo*, sketch detail (courtesy of the artist)	153
8.1	Yellow Crane Tower (Huanghe Lou), Wuhan, Hubei Province: after 1985 (photo by Zhang Tianjie) and before 1884	169
8.2	Central Pier, Hong Kong, after 2006	170
9.1	Qiu Zhijie, *A One-thousand-time Copy of Lantingxu*, 1990–1997 (courtesy of the artist)	181
9.2	The restricting metal wires on a *penzai* tree in Zhuozheng Yuan, Suzhou	184
9.3	Taihu stone in Wangshi Yuan, Suzhou	185
9.4	Tangerine Island, Changsha, Hunan Province	189
9.5	Text carved on rocks, Fuzhou, Fujian Province	191
9.6	Mao's poem 'Changsha' carved on stone, Tangerine Island, Changsha, Hunan Province	191
9.7	Xu Bing, *Landscript*, 2004 (courtesy of Xu Bing Studio)	192

9.8	Entrance to Yuelu College, Changsha, Hunan Province	193
9.9	A textual representation of the Humble Administrator's Garden (Zhuozheng Yuan), Suzhou	195
9.10	Entrance to Administrative Centre, Dongyang, Zhejiang Province	196
9.11	Nanmenkou shopping street, Changsha, Hunan Province	197
9.12	City centre of Dongyang, Zhejiang Province	203

Acknowledgements

If we must recast all inspiration, motivation, kindness, help, and love surrounding a book project as debt, my first debt is to places and people that grounded this book. To Singapore and Hong Kong, I am indebted to the fearless, resilient, and resourceful spirit of their inhabitants when all cultural traditions and ecological resources are placed under tremendous stress in their attempt to integrate with alien and dominating powers in the world. They first confused me, and then they showed me the way. To Esther, I am indebted to her love, aesthetic and intellectual companionship; many of the ideas in the book came up during our conversations, and many others emerged as we live through different conceptions of urban life together with endless fascination. To Esther's family, Anna, Peter, Florian, Martin, I am indebted to the mental and physical space they have given me so generously, sympathetically, and carefully, so that I have the privilege to be at home in dislocation. To Lauren, I am indebted to her love, joy, and optimism that give me the peace of mind to work that can never be attained in any other way. To my parents, sisters, and brother, I am indebted to their unconditional support, particularly when the experiences of life continue to drift us further apart following different courses; there is perhaps an important layer of materially embedded life that foregrounds all intellectualization. These make up a material and mental framework within which this book was conceived and written, and which, unlike debt, I will be unable to repay.

This book to describe the Chinese city prospered from friendship with two groups of inspiring people: first, in Singapore, Ryan Bishop and John Phillips, two fellow nomads, influenced the initial ambition of the book in a fundamental way. For us, life, design, and writing in Singapore, for many years, had been delightfully interlinked, and the extremities of our academic disciplines expanded the scope of the book from one of architectural design to one of city-making. With Ryan and John there is the larger framework of the Theory, Culture & Society Centre directed by Mike Featherstone and Couze Venn, who brought together – with great insight and energy – many stimulating and exciting ways of dealing with this complex topic of the city. The journals *Theory, Culture and Society* & *Cultural Politics* serve as headquarters of a global network of scholars; in many gatherings to discuss the city, I tested my first ideas of the book – in Singapore, Tokyo, Johannesburg, Hong Kong, and Beijing – benefiting enormously from these occasions. I have had the fortune to come to know scholars such as Chua Beng Huat, Andrew Benjamin, Eyal Weizman, AbdouMaliq Simone, and Wang Hui, whose works demonstrate courage and determination. For many years Michael Keith and Scott Lash shared with me, in various ways and in different places, their infectious enthusiasm for new ideas of urbanism, and their well-contextualized notion of a Chinese economic life; I value and treasure this privilege highly.

Second, in Melbourne, Leon van Schaik nurtured, for over thirty years, an extraordinary institution at the RMIT University; the School of Architecture and Design has been at the forefront of thinking and practice in architecture through a highly innovative formulation of higher degrees in design research. To research in the medium of design, and to evidence research through design, have been the foundations for this extraordinary endeavour; in the context of world circulation of generic design trends, the RMIT model has stood its ground in spatial intelligence. Through the experience of examining research degrees, I have come to know the inspiring people who made the RMIT model a reality: Richard Blythe, Peter Downton, Sand Helsel, Jon Tarry, Martyn Hook, Sue Anne Ware, Johan Verbeke, Nikos Papastergiadis, Jan van Schaik, Gretchen Wilkins, and many others. Associated with this institution in Melbourne there is a global network of outstanding people: the provocative Ranulph Glanville, the pensive Iain Low, and the fearless William Lim. Lim's intellectual rallies in Singapore calling for a theory of Asian architecture not only influenced generations of young Asian designers and theorists, but also offered several important opportunities for me to put some of the content of the book in front of critical juries.

Initially conceived in Singapore, this book was largely written in two places: Hong Kong and Charlottesville, perhaps two ends of what cities can be. I have relied on the generosity and kindness of many in these two places. At the Chinese University of Hong Kong, I am grateful to Director of the School of Architecture Puay-peng Ho, to Dean of Social Sciences Paul Lee, and to Head of Chung Chi College Leung Yuen-sang for their friendship and support. The endless wisdom of Nelson Chen and Christopher Law nurtured the

Acknowledgements

School and my teaching. Over countless lunches and teas, Andrew Li teased much content out of me through his interrogations; I owe deep gratitude and pleasure to his clarity of thought and quickness of wit. My other colleagues at the Chinese University of Hong Kong, Hendrik Tieben, Gu Daqing, Zhu Jingxiang, Bruce Lonnman, Bernard Lim, and many others, sustained an extraordinary level of productive energy and spirit of inquiry. In Hong Kong, I delighted in unforgettable friendship with many: Eymen Homsi and Sari Airola, Frank Vigneron and Chan Sin Man, Peter Gorer and Leng Woo, Saskia Witteborn and Tim Gruenewald, Joshua Bolchover and Jessica Pyman, Wang Weijen, Joseph Wong, Charlie Xue, Wong Suk-ying, Leo Ou-fan Lee, and Connie Kwong. By extraordinary coincidence, and in a most delightful and inspiring way, Jenny Lovell and Chris Fannin have become my links of friendship between Hong Kong and Charlottesville. At the School of Architecture, University of Virginia, I am deeply grateful for the generosity given to me by Dean Kim Tanzer, Chair of the Department of Architectural History Richard Wilson, and Chair of the Department of Architecture Iñaki Alday, allowing me to continue writing during a few demanding semesters. The energizing minds of Nana Last and Daniel Bluestone have given me great pleasure in responding to their comments on my writings; in an awe-inspiring intellectual environment anchored by great thinkers/doers such as Peter Waldman, Robin Dripps and Lucia Phinney, Edward Ford, and W. G. Clark, nourished by the extraordinary insights of Thomas Jefferson, animated by the productive minds at the School of Architecture, and challenged by the cross-cultural thinking at the East Asian Centre, I cannot ask for a larger mental space and a richer environment to work in. There are of course other cities: in Los Angeles, Dell Upton showed me the urban highlights in the midst of a continuing conversation on world history of architecture; in London, Iain Borden and Jonathan Hill at the Bartlett gave me an early chance to speak of figuration as a form of Chinese modernity; in Sheffield, Bryan Lawson, Kang Jian, and Peter Blundell Jones gave me great insights into the research and design of the architectural school; in Nanjing, I was thrilled to share a podium with Mark Cousins to speak on the figure as home; in Melbourne, Tom Kvan, Paul Walker, Zhu Jianfei, Anoma Pieris, and Lu Duanfang generously invited me to participate in their research events; in Brisbane, John Macarthur gave me a rewarding experience at Queensland University; in New Delhi, Anand Bhatt, seemingly nonchalantly, conceptualized cities of the world as well as New Delhi at the tea table; in Ahmedabad, Snehal Shah and K. B. Jain of the Centre for Environmental Planning and Technology (CEPT) indulged me, for a week and only delightfully interrupted by wedding banquets, to discuss with students on the fragile idea of Asian modernity.

I would like to thank the University Grants Committee of the Government of Hong Kong for a generous research fund to study the state-owned architectural design institutes in China; this research, and the larger research of the book, was conducted with the insights and generous help from many long-standing colleagues and friends in design institutes and universities in China. At the design institutes, Chen Yifeng, Huang Wei, Zhang Hua, and many others kindly responded to my interview requests and provided me with important research data; at universities in China and elsewhere, professors Liu Erming, Wu Jiang, Ding Wowo, Zhao Chen, Lu Yongyi, Chen Wei, Jeffrey Cody, Li Xiangning, Ge Ming, Li Hua, Lai Delin, Zhang Tianjie, Lu Andong, Liu Songfu, Xu Subin, Stanislaus Fung, and many others provided platforms of exchange and exploration that generated and substantiated many ideas. The Chinese city is both ancient and contemporary; in this sense, the pioneering works of contemporary Chinese architects outside the design institute system, such as Liu Xiaodu, Meng Yan, Wang Hui (Urbanus), Zhang Ke (Standardarchitecture), Eunice Seng, Koon Wee, Darren Zhou (Skew Collaborative), Doreen Lui Heng (NODE), Li Xiaodong, and Liu Yuyang, test the limits of Chinese architecture. I delighted, over many years and in a personal capacity, in the privilege to be at the scene of their explorations in research and design; their daily practice of architecture led me to many others who, like them, forge tirelessly a frontier of Chinese architecture that enlarges our understanding of an ancient tradition of city building.

Learning environment has been important to the book, from the germinating setting of Royston Landau and Micha Bandini at the AA School of Architecture, to the exploratory forums at various other universities. Jin Xiaomin at Nanjing University, Wang Ying, Mo Kar Him, and Jiang Boyuan at the Chinese University of Hong Kong have helped me obtain research data, prepare related classes, document interview recordings, photograph buildings and streets, and develop graphic illustrations; they have also assisted me, often beyond the call of duty, in solving perplexing problems in my life. At the University of Virginia, I am profoundly grateful to my first class, Bradley Allen, Kirstin Rouke, Justin Greving, Gu Lingyi, Jason Layel, and Zhan Haojun, who inspired me with their own delightful enquiries as we embarked on an unfamiliar journey in the Chinese city. I owe a deep gratitude to the students of my other classes – Architecture and Asia Trade, World Contemporary Architecture, and Summer in China Program – who have been endlessly resourceful and ingenuous as we find platforms for a redistributed understanding of world architecture. If the seasoned intellects of sinologists furnished the book its content, the vigorous minds of students gave the book its voice.

Introduction

The city as an object of knowledge not only stubbornly stakes its own category, but also cunningly undermines it through its sheer complexity. The physical and spatial city has a much slower metabolism compared with political and economic events taking place in it, appearing as layers of sedimentation – Freud used it as a metaphor to describe the unconscious – that often frustrate the attempts to understand it. Next to the enormously diligent and insightful accounts of cities, such as *The City in History* by Lewis Mumford and *Cities in Civilization* by Peter Hall, scholarship on the city builds up through dividing the city into a long list of smaller categories. There are cities of architects, politicians, planners, activists, historians, economists, philosophers, engineers, theorists, ecologists, biologists, feminists, geographers – the list is potentially without end. The notion of 'the Chinese city', even if it is sustained temporarily, gives us a chance to speculate on a distributed account of cities; this book seeks an equitable distribution of theory in the study of cities by tracing a set of key ideas – simultaneously ancient and contemporary – that appear to be deliberate choices made in relation to cities. The main contention here would be classificational: What if the Western categories of knowledge – well-rehearsed in the Greek thought and systematically practised in Western academia mapping the mental faculties constructed in a specific cultural context and language – were not primary in the formation of a large number of cities in the world?

This book outlines three imperatives in the formation of Chinese cities – there are doubtless more – that do not seem to have been derived from those in the West, although it is immensely illuminating when they are brought in relief against Western formulations, dislocated temporarily from the Chinese writing system in which they were first conceived. The first imperative concerns the ideal number of things and people in cities; in Chinese cities, there seems to be a moral and aesthetic demand for abundance and for it to be appropriately displayed. What determines the right number of things in cities? In *Timaeus*, Plato legislates a range of absolute quantities through the notion of proportion as the master key of all other quantities; the distributions of numbers, sizes, and distances are judged with strong connections to master keys like those found in mathematics, geometry, and music. While Plato regards some numbers to have higher intellectual status in the determination of quantities in cities, Shao Yong (1011–77), one of most accomplished scholars of the *Book of Changes*, allows each number to acquire significance in its own right. 'There is a thing of one thing. There is a thing of ten things. There is a thing of a hundred things. There is a thing of thousand things. There is a thing of ten-thousand things. There is a thing of a one hundred million things. There is a thing of a billion things.'[1] In his scheme of things, Shao Yong considers the human being as the 'thing of a billion things', an enormously complex amalgamation; if the Western ideal of an understanding of the human being lies in the genome map as the master key, then the Chinese ideal would be grounded in an acceptance of this immense entity of ever-changing flows of quantities. This part of the book characterizes Chinese cities as amalgamations of quantities that acquire their significance in their own rights; instead of being framed as having a corresponding relationship with a set of master quantities – a *utopia* that holds the key to all urban quantities, Chinese cities result from quantity control schemes that tend to accept the legitimacy of a wide range of quantities. More is more, and less is less; this foregrounds the moral and aesthetic foundations of the city of maximum quantities, and its accompanying city of labour.

The second imperative stems from the notion of prudence and its resultant corporeal and urban forms. The Chinese way of life, morally and aesthetically codified in the teachings of Confucius from the early stages of its formation, has often been described as 'sedentary'. Perhaps no one embodied this idea more deeply than the Ming emperor Hongwu (reigned 1368–98), whose vision of a contented peasant empire dedicated to the cultivation of land influenced all his imperial policies that relied heavily on strict hierarchical regulations. As a local official of the late Ming dynasty, Zhang Tao, described in detail, the ideal Ming life was one that 'every family was self-sufficient, with a house to live in, land to cultivate, hills from which to cut firewood, and gardens in which to grow vegetables'.[2] The prosperity, stability, and happiness of the Chinese empire would be ensured by this dedication to the cultivation of land. The persistent anxiety of the Chinese government is chaos (*luan*), and much of that anxiety came from the incessant assaults by the nomadic tribes on the steppe to the north and west of China, with the mounted archer as their most powerful weapon. This idealized Ming life can be seen as perhaps an epitome of Bertrand Russell's description of the prudent life rooted in the inherent demands of agriculture, complete with its emphasis on delayed gratification and endless endurance of toil.[3] Against this picture of safely guarded ideal life of prudence, the Greek conception of danger – as both an inevitability in life and a formative moral and aesthetic force – frames a dramatically different outlook: if the city can be seen to mediate between the body and danger, then the conception of danger gives rise to distinct mental and physical constructs in the city. This part of the book takes on the notion of the body in safety and danger by describing the resultant interior and exterior 'territories' constructed in response to real and imagined dangers. The body in safety in the Chinese cultural context can be seen to be actively engaged in pursuit of a large range of preservation regimens, demarcating boundaries around the conserved body, the protected home, and the walled village, defining spaces of intensive and regular care, and formulating dangerous and filthy spaces of non-recognition through the notion of *jianghu*. In the contemporary bacterially- and virally-challenged environment, this traditional scheme of spatial imagination is producing an intriguing layer of spaces that seem to have taken the hospital, and unwittingly the extraordinary achievements in hospital design and management as well as the corresponding writings of Florence Nightingale on hospitals, as its archetypal space analogous to the protected home and the walled village. As William McNeill shows in *Plagues and Peoples*, microparasites shape urban history powerfully;[4] in Chinese cities, they also shape it distinctively.

The third imperative concerns the way in which the Chinese writing system – through the strategy of mapping meaning with morphemic figures instead of phonetic alphabets – works as an archetype of human thought, both as a crystallization of the past and as a prophecy for the future. The alphabet-based Western languages function effectively as systems of representations rather than images of the 'external reality'; in its crucial formulations of syntax and semantics, the signifier and the signified, and the linguistic inside and the realistic outside in the defining works such as those of Ferdinand de Saussure, Ludwig Wittgenstein, and Claude Lévi-Strauss, the study of the alphabet-based language has served as an extraordinary model for immensely rich intellectual inquiries into meaning in the Western cultural context. It certainly gave rise to a 'linguistic imagination of the city' such as those of Kevin Lynch, Christopher Alexander, and Bill Hillier and Julienne Hanson; a city can be understood as having a set of parallel syntactic and semantic properties which can serve as the key to understanding. What would be the intellectual impact of the Chinese writing system – in which the signifier and the signified can be seen as one and the same, semantic content far outweighs syntactic rules, and the inside is far more important than the outside – on mental and physical constructs? If speech is sacrificed to writing – the aesthetic construction of the square words and the high incidents of homophones are certainly evidence for this sacrifice – then what does writing do to cities in this supremely dominant position? To think with Pablo Picasso and Xu Bing, do the Chinese write their cities? In three chapters, this part of the book first characterizes the world of writing in China – against that of speech – as a world of figuration, an endless procession of figures not only as representations but, more crucially, as themselves. The figure, like truth, says Philippe Lacoue-Labarthe, has 'an ontological status' of its own.[5] This ontologically constructed 'empire of figures' projects a tremendous plastic force to everything in the city; 'memory without location' is one of the most intriguing results of the nature of the figure, influencing in crucial ways the use and maintenance of the built heritage in Chinese cities. The protected home, private gardens, enclosed institutions, and encircled land all become colonies of this plastic power, appearing in their figurated forms to advance the interests of the empire of figures.

The nine chapters of the book depict indigenous intellectual frameworks in the Chinese city with regard to how to gather and keep things to sustain life, how to protect the body from danger, and how to articulate moral and aesthetic judgements on things in cities. All these, if we consider them carefully, possess their distinct features which are constructed differently from those of the Western city; they are the means through which we are granted access to an understanding of Chinese cities. However, the immensely complex city seems to haunt an enterprise like this; for more than 100 years, the Chinese city has been re-imagined and reconstructed to accommodate many features of the Western city resulting from a 'modernization' process. Across its vast territory and long history, the Chinese city responded to the rise and falls of intellectual trends, absorbed influences from the northern steppe and central and south Asia, and incorporated climatic conditions into the architectural and urban forms. It certainly cannot be taken for granted that there is formal and intellectual coherence in the notion of 'the Chinese city'. This vast body of seemingly loose amalgamations of Chinese cities is perhaps best held together by two important features: Confucianism and the Chinese writing system. For all the influences of Buddhism, Manichaeism, Nestorianism, Islam, Judaism, and Christianity in the history of China, Confucianism and the Chinese writing system transformed them into something closer to the intellectual conceptions of the Chinese culture. The Xianbeis, the Mongols, the Manchus, desiring as they were to sustain their non-Chinese steppe cultures, all to more or less extent accepted Confucianism and the Chinese writing system – and most of the resultant cultural and institutional structures primed for agriculture – as the most effective way to govern this vast empire. The Chinese city, in this sense, is not a racial, religious, and territorial definition, but one that can perhaps be understood as an intellectual construct. Confucianism and the Chinese writing system, despite the differences between the teachings of Confucius, the Han dynasty Confucian revival, the neo-Confucianism in the Song dynasty (960–1279), as well as complex semantic changes to the non-phonetic square words, can be seen as possessing a set of basic and distinctive features; they survived the great upheavals in the twentieth century, even though at moments – the iconoclasm of the May Fourth Movement, the delirious righteousness of the Cultural Revolution, and the proposal to abolish the Chinese writing system – the enthusiasm for change threatened their fundamental legitimacy. Like the English monarchy emerging much reformed from a crisis during the Civil War and the Commonwealth of Cromwell, Confucianism and the Chinese writing system came out of the radical changes during the May Fourth Movement and the Cultural Revolution with more accommodating features. They did not disappear under stress; they have been reconstituted for much changed political, social, and economic realities. Although the traditional rituals of Confucianism are much less important in today's China, the demand for hierarchical mental and physical constructs are highlighted by new functions and new rituals; the written Chinese today may have been changed extensively compared with that used in imperial China, but the square words survive despite modifications of form. It is questionable, as David Hall and Roger Ames remind us, to think that 'Karl Marx is more important than Confucius' in twentieth-century China;[6] it is important to regard twentieth-century China, despite all the dramatic changes that had taken place in the course of 100 years, as having maintained 'the order of the past' as Karl Jaspers observed. These chapters acknowledge a culture in rapid transformation as well as the endless ways in which the order of the past shapes the city.

The Western civilization seems to have considered the city as perhaps its single greatest achievement; this pride in the city, still quite visible in popular writings on cities by authors such as Joel Kotkin and Edward Glaeser, often moves authors to extoll the virtues of the Western city as universally desired.[7] Lewis Mumford speaks of the rise of the city above agriculture, the 'artificial creation of scarcity in the midst of increasing natural abundance' and 'an economy profoundly contrary to the mores of the village', as a historical certainty.[8] This does not seem to be the case with regard to Chinese cities. If the Western city is the triumph of its 'unnatural constructs' – public space, modernity, danger, and philosophy – with their artificiality vigorously defended, the Chinese city is necessary but subservient to the pursuit of the 'natural state of things' in family, abundance, safety, and figuration. Instead of the city, the Chinese civilization is more likely to point to its achievements in the Chinese writing system, calligraphy, painting, literature, and garden as having equal, if not greater, significance. This is perhaps why these areas are the traditional strengths of sinology, and why traditional representations of the city were difficult to find in China.[9] The imperial administrative structure indicated a broad conception: among the six ministries of the imperial administration – those of Personnel, Revenue, Rites, Works, Punishment, War – the Ministry of Works responsible for construction and cities ranked perhaps the lowest. From the founding era of the Chinese culture during the Han dynasty (206 BCE–220 CE), Confucian rites have been central to Chinese governance; this 'imperial Confuciansim'[10] monopolized the aesthetic realm in Chinese life, making it the physical manifestations of rites. It was the Ministry of Rites that masterminded the core moral and aesthetic values through its defining role in the formulation of Confucian rituals and the examination system. The Song dynasty (960–1279) brought an enormously important development to this imperial Confucianism through extensive re-establishment of ancient rites; the building document of the Ministry of Works of this era, the *Yingzao fashi* compiled by Li Jie in 1103, can be seen as a culmination of the materiality of rites; the eight ranks of structural timber usage determined material and spatial ritual orders in close parallel to the hierarchical ritual orders determined at the Ministry of Rites.[11] In the eighteenth-century imperial collection *Siku quanshu*, the *Yingzao fashi* as well as other building-related books were classified under the 'governance' (*zhengshulei*) section of the branch of 'histories' (*shibu*).[12] The Song dynasty assertion of Confucian rites through building was part of a much larger attempt to expel the mixing of Chinese culture with those of the steppe tribes; the love of riding-based games such as polo and hunting in the Tang era gave way to that of sedentary and contemplative learning.[13] It was perhaps an attempt to restore urban order when the traditional and strictly regulated 'ward and market' city was overwhelmed by the rapid growth of commerce that resulted in spontaneous construction of streets.[14] The knowledge of building construction never entered the curriculum of the highly developed education system of the Song era, with its specializations beyond Confucianism focusing on laws, medicine, the art of war, numerology, calligraphy, painting, and Daoist canons;[15] this absence of technical education remained a key feature in Chinese education until the fall of the Qing dynasty in the early twentieth century.[16] Song Yingxing, author of *The Exploitation of the Works of Nature* (*Tiangong kaiwu*, 1637), an amazing compendium of Ming technical achievements, began with an apology for elaborating on an 'insignificant' topic rather than one that is based on literary canons.[17] Liang Qichao (1873–1929), one of the liveliest intellects who wished to reform Chinese culture, was intrigued by the Western idea of the city and attempted to write a history of Chinese cities in 1927; in researching on this history, he was struck by the lack of verifiable facts and sites of Chinese cities, while the traditional attention seemed to him to have been paid largely to literary descriptions.[18] Although our knowledge of Chinese cities is much more advanced today, the study of the Chinese city has always been unsettled by this cultural conception. Connected with the condition of buildings as material rites is the equally perplexing problem of documenting the designers and builders; although biographies of architects working in early twentieth-century China have become more detailed, those working in the previous two millennia remain either mythical, such as that of Lu Ban, or sketchy, such as that of Li Jie. This cultural condition was at the start of twentieth-century research on Chinese buildings and cities at the research institute founded by Zhu Qiqian (1872–1964), as he embarked on an ambitious project of compiling biographies of 'philosophical craftsmen' (*zhejiang*) in China's past.[19] The exquisite building templates of the Lei family (Yangshi Lei) created in the late nineteenth century are a treasure trove of nineteenth-century designs of Chinese imperial palaces, but they speak dimly about the Leis as creators of personalized and creative knowledge of architecture.

The endeavours of the pioneering scholars of Chinese architecture in the twentieth century, to a large extent, were focused on retrofitting a realm of 'architecture' in this rites-based Chinese building tradition to match that of the Western conception of architecture. This seems to be the primary goal of the works of Osvald Sirén (1879–1966), Ito Chuta (1867–1954), Ernst Boerschmann (1873–1949), as well as those of the first generation of Chinese architects and scholars trained in the Western architectural tradition such as Liang Sicheng (1901–72), Lin Huiyin (1904–55), and Liu Dunzhen (1897–1968). As a result, social and political histories of Chinese architecture tend to concentrate on the twentieth century. One may argue that this 'history of architecture' gained tremendous momentum as a project of intellectual reform in twentieth-century China;[20] its accomplishment is remarkable. China's Building Industry Press, between 1999 and 2003, brought the achievement in the history of Chinese architecture to a great height by publishing a five-volume history of ancient Chinese architecture, all edited by eminent architectural historians in China, that gathered the research achievements of the twentieth century in China.[21] In parallel, Yale University Press brought out a volume written by the same set of Chinese scholars in 2002; in her introduction, Nancy Steinhardt calls for an 'expansive definition of architecture' – a possible revision of the Western notion of architecture – to guide the study of Chinese buildings and cities.[22] Steinhardt's call for rethinking, at the end of a century's effort to research in Chinese architecture, perhaps indicated that it is propitious to reposition the scholarship of Chinese buildings and cities. In reclassifying the Chinese material rites under the Western notion of architecture, a significant part of the scholarship in Chinese architecture in the twentieth century placed the Chinese building tradition in the context of the project of modern history inextricably linked to the rise of nation-states in Europe. This framework dislocates Chinese buildings from their own immanent political, social, and intellectual concerns that gave rise to their physical appearances. As Chinese buildings seem to misfit the framework of architecture, literati gardens appear to escape the notion of landscape; a blend of Marxist historical framework and a classification system inspired by typology in Western architecture dominated the writing of architectural history in twentieth-century China, and influenced crucially Chinese garden histories such as *History of Classical Chinese Gardens* written by Zhou Weiquan in 1990.[23] As if to anticipate this fate, Tong Jun's *Record of Gardens in Jiangnan*, written in 1937 and first published in 1963, passionately defended the literati garden from its fate of annexation into standard histories of linear progress and typological classifications. Tong Jun's work has now rightfully become a rallying point for young scholars to seek more illuminating ways to theorize the Chinese literati garden, although Tong Jun's retreat to traditional literary terms without a universal framework reduced the impact of his work significantly, and through his influence, those who rally around him. Neither the state function of Chinese buildings as material rites, nor the cultural function of Chinese gardens as an intellectual enterprise grounded in the Chinese writing system, could find their legitimate place in twentieth-century histories of Chinese architecture.

It is the overwhelming expansion of Chinese cities today and the viable economic life they accommodate that brought a pressing need for theory. The unexpected but compelling development of Chinese cities since the 1980s have aroused tremendous attention from the West outside the relative confines of sinology; there is a genuine sense that what is taking place in China could indeed become a common but unfamiliar future.[24] Rem Koolhaas and his colleagues presented selective features of the Chinese city as irreverent dismissals of long-cherished moral and aesthetical conventions in the West, sparking a long string of publications in similar veins.[25] Next to sinology, this new type of interest in Chinese cities seems to have a sustained critical potency in contemporary architectural thinking worldwide. Beyond the initial wonderment, groundbreaking contributions to the understanding of Chinese cities come from two unexpected, but logical, directions. The first is the government funded 'new urbanization' strategies contained in *China's New Urbanization Reports* of the Chinese Academy of Sciences since 2009,[26] and the *Annual Report on Urban Competitiveness* of the Chinese Academy of Social Sciences.[27] This economic policy research integrated countryside, cities, and economies in a single framework, and provided an economy of cities which grounds the Chinese city in one of its most solid foundations, linking the Chinese city to much wider urban and economic developments worldwide. The Chinese city seems to take shape in 'geography of money' – and the politics that both resulted from and shaped the geography – as we examine the economy of the Chinese city.[28] This line of investigation connected to a vast field of research on cities and economies; the far-reaching research enterprises of the London School of Economics on cities and the world economy bring us to enormously large scales of examinations.[29] However, in this larger field of research on cities and economies, there seems to be an abstraction of money and information in the works of such as Saskia Sassen and Manuel Castells – like the abstraction of labour in the works of Karl Marx – that illuminates and obscures in equal measures. The key issues here are not so much those of labour, money, and information, but their use. If Hannah Arendt staked a claim on the differences between different kinds of use of labour,[30] this book is framed within a set of distinctions in the use of labour, money, and information in the Chinese city. One of these distinctions is explained by Giovanni Arrighi in his argument that the use of money in China – a Chinese market economy rather than a capitalist one – has been conceived very differently from that of the West, resulting in a series of defining structural features in the Chinese economy which manifest in today's world.[31] The second contribution arises from a school of thought perhaps best captured by the works of Marcel Granet, David Hall and Roger Ames, François Jullien, and Wang Hui. Granet, Hall and Ames, and Jullien insist on seeing China on its own terms in order to understand it at all; too often the interpretive schemes of Western scholars reconstituted Chinese thoughts away from their situations and intentions.[32] Wang Hui took on the enormously demanding task of rethinking China's revolutions in the twentieth century by recontextualizing them in much longer stretches of intellectual, social, and political developments in China that fundamentally shared very little with those in the West.[33] Here, the China specialist converged with the Chinese public intellectual; both rejected simplistic accounts of Chinese thought as derived from a modernity rooted in the formation of nation-state in nineteenth-century Europe. In this sense, the student protests in Tiananmen Square in 1989 perhaps had a similar and profound impact on Chinese intellectuals as that on the French intellectuals following the 1968 student protests. Michael Keith, Scott Lash, Jakob Arnoldi, and Tyler Rooker return to the indigenous Chinese cultural framework – the Confucian rites (and rights) of economic life – in order to articulate the Chinese use of money and its impact on Chinese cities.[34] These insights into Chinese cities and economies bring contemporary Chinese cities to an illuminating context within which historians such as Timothy Brook and Craig Clunas have been tracing the links between Chinese cultural life and the structure of its economy in the Ming dynasty, a time when the size of China's economy was the largest in the world.[35]

The Chinese city appears to be a paradox; it seems to be simultaneously urban and anti-urban. In creating some of the largest amalgamations of buildings and people – in ancient capitals of Chang'an (Xi'an), Bianliang (Kaifeng), Lin'an (Hangzhou), Nanjing, Beijing – the Chinese city necessitated exchange; in walling all important social, cultural, and political institutions away from the scenes of exchange, the Chinese city turned its back on the scenes of exchange as the most profound sites for culture. In the thirty years between 1978 and 2008, the urbanization rate in China rose from 18 per cent to 45 per cent; this meant that 357 million farmers either moved to cities or transformed their villages into towns. The number of cities in China, over these thirty years, increased from 193 to 655.[36] The strategic future plan prepared by the Chinese Academy of Sciences suggests an urbanization rate of 70 per cent in the next forty years (2050), slightly lower than the current urbanization rate of developed countries, but a figure that is better calibrated for the cultural, geographical and economic conditions of China.[37] This would mean another 330 million farmers migrating from rural areas to emerging new cities and expanding existing cities. By any measure, these numbers are unprecedented in the history of human settlement; they underscore the importance of an understanding of the Chinese city. Like in the Song and Ming dynasties, the rise of Chinese cities today – resulting from the necessity of production and commerce – did not seem to have resulted in fundamental changes to deeply-rooted conceptions of the city; in today's Chinese cities, important political and economic decisions are made in hierarchical spaces – those of degrees of care – that are isolated and protected in the city. The Citizens' Centre in Shenzhen and Tiananmen Square in Beijing, as centrally important city spaces, seem to be contemporary reconstitutions of spaces of rites; their super-human scale and their deliberate avoidance of everyday use set them apart from the much smaller public squares in Western cities populated by cafes and restaurants, but they are in line with the enormous and ordered imperial spaces seen in the palatial and tomb projects. Everyday spaces in Chinese cities are much more of a consequence of functions even in those with strong Western influences, in the forms of shop-lined avenues and quick and easy street food. In Chinese cities today, drinking and eating alfresco may be seen to be fashionable, but they have never acquired a high social status; similarly, open spaces in Chinese cities may be interesting and useful, but they have not been conferred with features of empowerment rooted in everyday life.

The Chinese city imposes different orders of things from those in the West; this book outlines a set of important Chinese orders. Cities like Venice, Amsterdam, London, and New York serve as dominant centres both for money and politics, while cities like Beijing, Shanghai, Chongqing, and Guangzhou tend to fabricate enormous city-regions around them, as if to highlight their much more distributed importance. Like the Hongwu Emperor, Mao

Zedong regarded the countryside rather than the city as a more sustainable base for economic life; the city, left to its own devices, is perverse to the goals of life promotion: its wish for fertility slipped into pornography, its need for surplus food ballooned into gratuitous consumption, its pursuit of intelligence is accompanied by a culture of neurosis and suicide, and its instinct for security amplified into excessive machines of warfare. The city Mumford speaks of is a deliberate cultural construct; in the Western tradition, it has been constructed as the battleground of life with irresistible pleasures and excruciating pains. Chinese cities are prudent in their ideals; large and vibrant though they are, they are deeply committed to spinning safety zones which double up as social structures. The Chinese city is in some important measures the creation of what may be described as the agro-intellectual tradition which embraced a form of literacy focused on private writing and calligraphy instead of public speech, within the safety zone of the protected home instead of dangerous public spaces, weaving a spatial-social web of relational circles of immense complexity. Perhaps China's urbanization never contained Mumford's intellectual change; the Chinese city, instead of turning the world of the peasant upside down with syntactical ideals and capitalistic abstractions, perhaps always embraced the primary mode of production in agriculture and its inherent moral and aesthetic demands. Instead of seeing the Song dynasty as 'proto-capitalist' and the late Ming dynasty China as having narrowly missed a 'capitalist revolution' regularly recounted by economic historians, we should probably understand the Song and the late Ming as having resisted the alienation of the capital in its pursuit of what Adam Smith called a 'natural economy'. The Chinese city can certainly adapt to the necessities of international commerce and urban culture for its own continuous existence, but in each successive wave of adaptations with ever-expanding scopes – the Song with the steppe tribes, the Ming and Qing with European trade demands, the twentieth century with America-centred geopolitical strategies – the Chinese city seems to have always come back insisting on its indigenous intellectual and spatial conceptions. As Wang Hui observed, the Chinese order of things as formulated in the Song Confucianism (*tianli*, 'the heavenly principle') and the Western order of things (*gongli*, 'common reason'), instead of replacing each other in the long and complex Chinese twentieth century, have existed side by side with legitimate specific moral and political projects, both conservative and revolutionary.[38] The following chapters are interested in describing these aspects of the Chinese city as they appear both in the past and today, while being fully cognizant of new transformations appearing continuously as a result of unavoidable changes through time.

Notes

1. Shao Yong, *Huangji Jingshi Shu* (Book of Supreme Ordering Principles), annotated by Wei Shaosheng (Zhengzhou: Zhongzhou guji chubanshe, 2007), p.489.
2. Timothy Brook, *The Confusions of Pleasure: Commerce and Culture in Ming China* (Berkeley and London: University of California Press, 1998), p.17.
3. Bertrand Russell, *History of Western Philosophy* (London: Routledge, 1946/2000), pp.36–37.
4. William McNeill, *Plagues and Peoples* (New York: Anchor Press, 1976).
5. Philippe Lacoue-Labarthe, 'Oedipus as Figure', *Radical Philosophy* 118 (March/April 2003), pp.7–17.
6. David L. Hall and Roger T. Ames, *Anticipating China: Thinking Through the Narratives of Chinese and Western Culture* (New York: State University of New York Press, 1995), p.xv.
7. Joel Kotkin, *The City: A Global History* (New York: The Modern Library, 2005); Edward Glaeser, *Triumph of the City: How Our Greatest Invention Makes Us Richer, Smarter, Greener, Healthier, and Happier* (Harmondsworth: Penguin Books, 2012).
8. Lewis Mumford, *The City in History: Its Origins, Its Transformations, and Its Prospects* (New York and London: Harcourt Inc., 1961), p.36.
9. Susan Naquin, *Peking: Temples and City Life, 1400–1900* (Berkeley, Los Angeles, London: University of California Press, 2000), p.xxiii.
10. John King Fairbank and Merle Goldman, *China: A New History* (Cambridge MA: Harvard University Press, 1998), p.62.
11. Li Shiqiao, 'Reconstituting Chinese Building Tradition: The *Yingzao fashi* in the Early Twentieth Century', *Journal of the Society of Architectural Historians* 62:4 (2003), pp.470–89; earlier Song dynasty documents, such as *Sanlitu* by Nie Chongyi in 962 and the chapters in the Song encyclopedia *Taiping yulan* compiled in 983, convey an overarching concern for the restoration of rites – see Jiren Feng, *Chinese Architecture and Metaphor: Song Culture in the Yingzao Fashi Building Manual* (Honolulu and Hong Kong: University of Hawai'i Press, 2012).
12. Xu Subin, *Jindai Zhongguo jinazhuxue de dansheng* (The Beginning of Chinese Modern Architecture) (Tianjin: Tianjin daxue chubanshe, 2010), p.15.
13. Jacque Gernet, *A History of Chinese Civilization*, trans. J. R. Foster (Cambridge: Cambridge University Press, 1982), p.331.
14. Guo Daiheng, ed., *Zhongguo gudai jianzhu shi* (History of Ancient Chinese Architecture), volume 3 (Beijing: Zhongguo jianzhu gongye chubanshe, 2003), pp.16–59.

15 Yang Weisheng, *Liang Song wenhua shi* (History of Northern and Southern Song Dynasties) (Hangzhou: Zhejiang daxue chubanshe, 2008), p.387.
16 Xu Shubin, *Jindai Zhongguo jinazhuxue de dansheng* (The Beginning of Chinese Modern Architecture) (Tianjin: Tianjin daxue chubanshe, 2010).
17 Song Yingxing, *Tiangong kaiwu* (The Exploitation of the Works of Nature, 1637). Brook, *The Confusions of Pleasure*, p.168.
18 Liang Qichao, *Liang Qichao guanji* (The Complete Works of Liang Qichao) (Beijing: Beijing chubanshe, 1999), *Zhongguo wenhua shi* (History of Chinese Culture) Vol. 9, chapter on history of Chinese cities, p.5109.
19 The compilations of Zhu Qiqian and his colleagues were recently published, with additions added by Liu Dunzhen and Yang Yongsheng, as: Yang Yongsheng, ed., *Zhejiang Lu* (Record of Philosophical Craftsmen) (Beijing: Zhongguo jianzhu gongye chubanshe, 2004). For a general background of Zhu Qiqian, see Li Shiqiao, 'Reconstituting Chinese Building Tradition'.
20 Li Shiqiao, 'Writing a Modern Chinese Architectural History: Liang Sicheng and Liang Qichao', *Journal of Architectural Education* 56 (2002), pp.35–45.
21 *Zhongguo gudai jianzhu shi* (History of Ancient Chinese Architecture), in 5 volumes, eds Liu Xujie (v.1), Fu Xinian (v.2), Guo Daiheng (v.3), Pan Guxi (v.4), Sun Dazhang (v.5) (Zhongguo jiangong chubanshe, 1999–2003).
22 Fu Xinian, Guo Daiheng, Liu Xujie, Pan Guxi and Sun Dazhang, *Chinese Architecture* (Beijing, New Haven and London: Yale University Press, 2002), English text edited and expanded by Nancy Steinhardt.
23 Zhou Weiquan, *Zhongguo gudian yuanli shi* (History of Classical Chinese Gardens) (Beijing: Qinghua daxue chubanshe, 1990).
24 Thomas J. Campanella, *The Concrete Dragon: China's Urban Revolution and What It Means for the World* (New York: Princeton Architectural Press, 2008); John Friedmann, *China's Urban Transition* (Minneapolis: University of Minnesota Press, 2005).
25 Rem Koolhaas et al., *Mutations* (Barcelona: Actar, 2001) and Rem Koolhaas et al., *The Great Leap Forward* (Cologne: Taschen, 2002).
26 Niu Wenyuan, ed., *China's New Urbanization Report 2009, 2010, 2011* (Beijing: Science Press, 2009, 2010, 2011).
27 Ni Pengfei, ed., *Annual Report of Urban Competitiveness* (Beijing: Social Sciences Academic Press, since 2003).
28 You-tien Hsing, *The Great Urban Transformation: Politics of Land & Property in China* (New York: Oxford University Press, 2010).
29 Ricky Burdett and Deyan Sudjic, eds, *The Endless City* (London: Phaidon, 2007); Ilka and Andreas Ruby, eds, *Urban Transformation* (Berlin: Ruby Press, 2008).
30 Hannah Arendt, *The Human Condition* (Chicago and London: University of Chicago Press, 1958)
31 Giovanni Arrighi, *Adam Smith in Beijing: Lineages of the Twenty-first Century* (London and New York: Verso, 2007).

32 Marcel Granet, *Chinese Civilization* (New York: Alfred A. Knopf, 1930), *La Pensée chinoise* (Paris: La Renasissance du livre, 1934); David L. Hall and Roger Ames, *Thinking Through Confucius* (Albany, NY: State University of New York Press, 1987), *Anticipating China* (New York: State University of New York Press, 1995); François Jullien, *Detour and Access: Strategies of Meaning in China and Greece* (New York: Zone Books, 2004), *The Propensity of Things: Towards a History of Efficacy in China* (New York: Zone Books, 1999).

33 Wang Hui, *Xiandai Zhongguo sixiang de xingqi* (The Rise of Modern Chinese Thought), second edition (Beijing: SDX Joint Publishing Company, 2008).

34 Michael Keith, Scott Lash, Jakob Arnoldi and Tyler Rooker, *China Constructing Capitalism: Economic Life and Urban Change* (London and New York: Routledge, 2013).

35 Timothy Brook, *The Confusions of Pleasure*; Craig Clunas, *Empire of Great Brightness: Visual and Material Cultures of Ming China, 1368–1644* (Honolulu: University of Hawai'i Press, 2007).

36 Niu Wenyuan (ed.) *China's New Urbanization Report 2009*, pp.6–7.

37 Ibid., p.10.

38 Wang Hui, *Xiandai Zhongguo sixiang de xingqi*, pp.40–50.

豐盛

PART 1
Abundance

1
Quantity Control

Quantity regulation is spacing regulation; quantity control has a defining role to play in the forms of cities. Characters of cities are, in one important way, quantitative; the densely packed buildings of the urban centres in Hong Kong contrast strongly with the expansive orders of Tiananmen Square in Beijing. The ways of life in cities can be deeply influenced by the distributions of quantities. But the distributions of quantities in cities are not easily accounted for, as they seem to result from complex forces compounded together in response to diverse circumstances. Wealth and prosperity determine quantity distributions, as do famine, pestilence, plague, and war; power and privilege formulate their own ranked and hierarchical quantitative scales. The Chinese tendency to control quantities through systems of resident registration (*hukou*) orders quantities of people in cities in one way, the Western tendency to legislate quantities such as building regulations organizes quantities in cities in another way. Quantities are often 'out of control' in cities: migrants, slums, favelas, sprawls, as they trace the demand of the capital which tends to concentrate in cities. However, despite the complexity of quantity distributions, there seem to be consistent strategies that can be articulated; there are quantitative features that are 'in control'. In this sense, quantity regulation is intellectual; the number of things in cities results from deep philosophical contemplations. Chinese cities, as they respond to various external influences throughout their long history, seem to have maintained a series of numerical schemes that are grounded in intellectual understanding of the natural and human worlds. In conception and substance, these numerical schemes differ from those found in the Western city fundamentally; the Chinese numerical schemes – *yin* and *yang*, five elements, twelve temporal markers, sixty-four hexagrams – are often used in combination, which is very different from the notion of a singular numerical order – the One, duality, trinity, dialectics, harmonic proportions – espoused in Western thinking. The material consequences of this difference in cities as buildings take shape in response to these numerical schemes. It is clear that Chinese cities today are heavily influenced by rule-based planning and building regulations, but it is also worth emphasizing that the Chinese numerical schemes have not been displaced; they contribute to the character of Chinese cities as they appear and as they are experienced. Perhaps the most important feature of the Chinese city in relation to quantities is that more is more, and less is less; the moral and aesthetic legitimacy of quantities seems to be distributed across a wide spectrum of numbers, attributing a unique significance to quantities of each order of magnitude. If normative urbanism is managerial in relation to classification, possession, distribution, and movement of quantities, and to mediations between different stakeholders in the city, then this part of the book is about the agreement on quantity regulation before management. It is about the numerical footprints of cultures, and the way in which the city becomes one of the most important material measures of these footprints. Few quantities and their locations are innocent of ideas; they form structured surfaces that impose orders of things onto human and non-human centred entities. To unfold this complex condition under the term of density – still perhaps the most widely used description of quantities in cities – seems to be inadequate, as the notion of density hovers above the orders of things in abstraction.

From Two to Abundance

There seem to be two instincts about quantity. The first is the idea of possessing and displaying more than necessary: abundance. Abundance is important to life promotion and preservation; human communities have always valued the ability to gather resources many times more than is necessary for subsistence. The magnificent displays of resources – contrived through fashions – have been a consistent key to the construction of power and prestige; they have certainly been central to the formulation of social classes. It is clear that the desire for abundance is common to all cultures, and that power and resource distribution in the geopolitical context have always been inextricably linked together to produce a string of empires in history, from the Roman and the Han to the British and the American. These empires may indeed be seen as forced and unequal systems of distribution of resources, brought to reality through geopolitics and war. It should also be clear that cultures impose structured surfaces on the condition of abundance to form different orders of things, through quantity regulation. The same desire for abundance can be subject to different quantity regulation – different orders of things – which will have a decisive influence on how abundance is manifested in cultures, resulting in distinctive urban features.

In the Chinese order of things, abundance seems to be grounded in what may be described as the fertility principle: fertility is the ultimate source of unlimited additional quantities. Perhaps the most stable form of the fertility principle in the Chinese order of things is expressed as a productive binary: the *yin* and the *yang*; it is understood as the source for all possible things. This productive binary contains endless variety: the sun and the moon, the male and the female, the hot and the cold, the strong and the delicate, the dense and the sparse, and so on, are all derivatives of the first productive binary. This may appear to be similar to the formulations of duality in Western philosophy, but it differs in two important ways. First, this productive binary in the Chinese cultural context is expressed as a thing-based feature rather than a logic-based definition. Thing-based features cut through many categories that may seem to be illegitimate for Western philosophy to conceive. Second, while duality tends to define an antithetical relationship, pitching one against the other until one is eventually overcome by the other, productive binary assumes a legitimate and mutually dependent existence. The Chinese square word for abundance, *feng*, is made from symbols of cereal crops and beans; it suggests a strong bond between the meaning of abundance and agriculture. This single Chinese character symbolically unites abundance with agriculture through the fertility principle; the central tenets of Chinese governance never seem to have deviated from the substance of this symbolic union, even when narratives have shifted with time. This, subtly and decisively, formulated many moral and aesthetic frameworks in relation to the quantities of people and things in cities.

Spatial orders, and by implication chance narratives of the future, were established in early Chinese culture in a set of numbers derived from the *yin* and *yang* binary: four primary and four secondary directions, with each direction represented by a combination of three lines, or a trigram. A solid line represents the *yang* and a broken line represents the *yin*; with two layers of trigrams forming hexagrams, they come to sixty-four different combinations. The use of these sixty-four conditions is not limited to spatial characters; the hexagrams are used to explain almost all events in nature. This is the order outlined in the classic text *Book of Changes* (*Yi Jing*). These sixty-four hexagrams are annotated with descriptions that attempt to capture chance meanings in the sequences of *yin* and *yang* lines; Carl Jung described these hexagrams and the accompanying notes as ways of thinking through synchronicity (Chinese) rather than through causality (Western), indicating a possible 'method of exploring the unconscious'.[1] Temporal orders are in one way grounded in the four seasons,[2] and in another way grounded in five sets of numbers of twelve, popularly marked by twelve animals, representing twelve earthly branches (*zhi*), totalling sixty in number. The latter scheme has the virtue of marking generational divides, as sets of twelve years. These are used in combination with ten celestial stems (*gan*) to name each of the sixty temporal markers with two characters. But by far the most extensively referenced numerical scheme has been that of five. The productive binary of *yin* and *yang* is overlaid with five elements: metal, wood, water, fire, earth. They form the basis for an understanding of the human body as being made of five vital organs and senses, heaven as consisting of five planets, music as being constructed through a pentatonic scale, food as having five basic flavours, and colour as being made of five essential colours. Each element possesses a double role, simultaneously stronger and weaker than other elements, thus being productive and destructive at the same time: for instance, wood is stronger than earth but weaker than metal; wood is produced by water but produces fire, etc. In various combinations, these numbers influenced almost all material productions in China; from the orientation of buildings on sites to the distribution of wood and earth in buildings, these numerical schemes played decisive roles in traditional constructions.[3]

John King Fairbank and Merle Goldman thought that, compared with many other societies, the numerical schemes gained 'unusual currency in China and dominated thinking for an unusually long time'.[4] The persistence of these numerical schemes seems to be indicative of a framework of quantity control with deep intellectual roots.[5] It is perhaps the underlying fertility principle behind the numerical schemes that gave rise to their lasting and pervasive legitimacy in China. The eleventh-century scholar of the *Book of Changes*, Shao Yong (1011–77), mused that 'There is a thing of one thing. There is a thing of ten things. There is a thing of a hundred things. There is a thing of thousand things. There is a thing of ten-thousand things. There is a thing of a million things. There is a thing of a billion things.'[6] Each quantity, in this formulation, achieves a unique importance that is commensurate with that quantity; one might be tempted to describe this as numerical empiricism, but it is perhaps more fitting to describe it as a thing-based thought. Taken as such, the traditional Chinese numerical schemes may be seen as ways of understanding the world as being made of things: things can be events and moral principles, objects and subjects, natural processes and human practices.[7] 'Neither God nor Law' – Marcel Granet admired this Chinese unwillingness to build a transcendental world as 'resolutely humanist' in his masterful and sympathetic *La Pensée chinoise*.[8] In this cultural framework, ethics, aesthetics, and governance are not grounded in transcendental worlds, but in the number, nature, and propensity of things.[9]

The Chinese quantity regulation has a full spectrum; it ranges from two to abundance. It begins with two as the smallest number (*yin* and *yang*), but it has no limit to the largest number, except for the idea of abundance (*fengsheng, fanrong*) or completeness (*quan*), which is often judged to be sufficient in relation to specific conditions. Daoists work with small numbers; the Chinese literati tend to be influenced by this tendency to think through the fertility principle with fewer quantities. The paintings of the Ming scholar Wen Zhengming are compelling examples of this end of the spectrum of quantities. In his depictions of the literati garden Zhuozheng Yuan (1531), he used very few things and features to represent the garden as he saw it in the Ming dynasty, as well as the ideal nature as he imagined it. Each of his thirty-one painted scenes reiterates the productive binary in its many aspects: word and image, soft and hard, solid and void, close and far, human and nature (Figure 1.1). These were achieved through an exemplary economy of means in the distribution of things on paper; they are highly valued as literati art. Under the influence of Western art, we tend to discuss Wen Zhengming's art in terms of abstraction and minimalism, but this is misleading. The carefully controlled display of elements in literati paintings is neither abstract nor minimal; it is figural and sufficient. At the other end of the spectrum of quantity regulation, we can probably use *nianhua*, or Chinese New Year peasant paintings, as examples of abundance in larger quantities.[10] These paintings visualize greater ranges of colours, forms, symbols, and square words (Figure 1.2). Instead of focusing on essential elements, as in the paintings of the literati, *nianhua* presents a saturated collection of all: abundance in abundant display. The fertility principle is manifested more explicitly through fertility symbols (usually baby boys); their connections with the notion of abundance are immediate and accessible.

Understanding the Chinese City

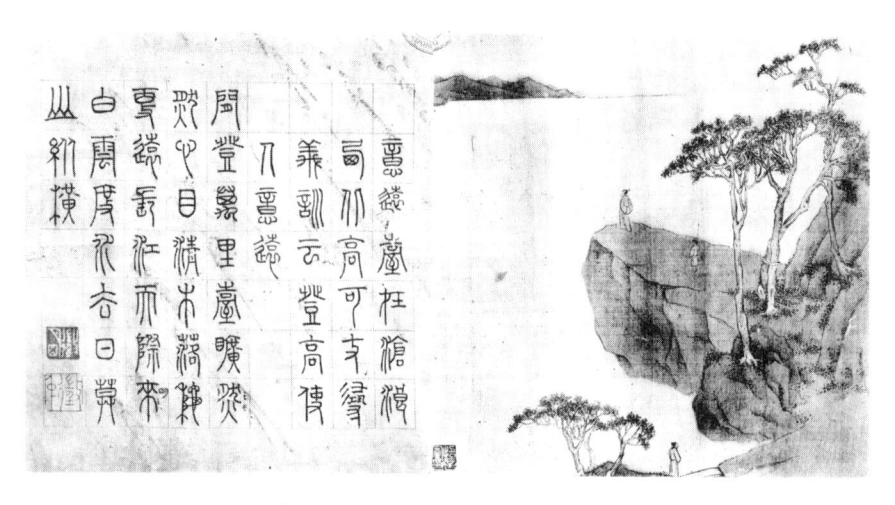

Figure 1.1 Terrace of Mental Distance, the Humble Administrator's Garden (Zhuozheng Yuan), by Wen Zhengming, 1531

Figure 1.2 Peasant painting from Yangliuqing, Tianjin

The Chinese language is filled with expressions of large numbers that indicate the significance of abundance: encyclopaedia is described as a book of 100 subjects (*baike*), diversity of views as those of 100 families (*baijia*), antiquity as 1,000 years old (*qiangu*), and years of longevity as 10,000 years (*wanshou*). The expression of 10,000 things has acquired a stable meaning for the largest inclusivity (*wanwu*). Intellectual achievements in this context are not primarily measured through 'views' which, despite their ability and promise to amplify amazing details, are often considered to have been derived from one perspective (*pianmian*) and therefore flawed; instead, the intelligent mind would strive for multiple accounts of a situation aiming to achieve a complete comprehension (*quanmian*). The intellectual landscape in China is crucially influenced by this method of conceptualizing the nature of knowing. In seeking the completeness of knowledge, the imperial administration gathered with great tenacity and righteousness large and complete collections of books. Among the well-known imperial book collections, the Song-dynasty *Taiping yulan*, or *Imperial Inspected Encyclopaedia of the Taiping Era* (977–983, 1,000 volumes), the Ming-dynasty *Yongle dadian*, or *The Great Canon of the Yongle Era* (1403–08, 11,095 volumes) and the Qing-dynasty *Siku quanshu*, or *The Complete Library in Four Branches of Literature* (1773–82, 36,381 volumes) are some of the best examples. In their sizes and methods of classification, these collections represent a very distinct tradition of managing quantities of information which differs fundamentally from that of the Western encyclopaedia. It was the imperial ambition to achieve completeness, as indicated by the words 'great canon' (*da*) and 'complete library' (*quan*) in the titles, that brought them legitimacy and authority. This is, as we can see in today's world of multi-media publications in China, still a much-desired status; the link between completeness and largeness on the one hand and legitimacy and authority on the other remains a very powerful one.

This relatively evenly distributed quantity regulation leads to an evenly distributed spacing regulation; we can perhaps describe this visual feature as spreading, an approximately even placing of spatial components. It is particularly interesting to note various well-known paintings of 100 things: the Tang-dynasty painter Wei Yan (eighth century) left us an extraordinary painting of 100 horses; the Italian Jesuit Giuseppe Castiglione (1688–1766) also painted a version of 100 horses for Qianlong Emperor. Both Wei Yan and Castiglione distributed their 100 horses evenly across the painting surfaces. Castiglione's spreading technique is particularly interesting because he had to rebel against his European landscape painting methods. Within the Baroque painting tradition that he learned in Rome, spreading would likely have been seen as a fault in composition, one of five important aspects of painting at the time. Here, Castiglione became a Chinese painter by depicting, with relatively equal emphasis, 100 horses spread along a very long scroll. From paintings to buildings, this spreading principle remains effective. The imperial Chinese city features the spread of courtyards surrounded by single-storeyed buildings. Although the concentric hierarchy of power maintains their own magnitudes of quantities, within each magnitude spreading seems to be the most consistent way to display quantities. While logic-based Western organization of quantities demands the display of the most representative of type, the thing-based Chinese organization of quantities insists on the equal significance of·each variety.

Taken as a whole, the Forbidden City in Beijing (Figure 1.3) can perhaps be seen as the epitome of numerical schemes. Built between 1406 and 1420, and with numerous minor renovations and changes made through its 490 years' usage as China's imperial court, the Forbidden City embodied the numerical schemes in their most elaborate and strict manifestations. The imperial regulations of the Ming dynasty, like its laws, were exceedingly detailed; it reflected the tradition of buildings as the embodiment of Confucian rites which remained largely unchanged in principle since the second century (Han dynasty).[11] The axis of the Forbidden City took its origin from the star positions in the northern sky, while the placement and the naming of the large range of buildings referred to ancient texts such as the *Book of Changes*. Prominent among the numerical schemes, the productive binary of the *yin* and the *yang*, the sixty-four hexagrams, the five elements, the twelve temporal markers, form an intricate web of carefully determined quantities. *Yin* and *yang* are indicated by many binary functions and names of buildings along the 8,000 metre axis, such as beginning/end (*qiankun*), sun/moon (*riyue*), spring/autumn (*chunqiu*), civil/military (*wenwu*), left/right (*zuoyou*).[12] Out of the *yang* numbers (odd numbers), five and nine are most valued; five is the mean and nine is the biggest. Further value of nine comes from the fact that 'nine' is the homonym of 'longevity' in Chinese. Five is highly valued because of its ability to function as the most powerful correlative number between the human body (five organs), the earth (five elements), and heaven (five planets). The imperial ruling quarters, the official halls, and the residential halls of the emperor are laid out as two groups of three halls (three in relation to nine), and the number of gates of the Forbidden City is nine; nine dominates decorative designs. The shape of the roofs, the height of podiums, the coloured paintings on timber structures, the number and sizes of beams and timber brackets are all determined by this set of numerical schemes. The concubine quarters of the Forbidden City are arranged as six (a *yin* number) on each side of the axis, forming a distribution of twelve concubine quarters which matches the number of temporal markers; this encapsulated a temporal regime of the emperor in relation to his imperial concubines. The sons of the emperor lived in quarters determined by the number five (again, a *yang* number). An example of a complex strategy of location would be that of civil and military offices: the civil office is located at the east of the axis for its association with the element of wood and the temporal marker of spring, to capture the energy of germination and growth, while the military office is located on the west side of the axis for its association with the element of metal and the temporal marker of autumn, to capture the energy of aggressiveness and termination. This is far from an exhaustive account of the numerical schemes of the Forbidden City,[13] but they can perhaps be seen as an indication of the crucial importance of numbers in the design and layout of buildings in Chinese imperial courts, of the various numerical schemes indicating cosmological orders, and of the intellectual conception of unique and distributed significance of the orders of quantities.

The Forbidden City features a spacing regulation that may be described as 'axial spreading', a numerically determined distribution of quantities along a long axis that reflects a distributed importance of each order of quantities. While the plan shape of the Forbidden City may resemble some examples of the European Baroque planning, axial spreading is fundamentally different from the 'scopic regime' that gave rise to the planning of Rome by Sixtus V and Dominico Fontana, or that of Versailles by Louis XIV and Jules Hardouin-Mansart, which tested the city and garden of vistas premised on the idea of scopic distance and the power and control that it implies.

Figure 1.3 The Forbidden City, Beijing

If the Forbidden City epitomizes carefully regulated numerical schemes, the Chinese market place perhaps represents an unregulated, but legitimate, notion of abundance. Market streets flourished during the Song dynasty (960–1279) at an unprecedented scale, even when the Song imperial court was deeply engaged in reformulating and imposing Confucian rites; commercial spaces poured out from previously confined quarters to form a new kind of Chinese city: that of maximum quantities. The Chinese imperial conception of commerce had always been ambivalent. Merchants were the lowest among the four categories of people: scholars (*shi*), peasants (*nong*), artisans (*gong*), merchants (*shang*). The rise of the market place in the Song dynasty may be seen to be compelled by the imperial court's need for commerce in response to the military threats of the Khitans, the Jurchens, and the Mongols in the northern Eurasian steppe.[14] Following a century of Mongol rule (1279–1368), the Ming dynasty re-established perhaps the strictest social order, and discouraged trade in the early stages of the dynasty. The market place nevertheless flourished again in the late Ming (first half of the seventeenth century) to surpass that of the Song dynasty. In the absence of a strict imposition of rites – resulting perhaps from both an imperial neglect and an imperative of trade – market places in Chinese cities seem to have operated with many numerical schemes simultaneously without an overarching and dominant framework such as that of proportion. An extraordinary painting by Zhang Zeduan (1085–1145) entitled *Along the River during Qingming Festival* depicts, in the form of a long scroll, detailed scenes of a market place in the twelfth-century Song capital city of Bianliang (Kaifeng). While the imperial Confucianism demanded buildings as observance of rites, the market place gave rise to material abundance through its multitude of numerical schemes all competing for prominence and influence.

How does abundance – with all its intellectual conceptions and numerical schemes vividly demonstrated in imperial Chinese cities – appear in today's cities in China? In many ways, and despite the extensive use of contemporary typologies, materials and technologies derived from the West, Chinese cities remain vigorously engaged, implicitly and explicitly, with numerical narratives of the past. Perhaps the greatest difference between the numerical schemes in contemporary Chinese cities and those in the past is that they lost their status as grand narratives; they nevertheless sustain a powerful position as fragmented small narratives. In certain spheres of Chinese life such as health care, the traditional numerical schemes of the five elements still anchor Chinese medicine and the Chinese corporeal preservation regimens. In Beijing, along the imperial axis of the Forbidden City, two important additions were made in the twentieth century. The first was constructed at the tenth anniversary of the founding of the People's Republic of China in 1949; this included Tiananmen Square and two of the ten grand projects – the Museum of Revolutionary History and Great Hall of the People flanking the imperial axis – built to celebrate this occasion. The second was built for the 2008 Beijing Olympic Games; for this event, two central venues – the Olympic Stadium and the National Aquatic Centre – were again laid out to straddle the imperial axis (Figure 1.4). The twentieth-century additions extend the numerical schemes of the imperial city: the past and the future, the emperor and the people, the square and the round, the blue and the red, the aquatic and the terrestrial all conspire to invoke an ancient sensibility of the productive binary. Whereas the names of the architects responsible for these monumental structures may escape the attention of the general population in China, the significance of the forms and locations of the buildings certainly hold an immediate and strong power deeply rooted in China. When cities such as Shenzhen and Guangzhou build their grand new city centres in Futian District (Figure 1.5) and in Zhujiang New City, their urban visions may be partially inspired by Baroque Rome and Parisien Beaux-Arts planning, and Soviet Socialist Realism, but they are, more importantly, products of ancient schemes of quantities based on the productive binary, brought out through the technique of axial spreading.

Figure 1.4 Olympic Village, Beijing

Figure 1.5 Shenzhen city centre, Shenzhen

If the Forbidden City serves as the epitome of ordered Chinese numerical schemes, Hong Kong stands as an exemplar for the city of maximum quantities, resulting from a multitude of competing numerical schemes all seeking their materializations to the greatest extent possible. It is with good reason that Zhang Zeduan's painting – and not those of Wen Zhengming who would have dismissed the Song commercialism as a low life form – was on loan to Hong Kong when the city celebrated the first ten-year anniversary under Chinese sovereignty in 2007. Hong Kong is perhaps a city that most resembles the spirit of the Song-dynasty painting in today's China. Hong Kong is a city of abundance in abundant display, a visual character similar to that in *nianhua*. Hong Kong's abundance is not limited by absolute numbers, but by standards of hygiene and safety as a human settlement. Most Chinese cities develop along the spectrum of quantities, with the Forbidden City and Hong Kong as its extremities.

The Just Right

The second instinct in relation to quantity seeks, in its ideal formulations, not abundance but the just right. The moral and aesthetic judgement on what is not enough and what is too much is not easily made in the Chinese city; it all depends. In the Western city, it is possible; at least in a string of foundational texts in architecture – Vitruvius's *Ten Books on Architecture,* Palladio's *Four Books of Architecture,* and Le Corbusier's *Towards a New Architecture* – the importance of the right amount of things in the right dimensions is clearly legislated. In architectural practice, creating the just right quantities – in terms of both amount and relationships – is a highly valued skill; like the Chinese numerical schemes, this Western sensibility has a deep intellectual connection. Perhaps the first and most illustrative work of this tradition is Plato's *Timaeus,* although the central doctrine contained in this book is widely disseminated through a range of works. In relation to the Chinese conception of the productive binary, the most important intellectual difference is Plato's conception of the third; the third, in the form of the mean, has a precise and identical relationship with both the first and the second: 'It is not possible to combine two things properly without a third to act as a bond to hold them together.'[15] When Plato speculated on a model of the universe as consisting of 'on one hand an intelligible and unchanging model and on the other a visible and changing copy of it', he thought the third condition, a 'receptacle' and a 'nurse of all becoming and change' (*chora*), must be imagined.[16] Unlike the two distinct states (*yin* and *yang*) in the Chinese imagination, Plato postulates three forces (being, space, becoming), with the third force operating on a separate and more powerful plane. Unlike the Chinese elemental thinking on the five elements of interconnected equal status and importance, Plato considers water and air as proportionally in the middle of fire and earth as 'the third conditions'; if two is the smallest number for abundance in the Chinese conception, three would be the smallest number in Plato's understanding of a dynamic condition. It allows 'proportion' – precise, constant, irreducible numerical schemes – that frames and bonds all things like a set of master keys. Proportion can be mathematical, geometrical, and moral. Proportion is the first great iteration of *chora*. 'The best bond is one that effects the closest unity between itself and the terms it is combining; and this is best done by a continued geometrical proportion.' 'So by these means and from these four constituents the body of the universe was created to be at unity owing to proportions; in consequence it acquired concord, so that having once come together in unity with itself it is indissoluble by any but its compounder.'[17] Speculating on the things that make up the universe, Plato suggests that 'these things were in disorder till god introduced measurable relations, internal and external, among them, to the degree and extent that they were capable of proportion and measurement'.[18]

The Chinese notion of *qi* comes close to the notion of *chora* in its capture of an invisible form of vitality, but the similarity quickly ends. Qi exists in all numerical schemes of quantities in the Chinese cultural tradition: the *yin* and *yang* (two), the elements (five), the biggest yang number (nine), the temporal order (twelve), the hexagrams in the *Book of Changes* (sixty-four). Qi is elemental while *chora* is mathematical; *qi* is distributed while *chora* is reductive; *qi* is vital while *chora* is enlivening. The account of *qi* is perhaps most vivid when it is applied to the human body; the intake and discharge, the up and down of the various different types of *qi* within the body link it to environmental elements and justify analogous medicinal interventions to regulate the body in relation to its *qi* balance. The account of *qi* in the environment, often seen in the practice of *fengshui*, demonstrates a traditional connection between the notion of *qi* and the constructed environment. The Confucianist 'doctrine of the mean' may also appear to be similar to *chora*, but it is far from mathematical; it is an ethical doctrine of moderation rather than an epistemological doctrine of the precise middle ('one exceeding one extreme and being exceeded by the other by the same fraction of the extremes'[19]). The Platonic numerical sequences outlined in *Timaeus*, 1:3:9:27 and 1:2:4:8, do not go beyond 27;[20] this speculation on the material constitution of the world through small integers exemplifies the nature of Western knowledge as classificational, categorical and typological. Knowledge hinges on the formulation of a set of master keys; it is premised on the notion that the large is understandable through the small, the large is constructed with the small in numerical relationships. Alberti claims that 'Nature is composed of threes all philosophers agree'.[21] While each element, each colour, each sound, each order of magnitude within the numerical schemes in the Chinese order of things possess *qi* and therefore values are placed in the fullness of these elements, resulting in distinct formal, colouring, and musical features, the Platonic *chora* demands proportion between forms, colours, and sounds. Western arts deviate from this point to proceed on a very different path; the dilution and mixing of colours in the search for proportional relationships in the mixing behaviour of colours would have been seen in the Chinese conception of colours as having weakened the *qi* of the five colours.

In Renaissance Italy, the intellectual and artistic circle of the Medici family in Florence was very enterprising with the discovery of Plato's *Timaeus*. Giorgio Vasari was scornful of the excessive amount of architectural detail in Gothic architecture, denouncing it as lacking in proportion. Raphael depicted Plato, in *School of Athens*, as holding *Timaeus* in his left hand; Raphael's painting is exemplary in visualizing the idea of proportion as the universal bond through careful composition, and through the depiction of architecture as if it is that very well-proportioned universal bond that nurses knowledge and beauty. Vasari and Raphael, in words and images, crystallized a long period of searching for ideal architectural forms based on proportion. Alberti's notion of *concinnitas*, a force that 'molds the whole of Nature' as the true source of beauty, reproduces Plato's 'receptacle' and 'nurse' metaphor.[22] 'The greatest glory in the art of building is to have a good sense of what is appropriate. For to build is a matter of necessity; but to build something praised by the magnificent, yet not rejected by the frugal, is the province only of an artist of experience, wisdom, and thorough deliberation'.[23] Perhaps the most important aspect of this revival of Platonic numerical order is its moral implication; 'propriety', as the 'just right conduct' – for instance courage as the proportional middle between cowardice and rashness – of the cultivated members of society, can probably be seen as a parallel quality to the just right numerical order. We can find this moralization of conduct in Baldassare Castiglione's *Il Cortegiano* in 1528. As early as Vasari's *Lives of the Most Excellent Painters, Sculptors and Architects* in 1550, this coupling of proportion and morality served as one of the central convictions in theorizing art and architecture. *The Painting of the Ancients* by Franciscus Junius in 1637, *Characteristicks of Men, Manners, Opinions, Times* by Shaftesbury in 1711, *Aesthetica* by Alexander Baumgarten in 1750, *Critique of Judgment* by Immanuel Kant in 1790, progressively developed the idea of taste – a crucial ability to sense the beauty in correct proportions in the arts and in human conduct – as a quality of good cultivation. If the European eighteenth century is one of politeness,[24] then this politeness is materialized in the legislation of quantities in art and architecture – a spacing regulation of politeness, so to speak. European colonization of other parts of the world since the extraordinary Portuguese navigation in the 1590s around the Cape of Good Hope to the west coast of India, brought the European notion of taste to influence other cultures. This moral discourse based in a set of numerical schemes of the just right is far from being a normative framework in relation to quantities; on the contrary, like so many cultural features in the West, the cultivation of the just right appears to be an artificial construct of scarcity against the natural tendency to desire abundance.

If proportionality can be understood as one of the most crucial manifestations of *chora*, then foundational architectural texts in the Western tradition by Vitruvius, Alberti, Palladio, and Le Corbusier are crucial moral battles against excessive and miscalculated quantities, be they Roman eclecticism, medieval Romanesque mixtures, or French Beaux-Arts amalgamation of styles. All the writers of these treatises take the moral high ground of abstinence; they offer prescriptive methods in the form of proportional schemes that guarantee good taste. The proportional schemes are, as Alberti maintains, ways of the just right so that nothing can be added and nothing can be taken away without making the design worse.

The construct of the proportional mean enables two kinds of dependent states: less and more. It also creates one moral principle: less is more. There seems to be a dialectics of quantities between less, more, and the just right. When it is less, it presents an aesthetic of artificial scarcity and a moral will to abstain from the allures of abundance. We find this in early Christian architecture, in Cistercian churches, and in Classicism. Today, we find it in minimalist designs and starving fashion models: the sterile environment and malnourished bodies certainly do not convey any sense of fertility or life-promotion; they seem to represent life's martyrdom in the battle against abundance, an impulse – simultaneously Platonic, Christian, and modern – to control quantities severely, as if to intensify the aesthetic potential of the moral power of quantity control within an environment of abundant provisions. It is, as Mumford observes, the principles of life promotion rooted in agriculture which the Western city subverts and abandons.[25] When it is more, it is manifested as a willed excess, a rebellious eruption of repressed desires for more. Much of the critique of the Baroque resulted from the condemnation of the state of too much and its associated moral decline: licentiousness, looseness, promiscuity, decadence, etc. Much of the enjoyment of the Baroque came in the form of guilty pleasure. In eighteenth-century Europe, for those who sought cultivation in classical antiquity which governed both the aesthetic state of things and the moral state of human beings, the Baroque exhibited a lack of taste. Chinese influences on Western art in the eighteenth century, *chinoiserie*, injected a bold and liberating imagination of quantities which placed the Western order of quantities under stress.

The New *Chora*: Machine, Language, Data

While *chinoiserie* may be playful, it did not pose a real challenge to the Western quantity control strategy rooted in proportionality. It was the rise of Western science that first mounted a devastating attack on proportions. Francis Bacon (1561–1626) was perhaps the most notable among them. In an essay called 'Of Beauty', Bacon dismissed proportional ideals as the best way to achieve beauty. Referring to the proportional methods of Dürer and the legend of Zeuxis having painted a cult beauty of Helen by combining the five most beautiful girls in the body of one, Bacon wrote:

> A man cannot tell whether Apelles or Albert Durer were the more trifler; whereof the one would make a personage by geometrical proportions, the other, by taking the best parts out of divers faces, to make one excellent. Such personages, I think, would please nobody but the painter that made them. Not but I think a painter may make a better face than ever was; but he must do it by a kind of felicity (as a musician that maketh an excellent air in music), and not by rule.[26]

Instead, Bacon suggested that 'There is no excellent beauty that hath not some strangeness in the proportion'.[27] Bacon's comments on beauty were not incidental; they were part of an ambitious knowledge reform programme. He argued that at the heart of the Renaissance pursuit of beauty was a fundamental misconception of the form and objective of knowledge. The Renaissance was misguided by a vanity of the mind to pursue 'delicate knowledge', while the true meaning of knowledge lies in its empirical dimension and its usefulness. The Renaissance love of beauty, Bacon wrote,

> grew speedily to an excess; for men began to hunt more after words than matter; more after the choiceness of the phrase, and the round and clean composition of the sentence, and the sweet falling of the clauses, and the varying and illustration of their works with tropes and figures, than after the weight of matter, worth of subject, soundness of argument, life of invention or depth of judgment.[28]

The 'weight of matter' is significant; it is the notion of external truths that captured the imagination of Bacon and that of a generation of scholars in Europe who contributed towards the 'scientific revolution' by focusing on facts and functions. In France, Claude Perrault (1613–88) considered some of the proportional schemes practised in Greek architecture as 'arbitrary', and turned his

21

translation of Vitruvius into a critique, while in England, Christopher Wren (1632–1723) thought proportional schemes to be 'customary', a habit of time rather than a truth; both denied their role in the production of good architectural designs.[29]

How did the tradition of working with proportions in art and architecture survive this onslaught? It was held together temporarily by the ingenious framework of the European Enlightenment, through works such as those of Shaftesbury and Kant. Their argument was that the beautiful, the good, and the moral are different manifestations of the same power; this power is Plato's universal bond understood as a moral imperative. The goodness of nature as a whole compels human beings to formulate their moral and aesthetic practices – still largely inherited from the Renaissance Platonic enterprise – according to good judgement, one that is able to recognize the just right as a mark of good taste.[30] Shaftesbury defended the Renaissance, and argued against the scientists whom he regarded as having been too pedantic with empirical details. Instead, proportion is a shadow of virtue and evidence of manner and taste, qualities essential to a human ideal in the character of the virtuoso, an eighteenth-century answer to Castiglione's courtier in Renaissance Italy. Fragile as it was, this moral and aesthetic enterprise – manifested in the eighteenth century as a culture of politeness – was crucial to the rise of the economic middle class, which made good use of this immensely rich cultural tradition as a mark of class distinction.[31] Here, the Platonic *chora* shifted from mathematical precision to a 'moral sense' which found its physical forms in, among other features, proportionality.

In the middle of the twentieth century, two important publications concerning proportion appeared: Colin Rowe's 'The Mathematics of the Ideal Villa' (1947)[32] and Rudolf Wittkower's *Architectural Principles in the Age of Humanism* (1949);[33] in revealing the deeper mathematical roots of proportions and broader application of their rules in designs, and in tracing the decline of proportions since the rise of Western science, these essays can be understood as obituaries of proportion. Wittkower suggested that the decline of proportion was due to the increasing importance of the psychology of creativity, affirming that the seventeenth-century critique of proportion was the starting point of its decline.[34] However, Wittkower perhaps misjudged the successor to proportion. The triumph of science since the seventeenth century was not accompanied by the surge of the psychology of creativity, but by the rise of facts and functions in design. Three metaphors seem to have appeared to suggest new ways of understanding *chora* in design. The first is the functional machine, a notion that influenced early twentieth-century modern architecture, but it can be traced back to its use by Thomas Hobbes in relation to a social form that was deeply inspired by seventeenth-century science; this appeal to the causality of the mechanical – as that of materials and forms – gained tremendous power in the first half of the twentieth century. The second is language, a metaphor for architecture through the idea of an invisible force that produces meanings; this mapping of design onto syntactical rules and semantic conventions provided an attractive ontology for architecture. From shape grammar and space syntax to semiology and deconstruction, the linguistic metaphor energized the theory of architecture for much of the second half of the twentieth century. The third is data indexing; this is most dramatically demonstrated by one of the greatest data spectacles of our age – the Google Search – in which indexed data and the fast feedback loop have pushed the management of data into an aesthetic project. Now, it seems, data are able to reconstitute all human activities: sociality now becomes mappings of movements of data in social media, viability of society becomes consumer confidence index, quality turns into graphs of data indicating customer satisfaction. Algorithm seems to have the power to contend for the status of the new *chora*.

As contrasting as architectural publications can possibly be, Richard Padovan's *Proportion* (1999)[35] and Rem Koolhaas's *S,M,L,XL* (1995)[36] could nevertheless be seen as two sides of the same coin in relation to the design heritage of proportioned quantities. Padovan defends proportion on the ground of our 'natural' intellectual behaviour, resulting from both empathy and abstraction, two modes of functioning of the human mind: projecting its intellectual conception onto the environment, and understanding the environment through rational schemes of abstraction. Koolhaas internalizes the shock of a Western architect by the apparent disregard of its tradition of quantity management in other parts of the world (Singapore, Pearl River Delta), and turns the Western heritage of quantity management on its head. Between these two kinds of assertions, the power that Plato described as the universal bond finds its successive forms: the mechanical, the linguistic, the parametric, and the ecological. What is common to all of them is the assumption of a singular overarching logical/numerical framework that regulates, distributes, aestheticizes, and moralizes. They emerged as alternatives to proportion as the most fundamental framework of quantity regulation, but more importantly, they appear as reconstitutions of many of the central features of the Platonic *chora*.

The quantity regulation of the Chinese city, with which we began this chapter, is different in fundamental ways from that of the Western city, and must be contextualized within Western numerical strategies in order to place both the Chinese city and the Western city within a larger critical framework. The seemingly endless parade of quantities in the Chinese city – from the productive binary to complex and grand numerical schemes, from politics to community, from food to medicine, from ornaments to buildings, from the late Ming dynasty to the twenty-first century – is potentially disorientating without a set of master quantities; we must see that the parade of quantities is the parade of all orders of things (*wanwu*), with the nature of each order of magnitude manifested in the display of quantities. In resisting abstraction in the idea of master keys, the parade of quantities in the Chinese city conveys meanings in material ways and produces the city through distributed material orders. With each additional appearance of a thing, even when it is identical to a previous appearance – a common practice in the use of Chinese square words – meanings change. In the Chinese city, the twos, the fours, the fives, the eights, the nines, the tens, the twelves, the one hundreds, the one thousands, the ten thousands, continue to have their persuasive power in the realization of projects, both as real estate speculation and as grand constructions symbolizing culture and nation, both as the way in which building materials are used, and as the way in which cities are laid out. These quantities exist as both original quantities and those making a second appearance following their first appearances elsewhere, as acts of confirmation, solidarity, emulation, tribute, and respect; this is in line with similar practices in calligraphy, literature, painting, and gardening. Shao Yong's speculation on the nature of the number of things stops at the thing of a billion things, which he considered as the order of magnitude of a human being ('isn't the human being the thing of a billion things?'); if he is be taken as a start, what would be a city of a billion things? To follow Shao Yong's thoughts, this city of a billion things would be an amalgamation – without abstracted master quantities – of countless orders of magnitude of quantities, all moving and changing with their propensity, all seeking their materialization to the greatest extent possible. This would be a city of immense complexity. This would be an important understanding of the Chinese city, not so much when it is in the form of the Forbidden City with strictly regulated quantities, but when it is in the form of Hong Kong with its complex amalgamations of economies and ecologies, of systems of languages, transportation, habitation, and consumption, of narratives of past, present, and future. This is a way to understand the fast-growing Chinese cities today, when many of them have, with or without intention, traced the path of development of Hong Kong, an exemplar city that combines orderly life with a high concentration of buildings and people, and that incorporates all external influences into its existing orders of quantities. This is the city of maximum quantities.

Notes

1 Carl Jung, 'Foreword', *I Ching*, trans. Richard Wilhelm (Princeton: Princeton University Press, 1967).
2 Craig Clunas, *Empire of Great Brightness: Visual and Material Cultures of Ming China, 1368–1644* (Honolulu: University of Hawai'i Press, 2007), pp.21–52.
3 Klaas Ruitenbeek, *Carpentry and Building in Late Imperial China: A Study of the Fifteenth-century Carpenter's Manual* Lu Ban Jing (Leiden: Brill, 1996).
4 John King Fairbank and Merle Goldman, *China: A New History* (Cambridge MA: Harvard University Press, 1998), p.65.
5 Joseph Needham, *Science and Civilization in China*, Vol. 2 (Cambridge: Cambridge University Press, 1956); Ho Peng Yoke, *Li, Qi and Shu: An Introduction to Science and Civilization in China* (Hong Kong: Hong Kong University Press, 1985).
6 Shao Yong, *Huangji Jingshi Shu* (Book of Supreme Ordering Principles), annotated by Wei Shaosheng (Zhengzhou: Zhongzhou guji chubanshe, 2007), p.489. On Shao Yong see Don J. Wyatt, *The Recluse of Loyang: Shao Yung and the Moral Evolution of Early Sung Thought* (Honolulu: University of Hawai'i Press, 1996).
7 Wang Hui, *Xiandai Zhongguo sixiang de xingqi* (The Rise of Modern Chinese Thought), second edition (Beijing: SDX Joint Publishing Company, 2008), p.62.
8 Maurice Freedman, Editorial notes on his translation of Marcel Granet, *The Religion of the Chinese People* (New York: Harper & Row, 1975), pp.176–77.
9 François Jullien, *The Propensity of Things: Towards a History of Efficacy in China* (New York: Zone Books, 1995).
10 James A. Flath, *The Cult of Happiness: Nianhua, Art, and History in Rural North China* (Vancouver: University of British Columbia Press, 2004).
11 Sun Dazhang, ed., *Zhongguo gudai jianzhu shi* (History of Ancient Chinese Architecture), Vol. 5 (Beijing: Zhongguo jiangong chubanshe, 2002). Meng Fanren, *Mingdai gongting jianzhu shi* (History of Palace Architecture of the Ming Dynasty) (Beijing: Zijincheng chubanshe, 2010), Chapter 9.

12 Sun Dazhang, ed., *Zhongguo gudai jianzhu shi*, p.37.
13 A more detailed account of the measurements of the Forbidden City can be found in Fu Xinian, 'Mingdai gongdian tanmiao deng da jianzhuqun zongti guihua shoufa de tedian' (The characteristics of the planning of large building groups in the Ming dynasty), in *Jianzhu lilun lishi wenku* (Compendium of Essays in History and Theory of Architecture) (Beijing: Zhongguo jianzhu gongye chubanshe, 2010), pp.85–106.
14 Guo Daiheng, ed., *Zhongguo gudai jianzhu shi* (History of Ancient Chinese Architecture), Vol. 3 (Beijing: Zhongguo jiangong chubanshe, 2003). Jacques Gernet, *Daily Life in China on the Eve of the Mongol Invasion, 1250–1276*, trans. H. M. Wright (London: George Allen & Unwin, 1962).
15 Plato, *Timaeus and Critias*, trans. Desmond Lee (London: Penguin Books, 1977), p.44.
16 Ibid., p.67.
17 Ibid., p.44.
18 Ibid., p.96.
19 Ibid., p.48.
20 Rudolf Wittkower, 'The problem of harmonic proportion in architecture', *Architectural Principles in the Age of Humanism* (London and New York: W. W. Norton, 1971).
21 Leon Battista Alberti, *On the Art of Building in Ten Books*, trans. Joseph Rykwert, Neil Leach and Robert Tavernor (Cambridge MA: The MIT Press, 1988), Book 9, p.304.
22 Ibid., pp.302–03.
23 Ibid., p.315.
24 Lawrence E. Klein, *Shaftesbury and the Culture of Politeness: Moral Discourse and Cultural Politics in Early Eighteenth-century England* (Cambridge: Cambridge University Press, 1994).
25 Lewis Mumford, *The City in History: Its Origins, Its Transformations, and Its Prospects* (San Diego, New York and London: Harvest Books, 1961), p.37.
26 He refers to the proportional methods of Dürer and the legend of Zeuxis having painted a cult beauty of Helen by combining the five most beautiful girls in the body of one. Francis Bacon, *The Philosophical Works of Francis Bacon*, ed. John M. Robertson (London: George Routledge, 1905), p.788.
27 Ibid.
28 Francis Bacon, *The Advancement of Learning*, Book I, Chapter IV, Section 2 (London: J. M. Dent & Sons Ltd, 1973).
29 Li Shiqiao, *Power and Virtue: Architecture and Intellectual Change in England, 1660–1730* (London and New York: Routledge, 2006).
30 Shaftesbury, *Characteristicks of Men, Manners, Opinions, Times*, in 3 volumes (London, 1714).
31 Klein, *Shaftesbury and the Culture of Politeness*.

32 Colin Rowe, 'The Mathematics of the Ideal Villa: Palladio and Le Corbusier Compared', *Architectural Review* (March, 1947), pp.101–104.
33 Rudolf Wittkower *Architectural Principles in the Age of Humanism* (London: The Warburg Institute, 1949).
34 Rudolf Wittkower, 'The Changing Concept of Proportion', *Idea and Image: Studies in the Italian Renaissance* (New York: Thames and Hudson, 1978), p.121.
35 Richard Padovan, *Proportion: Science, Philosophy, Architecture* (London and New York: E & FN Spon, 1999).
36 Rem Koolhaas, Bruce Mau, Hans Werlemann, Office for Metropolitan Architecture, *S,M,L,XL* (New York: Monacelli Press, 1995).

2
The City of Maximum Quantities

Hong Kong as a city of a billion things – encapsulating the notion of abundance in all its aspects – is one of the most notable results of the Chinese framework of quantity management; two cities perhaps invite comparisons with Hong Kong, and they may be considered as superseded cities of maximum quantities. The first is Venice. In different eras, Venice and Hong Kong straddle between vastly different ideological, cultural, and economic worlds and thrived despite, or because of, these differences. However, beneath the display of sensual delight in the fashionable and hybridized architecture, Venice had a serious side that seems to be absent in Hong Kong: from the Renaissance on, Venice was committed to Greek and Roman intellectual ideals; Daniele Barbaro propagated Roman virtues in art and architecture, and Andrea Palladio published correct rules of architectural design more accessible to the rich and practical merchants of Veneto than to the bankers and Popes in Florence and Rome. The second superseded city of maximum quantities is New York. Both New York and Hong Kong are fiercely dedicated to commerce, and have striven to do more with less, create more floor area with less land. New York was the new Western frontier of quantities, a city that made the best use of tall buildings – the ruthless vertical extrusion of floor space enabled by Elisha Otis's invention of the elevator – in Manhattan. Like Venice, New York is perhaps not as radical as it appears to be: its grid was already prefigured in Robert Hooke's design for London after the Fire in 1666,[1] and its architecture tried, and succeeded, in imposing proportional control, like in the case of the Flatiron Building completed in 1902. The 1916 Zoning Law, ostensibly based on the form of the Woolworth Building, appears to be grounded in the traditional typologies of European cathedrals. When Hugh Ferriss published his manifesto of the skyscraper, *The Metropolis of Tomorrow* (1929), both classical and Gothic cathedrals were depicted on the dust jacket as distant predecessors of the skyscraper in a progression of building types.[2]

Both in the form of the Renaissance city and that of the modern gridiron city, Venice and New York seem to have been influenced by the invisible force of proportionality: it found moments of clarity in churches, urban squares, blocks and gridded streets. It reached its full expressiveness in Palladio's *Four Books of Architecture* (1570) and Ferriss's *The Metropolis of Tomorrow*. Their method of accommodating quantities, therefore, may still be understood as fundamentally proportional, examples of what Lewis Mumford considers as the result of 'geometric clarification',[3] leading to an evaluation of the geometric figure above urban functions. The open grid is its ultimate achievement. Against this heritage, Hong Kong never conceived such invisible force of proportional control; its quantities are functional (but not functionalist), a system of utilitarian connections without visual purification. There are perhaps two levels from which we can understand the differences between Venice/New York and Hong Kong. First, despite the similar-looking features of density and tall buildings, the differences in Hong Kong are most visible at the human scale; proportional quantities at the human scale are readable, while functional quantities are saturated. Proportional quantities are intentional and rule-based, and functional quantities are resultant and thing-based. Proportional quantities are like a greenhouse, while functional quantities are like a jungle. In New York, skyscrapers maintain some form of integrity on the street level, while in Hong Kong, tall buildings melt into a sea of densely packed signage and movement on the ground. The intellectual formulation of abundance and the resultant amalgamations of functional quantities are what make the city of maximum quantities possible. Second, in Hong Kong, the city of maximum quantities is also the city of minimum dimensions. Things in the city – seats, beds, corridors, rooms, pavements, footbridges, shops – are minimally dimensioned, not for aesthetic effect, but in the interest of maximum quantities.[4]

Hong Kong owes its existence to a series of amazing historical accidents. It was created as the result of a trade war in the mid-nineteenth century, known as the Opium War, between the British Empire and the Qing Empire in China. Militarily weak, the Qing Empire lost the war and ceded Hong Kong in perpetuity to Britain in 1842, through the Treaty of Nanjing, as part of war reparation. Under the British rule, which was interrupted by Japanese occupation between 1941 and 1945, Hong Kong played the role of an *entrepôt*, with exceptional freedom of trade and low taxation, a trait that continues to be maintained today. Hong Kong has been ranked the world's freest economy for eighteen consecutive years, for as long as the ranking has existed, published jointly by *The Wall Street Journal* and the Heritage Foundation.[5] This extraordinary heritage of Hong Kong includes a minimum government, no particular industrial policy, little import and export controls, and no military force. Since the transfer of sovereignty in 1997 from Britain to China, Hong Kong's traditional role as an *entrepôt* appears to have strengthened considerably. Hong Kong government spends less than 15 per cent of its gross domestic product (GDP), while the US government spends over 40 per cent. The economist Milton Friedman considered Hong Kong as a radical economic experiment over a period of fifty years from 1947 to 1997, with control samples found in Britain, Israel, and the United States. Friedman argues that Hong Kong's per capita income grew most dramatically among them and this proves the inherent intelligence of the market place over planning.[6] However, in this neoliberalist reading of Hong Kong, the role played by the traditional cultural conceptions of the city as a market place, and the countless numerical schemes that competed for domination and influence in the city, are not considered at all. The city of Hong Kong boasts the highest number of US dollar millionaires in the world, but over 18 per cent of its population (estimated at 1.26 million in 2011) is considered to live below the poverty line (although the Hong Kong government does not have an official poverty line).[7] It did not even have a minimum wage until 2011, when legislation set the minimum wage at 28 Hong Kong dollars (about 3.6 US dollars) per hour. Because of the freedom of trade and the lack of industrial policy, Hong Kong's traditional labour-intensive industries moved to China, and over 90 per cent of Hong Kong's economic activities consist of 'services', the handling of goods and money in transit and in consummation, as well as the infrastructure that sustains this market place.

The City of Speculators

Among the 'service sector' of Hong Kong, which makes up 90 per cent of its economic activities, a large proportion – around a quarter[8] – is the value derived from the unmovable assets on the land, the material elements that make up the city. The real estate and construction sectors represented 45 per cent of Hong Kong's stock market capitalization; this is extraordinarily high when compared with that in the US (5 per cent), the UK (10 per cent), and other Asian economies (between 10 and 20 per cent).[9] Hong Kong has an extraordinary scheme of land valuation and speculation. Except for a tiny piece of land belong to St John's Cathedral, all land in Hong Kong was owned by the colonial government and this government-based land ownership continued into the post-1997 era. While in traditional European cities such as

London real estate speculations were moderated by feudal holdings on long leases, Hong Kong has never been limited by this condition. Historically, there has been an extraordinary alliance between the supply of land and the value of real estate; it was played out in the most dramatic fashion in 1984 when the Sino–British Joint Declaration attempted to shore up confidence and stabilize the property market by limiting the supply of land to 50 hectares per year; as a result, the property price rose dramatically from 1985 to 1997. The basic aim of this land control is to maintain a relatively high land value and high real estate prices. To a certain degree, the government controls the price level of the real estate through the volume of land supply, balancing the appetite of property developers, its financial viability, and the welfare of the population. Hong Kong's real estate is priced often among the highest in the world, if not the highest.

The government has a structural interest in maintaining a high real estate price. The low taxation policy in Hong Kong is only possible because about 33 per cent of government income comes from real estate and construction sectors and about 35 per cent of its expenditure is in the same sectors.[10] The income includes land sales, land premium, and stamp duty. What is sold in these 'land sales' is not ownership but development rights; it is invariably highly priced. Land premium is a differential sum between the original land use (already determined by government through the statutory Outline Zoning Plan) and proposed alteration of land use by developers; it is an estimated amount which is paid to the government prior to development. Stamp duty, which averages 3 per cent, is the 'resale tax' imposed on the second-hand property sales. These incomes, in addition to taxation, are used by the government to subsidize its public housing programme, which consists of about 50 per cent of the housing units in Hong Kong. This high degree of dependency on the real estate market perhaps pushed the government – otherwise deeply committed to competition of the market place – to accept reluctantly a virtual monopoly of large property developers to keep property prices high. The property developers cultivate a strategy of combining controlling investments in real estate, utility companies (telecommunication, electricity, and gas), public infrastructure (railways and bus services), and supermarkets; this amazing grip on almost all aspects of essential living has been astonishingly successful in Hong Kong.[11] By taking advantage of the low rent in government housing, the low-income population has a chance to accumulate capital to make their foray into the expensive private housing market, where profits are lucrative and risks are high. Buying private property in Hong Kong is often referred to as 'getting on the vehicle' (*shangche*) – an expressive term that vividly describes both the run-away property prices and the consequences of people left out of the speculative cycle. An important feature of this economy is that while developers monopolize, contractors decentralize; the average size of contractors in Hong Kong is fewer than eight workers, allowing efficient subcontracting to take place competitively.[12] The general population, the property developers, and the government all stand to gain from this high real estate price; all parties work together to ensure that property sales are amazingly smooth and fast in Hong Kong, and contractual works are efficient and affordable. In Hong Kong, purchasing a property is basically as easy as purchasing any other goods. The city is whipped into a constant frenzy of property speculation by the lively media.

What emerges from this extraordinary and unique combination of land ownership, government policy, mass participation, and the investment patterns of developers in Hong Kong is an architecture and a city that test the limits of hygiene and safety, and not those of aesthetic and moral propriety. Hong Kong has very high plot ratios – the ratio between the sum total of floor areas of a development and its site area – compared with other big cities in the world, on average eight for residential developments and twelve for commercial ones; this contributes to the basic quantities of floor areas to be constructed. Aesthetics and its moralization, so fundamental to the mental and physical make-up of so many cities in the world, is largely irrelevant in Hong Kong; it seems that no building has ever been turned down by the Buildings Department just because it is considered to be unsightly. The picture of abundance in Hong Kong is therefore constructed with building schemes pushing the boundaries of livability; these are vulnerable boundaries, as the 1894 bubonic plague and the 2003 SARS outbreaks demonstrate vividly. However, Hong Kong is deeply committed to its urban choice despite its inherent risks; the economic imperatives of this city and the benefits it brings – quick profit, proximity, convenience, chance events, safety in uniformity – ensure great devotion of its citizens to the way of life in Hong Kong.

As an epitome in place of an archetype of a Hong Kong development, Kowloon Walled City embodied in the most fascinating ways some crucial aspects of the city of maximum quantities (Figure 2.1). Kowloon Walled City was an administrative anomaly; at the time of leasing the New Territories to the British for ninety-nine years in 1898, the Chinese, with the reluctant consent of the British, kept their rights to control a small piece of land traditionally used as a military defence post. This curious clause in the Peking Convention

The City of Maximum Quantities

Figure 2.1 Kowloon Walled City before demolition (photo by Ian Lambot)

for the Extension of Hong Kong (1898) would begin an exceptional history of self-organization of a tiny piece of land. It is this self-organizing nature of Kowloon Walled City that embodied the principles of functional quantities in the Chinese cultural context. Within a year of occupation of the New Territories, the British declared unilaterally that they were to assume jurisdiction over Kowloon Walled City; in practice, neither the Chinese nor the British established any form of administration over the City. In 1940, after a long period of hesitation, the British administration finally demolished part of the city and the Japanese demolished the wall itself during their brief period of occupation of Hong Kong. After the Second World War, the Chinese continued to assert sovereignty over Kowloon Walled City and, following protests in China over planned British interventions, the British administration left the place to its own devices.[13] Before it was demolished in 1993, Kowloon Walled City was a huge block of buildings ranging from ten to fourteen floors, housing approximately a population of 35,000 people, on a site of 2.2 hectares. This made Kowloon Walled City easily the densest human habitation in the world, encompassing systems of supply of water and discharge of sewage, production of food, and provision of health care and education; it housed secret societies and congregations of religious worship, parlours of the game mah-jong, and halls of good food. Over the centuries, the British administration and the general media have tended to sensationalize its crime and filth: 'a cesspool of iniquity, with heroin divans, brothels and everything unsavoury' as the twenty-second Governor, Sir Alexander Grantham, would describe it.[14] The crime and filth, if one considers the unique legal circumstances of the place, can perhaps be considered as incidental features; it is not an unavoidable consequence of the high concentration of buildings and people.

The crime and filth may have failed Kowloon Walled City in the late-twentieth century, but its spirit of maximum quantities lives on in Hong Kong, in new towns such as Tin Shui Wai, built from 1987. With a population of 270,000 in an area of 4.3 square kilometres, Tin Shui Wai has a population density of 63,000 per square kilometre, and uncannily resembles Kowloon Walled City in its image: a seemingly impenetrable mass of small housing units from a distance (Figure 2.2). The average population per square kilometre in Europe is 3,050 and in the United States is 1,150; in Asia, this figure is 4,800 for Japan and 7,600 for the rest of Asia.[15] Tin Shui Wai, among many other similar urban scale developments in Hong Kong, possesses several key components that made its existence possible: a light rail line and a range of public and

Figure 2.2 Tin Shui Wai, Hong Kong

private transport facilities, a mixture of private and public housing projects, and a range of provisions of municipal facilities such as open space, schools, markets, sports grounds, and cultural facilities. Most of the residents live on public housing estates, and the largest private development is Kingswood Villa developed by Cheung Kong Holdings in the late 1990s, with over 15,000 units in fifty-eight residential towers. Despite its reputation of high rates of suicides and unemployment, Tin Shui Wai has dramatically improved levels of hygiene and safety compared with Kowloon Walled City; it is an amazing accomplishment in the concentration of buildings and people in the contemporary context.

In the rapid production of floor space, standardization is the key. Here, architecture's aspiration to the status of commodity is unmitigated: successful architectural projects feature tried and tested standard apartment and office layouts. The formulaic layouts – considered to be over-simplified in many other cities – allow the participation of people with no architectural training in the real estate business, from development managers, skilled draftsmen in architectural offices, to real estate agents and speculators, dramatically increasing the ease of access to property speculation and speeding up the return on investment. The premium status of habitation lies in price differentiations which, in this context, are not embodied in design but indicated by quantity: sizes, material costs, branded goods, significations of exotic lifestyles. A property development such as The Palazzo, designed by Ronald Lu and Partners in 2009, embodies these differentiations aggressively, and its high prices are almost entirely justified on the basis of these differentiations. The developer, Sino Land, promoted the standard Die Dietrich kitchen appliances, as well as the architectural references to the Roman bath and Borghese Gardens. It also leverages heavily on the fact that the development has an oblique view of the Shatin Race Course, through its references to the Hong Kong Derby, an event that is associated with the rich and powerful in England and Hong Kong. Sino Land also claims that the architecture of The Palazzo is inspired by its Fullerton Hotel project in Singapore in 2001, an adaptive reuse of a former nineteenth-century General Post Office building on the waterfront of the Singapore River. The fact that The Palazzo is located on a sliver of land between a railway line (East Rail) and a highway (Tolo Harbour Highway) (Figure 2.3) is loudly drowned in aggressive advertising and elaborately disguised behind an amalgamation of generic Western classical details (Figure 2.4).[16]

The Palazzo comes from a lineage of developments that is vividly demonstrated by its neighbouring residential projects Jubilee Gardens (1985–1986) and Royal Ascot (1995–1997) (Figure 2.5); on the

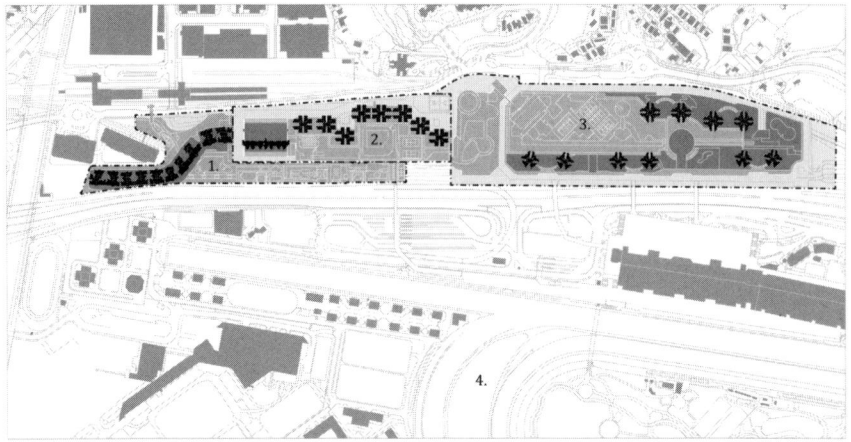

Fotan Railway Properties Development: Plan at Podium Level

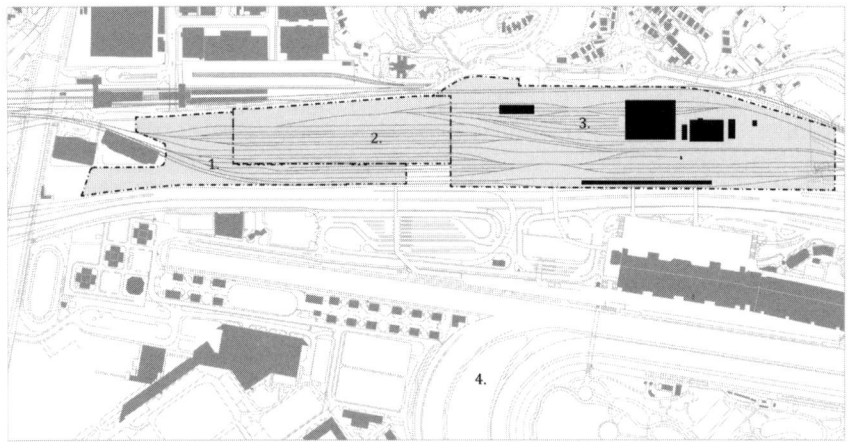

Fotan Railway Properties Development: Plan at Track Level

Name of Properties and Places:
1. The Palazzo (2009)
2. Jubilee Garden (1986)
3. Royal Ascot (1997)
4. Shatin Racecourse

Figure 2.3 The site plan of The Palazzo, Jubilee Gardens, and Royal Ascot, Shatin, Hong Kong

same sliver of land between the East Rail and Tolo Harbour Highway, these two earlier developments illustrate two developmental stages for The Palazzo in their basic strategy to provide a car park, podium garden, and vertically extruded apartment units (Figure 2.6). While the basic strategy remained similar, the thematic content grew progressively from Jubilee Gardens, to Royal Ascot, and finally to The Palazzo; correspondingly, the proportion between useful floor area and total building floor area (the floor efficiency ratio) declined

Figure 2.4 An advertised image of The Palazzo

1. The Palazzo (2009) 2. Jubilee Garden (1986) 3. Royal Ascot (1997)

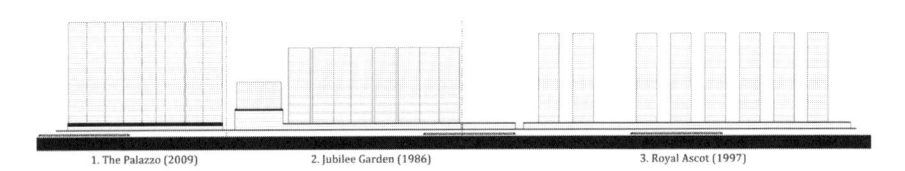

Figure 2.5 Section of The Palazzo, Jubilee Gardens, and Royal Ascot

from over 80 per cent for Jubilee Gardens and Royal Ascot to 77 per cent for The Palazzo. The Palazzo has distributed more floor areas to a 'club house' loosely based on Italianate Renaissance gardens; while reducing the floor efficiency of the development, this strategy

Figure 2.6 The view of The Palazzo, Jubilee Gardens, and Royal Ascot

increased the value of the property by a great margin: The Palazzo is able to command higher prices (10,000 Hong Kong dollars per square foot; price information in 2011) than both Jubilee Gardens (4,960 Hong Kong dollars) and Royal Ascot (7,500 Hong Kong dollars). Presented as 'a classic above it all', The Palazzo invests heavily in a narrative of high life through associations of Italianate Renaissance gardens and horse racing, sustaining high property prices despite its standard apartment layouts. The Palazzo brought together a series of key innovations in real estate developments: mass transportation, the legal notion of strata title, standardization of design for the market place, the motorized vehicle, the elevator, and air-conditioning. All these conspired to invent a new city in the Chinese cultural context.

The architectural profession in Hong Kong has adapted to this condition remarkably; it is fiercely loyal to the ways of the speculator rather than to the central aesthetic and moral tenants of architecture. The term 'design' in Hong Kong seems to be all but a ghost of Giorgio Vasari's *disegno*. In Hong Kong, design appears to be rehearsals of routines of functional amalgamations and resolutions, often with great ingenuity, of problems inherent to these amalgamations. Financially successful architectural practices in Hong Kong are marked by their characteristic patterns of long working hours, short notices of design change, and highly flexible design principles. Tuned to such ruthless singularity, Hong Kong's architectural profession is unmatched in its ability to produce designs that maximize profit opportunities in minimum time. By the same token, it is also inexperienced in designing effective civil spaces with the cultural sophistication commonly expected in many other cities in the world. This condition has a visible impact on the pecking order of most of the architectural practices in Hong Kong. At the top are quantity managers (project architects) who are highly experienced with the demands of the developer, the intricacies of the building and planning regulations, including the latest regulatory decisions detailed in the Practice Notes for Authorized Persons, and forms of contracts; the design team, often staffed with inexperienced young graduates and non-local architects, seems to be an embodiment of the low status of design. Hong Kong's young architectural graduates aspire to work in the 'project team' to learn the skills of managing quantities; the archaic and impenetrable nineteenth-century English language of Hong Kong's building regulation known as Chapter 123 of the Building Ordinance provides a curious twist to this 'regulation fetish' – an inevitable phenomenon in the city of maximum quantities. Hong Kong's public sector does not seem to offer significant design opportunities; government projects are awarded with a tender system that erects an almost impossible barrier for small design firms, which often harbour, in many other cities, new ideas of architectural design. Once invited to tender for government projects, the lowest bidder usually gets the job; this is yet another exclusion of architectural design as an important judgement criterion. In these intricate operations, design seems to have become an inconsequential notion; it is finance – disguised as designs and project management – that determines decisions concerning the constructed environment in Hong Kong. Although only about 35 per cent of the land of Hong Kong is developed, it is one of the best examples in which the mechanisms of the real estate market reinvent the art of building, challenging the perennial values harboured by the ideals of architecture as a distinct discipline of human knowledge.

Terminal Developments

At the apex of the real estate speculation in Hong Kong rest the extraordinary 'terminal developments'. This is a form of developments in cities where large self-contained and multifunctional complexes – often stretched to the limit of quantity concentration and urban infrastructure in Hong Kong – grow rapidly along mass transit railway lines. These are not small towns but made of singular developments, comprising elements of retail, entertainment, offices and hotels, and residential units, often created on relatively small sites. A prime example of a terminal development is Kowloon Station in Hong Kong (Figure 2.7). Kowloon Station is, instead of a case of 'finance of architecture', an extraordinary example of 'architecture of finance'. At the confluence of Mass Transit Railway and Airport Express Rail, as well as situated next to the high-speed rail terminal linking to the high-speed rail network in China, the 13.54 hectare site is owned by the Mass Transit Railway Corporation (MTRC), a government institution established in 1975 which has, since

Understanding the Chinese City

Figure 2.7 Kowloon Station, Hong Kong

Figure 2.8 Sales graphics, Kowloon Station, Hong Kong (photo by Esther Lorenz)

2000, been corporatized and listed on the Hong Kong Stock Exchange with 23 per cent of its shares owned by private investors. The MTRC has always been run like a business entity, with 'government subsidies' primarily in the form of development rights.[17] Kowloon Station creates 1.06 million square metres of highly valued real estate: sixteen residential towers (8,809 residential units), two hotel and serviced apartment towers, a 118-storey premium office tower of 231,778 square metres of rentable space, a themed shopping mall of 82,750 square metres, 5,400 parking spaces, and other associated facilities (Figure 2.8). All these development components are divided into seven packages, taken up by developers either on their own or in the form of consortia. The station was opened in 1998, and the shopping mall was opened in 2007; the last package, featuring one of the world's tallest towers, was completed in 2011. With a master plan developed by the British architect Terry Farrell and iconic office and hotel towers designed by the American architectural firm Kohn Pedersen Fox – much of these made possible by the rich experiences and astute skills of Wong & Ouyang of Hong Kong – this development has become one of the most desired locations in Hong Kong for shopping, living, and working. By 2010, the highest property price for the Cullinan – its high-end residential towers – reached 70,000 Hong Kong dollars (9,000 US dollars) per square foot, a historical record high. The Kowloon Station development model is a culmination of a process of experiments that produced, over a period of thirty years, other less exaggerated, but equally compelling, examples: New Town Plaza in Shatin, Marina Square in Tsing Yi, Times Square in Causeway Bay, Pacific Place in Admiralty, Gateway in Tsim Sha Tsui, Taikoo Place and Cityplaza in Tai Koo Shing, Sunshine City in Ma On Shan, Festival Walk in Kowloon Tong, Langham Place in Mongkok. All these developments rely heavily on mass transit rail links supplemented by other forms of public transport, and mixed developments as destinations. All of them have been very successful in generating profit on the one hand and a form of life on the other; despite stylistic difference, they feature similar deliberate isolation from the city as terminal developments. Major Hong Kong developers, such as Wharf Holdings, Hong Kong Land, Henderson Land, Sino Land, Cheung Kong Properties, Sun Hung Kai Properties, New World Development, have significant property developments in China; many of them follow the successful formula refined over a long period of time in Hong Kong.

The basic enabling factor that produced terminal developments is similar to that which formed the development of urban areas such as Golders Green in London in the early twentieth century, when the expansion of an urban railway gave rise to the possibility of new settlement areas. This was a particular kind of 'new town' settlements, which followed a development logic perhaps first practised systematically through the colonial settlements of ancient Greek cities. Hong Kong has adopted many strategies developed during the New Town and Garden City movements in the early twentieth century, when, from the 1950s, mass migration from China caused acute housing shortages. Here, mass transit is the key; while aiming to move a large amount of people fast and cheaply, mass transit creates new development opportunities. The combination of mass transit railway and shopping perhaps first emerged in Tokyo in the early twentieth century when department stores began to offer the construction of railway stations that are directly connected to, and bear the names of, the department stores. In Hong Kong, these first experiments have been expanded tremendously. In particular, several conditions conspired to create Kowloon Station as an epitome of the station-based real estate ideal: the capacity of developers in Hong Kong to gather large amounts of capital to develop sites along a mass transit railway, the desire to create a new airport by the last British administration before the handover in 1997, Hong Kong government's 'state capitalism' embedded in the institution of the MTRC, and the extraordinarily high level of public participation in real estate speculation in Hong Kong. Kowloon Station resulted, in crucial ways, from the creation and maintenance of ever-larger systems of urban functions as capital investment instead of public welfare, as both a need and a consequence of international finance. Kowloon Station is a crucial part of the Airport Core Programme (ACP), first conceived by the Hong Kong government in May 1989 in the wake of the 1984 negotiations between China and Britain over Hong Kong's post-1997 future. The ACP aimed at upgrading Hong Kong's infrastructure as part of an enormous 'revamp' of Hong Kong; it was a massive infrastructural development which included a new airport, two railway lines linking the city and the airport (31.1 and 34.8 kilometres respectively), and five stations with commercial development potentials (Hong Kong Central, Kowloon, Olympic, Tsing Yi, Tung Chung). Among the stations, Kowloon Station is without doubt the most outstanding in scale and complexity. The MTRC secured government consent with regard to the use of airspace above stations, and was free to enter into agreements with property developers who would develop according to design standards established by the MTRC, and who share the profit with the MTRC when property was sold. The total area for commercial development of the ACP is 63 hectares, which results in approximately 3.5 million square metres of real estate space. The Hong Kong government, in the process, collected large premiums on the land/airspace sales in the order of over 40 billion dollars.[18] The five development sites around five stations contributed 28,000 residential units, eight office towers, six shopping centres and almost 3,000 hotel rooms.[19] As expected by the Hong Kong government, the government and MTRC development costs of these sites were reimbursed by property developers as up-front cash payments when development packages were awarded; this reimbursement was then credited into the property development.

As a government-owned and listed transportation company, the MTRC, in the years straddling the handover of Hong Kong in 1997, was catapulted to the key role to reinvent Hong Kong. From inception, the MTRC achieved its financial viability through unregulated train fares, focus on high volume and profit margin rail developments, a high degree of managerial autonomy despite its being a government-owned corporation, and privileged access to real estate development rights.[20] Despite the public disputes between suspicious Chinese and British governments over the financing of the ACP projects for many years before the 1997 handover, the MTRC had skilfully secured a profitable future for all the developments along the airport rail lines, with the help of credits from more than 170 local and internal financial institutions and banks.[21] In this sense, the MTRC is an extraordinary example of neoliberalism: a government utilities company that managed to be profitable throughout its existence.

In the larger scheme of things, particularly from a perspective of finance, Hong Kong's Mass Transit Railway Corporation does not seem to care if there is a 'station' at all in urban and architectural terms, unlike those in the era when train stations such as King's Cross, Paddington, Central Station, among countless others, commanded a strong and unmistakable urban and spatial presence. Kowloon Station, for all its grand claims, functional efficiency, and technological sophistication, is architecturally nothing but a name; its subterranean existence has been reduced to the minimum in the forms of information boards, mechanized barriers, electro-magnetic payment systems and signage. Although terminal developments are located in the city, they do not seem to be interested in the city; they aim to capture the travelling mass for as long as possible within the development. In this sense, terminal developments are very different from the American suburban shopping mall, which, for all its predictable banality, is a clear spatial construct – a standalone monumentality of shopping surrounded by dedicated road and parking spaces. A terminal development in Hong Kong is a set of signage-enabled internal circulation routes linking many different functions. One has little direct spatial sense as to where one enters the development and where one parks the car: everything seems to need a barcode and a user's manual. The architecture of terminal developments conspires to reinvent this spatial obfuscation enthusiastically; the inward-looking nature of the development is highly exaggerated by the architecture that exposes to the city, without aesthetic pretension, its mechanical supply, operative and discharge systems – transformer rooms, car park entrances, HVAC (heating, ventilating, and air conditioning) exhausts, loading and unloading bays, drop-off and pick-up zones. This feature is both a result of building regulations demanding street accesses to mechanical facilities and a strategy to replace street life with interior malls. It does not need a city in order to work, just like in a hydroponic farm where plants do not need soil to grow.

The act of design, in the normative sense, is progressively replaced by what may be described as quantity management, a crucial activity that begins and ends with financial calculations. The framework for calculation is largely defined by maximum allowable quantities of real estate, and an estimated level of pricing of real estate. Under Hong Kong's planning law, the Outline Zoning Plan (OZP), Kowloon Station is given the status of a 'comprehensive development', where multi-functional developments at a quantity of an average of approximately eight times the site area (average plot ratio of eight) can be constructed; here the complex amalgamation of apartment units, podium clubhouses, hotels, office towers, premium shopping malls are mixed carefully; mass transit links, public buses, mini-buses, taxis, and private cars are integrated into the calculation as the number of people and the feasibility of the development are intimately connected. All these numbers are calculated to respond to market conditions: sizes, quantity, and grades of finishing of apartment units, offices, hotels, shopping malls. All these decisions – long before architects begin to 'design' – are guided by myriad consultants specializing in quantity management. Following these quantity-based decisions, the primary task of architectural design is one that invents circulations – perhaps duplicating the circulation of capital as its fundamental logic – in this maze of calculated quantities while fulfilling environmental, hygienic, and fire safety regulations in Hong Kong. If 'community' featured as one of the highest design ideals for the architectural profession for much of its long history, 'circulation' has now taken over community as the new design ideal, one that takes architecture not as enabling settings for social life, but as a crucial instrument to scale up and speed up financial transactions. Despite its height, the office tower called International Commerce Centre (ICC) is extruded from standard, formulaic, and conventional office and hotel layouts. Perhaps the deepest impact of this design by quantity management can be found in the apartment units. The sizes and grades of finishing of apartment units are very sensitive to market fluctuations, and are often controlled tightly; for Kowloon Station, the packages with apartment buildings are all designed by local architectural firms with deep knowledge and experience of the real estate market in Hong Kong. Again, standardization is the key; it is the key feature that turns architecture into a financial product, with pricing levels responding to key standard indicators such as the number of rooms, floor-to-floor heights, direction and type of views, as well as the number of facilities offered in the clubhouses, such as swimming pools, sports courts, dining and entertainment facilities. This is architecture's approximation of the manufactured goods as a system, which, since the Industrial Revolution, 'imposes its own coherence and thus acquires the capacity to fashion an entire society'.[22] At Kowloon Station, this capacity to fashion an entire society reached an extraordinary level. The numerical accounting of the quantity of provision far outweighs any qualitative descriptions of spatial design; it certainly has a much stronger and immediate impact on the pricing levels of apartment units. On the other hand, standardization reduces construction cost and time, which is crucially important to the return on investment; relentless vertical extrusion, in this sense, is designed by financial calculation rather than by the profession of architecture. The resulting skeleton from these quantity management activities predetermines the design of architecture.

Alan Colquhoun characterized the architecture of finance in the 1970s as the rise of the 'superblock', large and homogenous blocks of structures in cities that no longer saw human community as their primary concern. Superblocks, Colquhoun says, are a 'fact of the modern capitalist state'; 'it is not simply a new type to be added to the repertoire of the city but a type of types, whose presence is rapidly destroying the traditional city'.[23] If Colquhoun sensed with great discomfort the rise of capital in architecture, Kowloon Station signals the final triumph of capital's colonization of architecture. Kowloon Station provides an early twenty-first-century version of the superblock, with a single project of 1.06 million square metres of space (approximately the size of Canary Wharf in London), forming part of a gigantic airport infrastructural project costing 35.1 billion Hong Kong dollars (approximately 4.5 billion US dollars), an enormous sum raised through a combination of government funding, developers' upfront premium payments, and loans raised from more than 170 international financial institutions and banks.

Terminal developments are terminal in three ways: as destinations, barriers, and a possible end of architecture. As destinations, it is apparent that terminal developments are focused on providing a complete set of functions of life artificially – from air to subjectivity – which blends realities with simulations. As barriers, terminal developments imagine themselves urbanistically as gigantic intake and discharge machines, drawing in motivated and pre-prepared consumers on the one hand, and spitting out dirty and hot air, traffic, consumption and human waste, tired and satisfied consumers on the other hand. As a possible end of architecture, terminal development in Hong Kong enjoys enormous success, and reproduces its basic form and strategy in the city with or without the involvement of architects. If capital drives urban developments, and succeeds most dramatically in terminal developments in Chinese cities, then we are confronted with a critically important emerging urban reality.

The City of Economic Specialization

If Hong Kong is an experiment, China offers many chances of application. What made this application a reality was an amendment in 1988 to the Chinese Constitution: prior to the amendment, the Constitution (Article 10) and the Land Management Law stated that all urban land belongs to the state; land in the countryside and in suburban areas is under collective ownership. The 1988 amendment, without abandoning this principle, allowed the transfer of land-use rights. On paper, this momentous change effectively put China under a similar condition as prevailed in Hong Kong: the government owns the land and creates the opportunity to profit from its development. In practice, it unleashed enormous uncertainties and created numerous unforeseen consequences. This was part of several important changes that include a shift from planned economy to market economy, and decentralization from central government to local government.[24] Endlessly fluid, this release of land from non-commercial possession to the possibility of sale and rent has generated a huge level of enthusiasm and grievances connected to financial gain and loss. The landscape of power in China has decisively shifted because of this change; more importantly, it has shifted in the form of city building. During the thirty years between 1978 and 2008, the urbanization rate in China rose from 18 per cent to 45 per cent; this meant that 357 million farmers either moved to cities or transformed their villages into towns. The number of cities in China, over these thirty years, increased from 193 to 655.[25] In traditional urban areas, although the neatness of the laboratory conditions of Hong Kong are absent in China, there are many features of urban development in China that are rooted in the principle of maximum quantities already discussed in relation to Hong Kong. State ownership of urban areas is dominant in most large cities, and the ways in which various power centres have built up 'land banks' – essential for regulating price levels of real estate and for creating a buffer zone when government policies change – are surprisingly similar to practices of Hong Kong developers; only here the stakes are much higher and the methods are more rooted in the culture of connections (*guanxi*). Overseas Chinese investments were crucial in the early days of the market reform in China. Almost all Hong Kong and Singapore listed property developers, such as Cheung Kong Holdings, New World Development, Sun Hung Kai Properties, Capital Land, etc., have eagerly participated in purchasing land-use rights and developed huge commercial real estate projects. Sun Hung Kai's Dong An Market and Cheung Kong's Oriental Plaza, both in Beijing, boasted the most desirable locations of Wangfujing Street, while Capital Land's Ruffles Square in Chengdu touted a design by Steven Holl. These projects followed closely their well-tested experiences and development formula in Hong Kong and Singapore, and served as important lessons for the fast-growing Chinese developers. With the virtual abandonment of the public housing programme in China, private housing development now occupies 70 per cent of the real estate market.[26] As in Hong Kong, the government – both central and local – balances precariously between fuelling and cooling speculation to achieve a balance between income and social discontent.

It is on the urban fringe that the Chinese urbanization process departs from the Hong Kong and Singapore models. In a move in 2001 that inspired an enormous trend in China, Shanghai decided to develop a new city called Songjiang about 30 kilometres southwest of the traditional city centre, combining a series of development components including industry, a university town (an enormous walled compound 'campus' enclosing seven universities), a themed development (Thames Town), and a huge amount of real estate (Figure 2.9). This is known as the One City, Nine Towns Development Plan. Thames Town, which houses the exhibition hall of the whole Songjiang new city, is clearly presented as its star attraction, and the universities are its anchor tenants. Songjiang, with Thames Town and the universities at its heart, is strategically planned with another nine smaller themed towns – Italian, German, Dutch, French, American, local waterway towns – as parts of an enormous web of urbanization. This development, which is now imitated in many other cities in China, achieved a much higher level of financial success than both the inner city re-development and the industry-based 'development zones' in the 1990s.[27] Songjiang's transportation links are excellent, combining highway, mass transit rail, and

Understanding the Chinese City

Figure 2.9 Model of Songjiang, Shanghai

high speed train line. Its success was indicated by the decision in 2011 of the Songjiang government to expand the population of the new city from the original 600,000 to 1.1 million, and its area from 60 to 160 square kilometres.[28] For the rest of China, this 'new city movement' takes many different forms: new government headquarters, central business districts, zones for major international events such as the 2008 Olympic Games and 2010 Asian Games, and World Exposition.

What emerged from this rapid development at the urban fringe is what may be described as the village of maximum quantities, a phenomenon more clearly seen in Southern China, where villages were skilled in their negotiation of land rights with municipal governments when their village land was forced to be 'sold' for new developments. As a result and over time, some villages lost their farm land but kept their village area; they are surrounded by much larger and taller buildings in cities. Villagers formed shareholding companies and engaged in many forms of property development, riding on the rising property prices brought about by the transformation of rural land into urban areas around them. Villagers built ferociously on their small lots with tall buildings, in a way perhaps matched only by Kowloon Walled City in Hong Kong; Shenzhen by 2004 had a village population density of 230,000 per square kilometre.[29] These buildings are known as 'handshaking buildings' as the narrowness of the gaps between buildings enabled higher-floor residents in neighbouring buildings to touch one another. They were built in this way to increase total rentable areas and to secure resale values through the increased total floor areas, mirroring the way in which municipal governments treated their land. Already, the urban villages around the Pearl River Delta, with their proximity to the city and their newly added floor areas, specialized in certain areas to find an economic role. Rental income is the usual starting point, but there are also extraordinary examples, such as Dafen Village in Shenzhen where in 1989 a Hong Kong businessman named Huang Jiang started an oil painting workshop to produce commercial oil paintings, as well as to provide training for villagers to learn how to paint in oil. In 2008, the village transformed from its original 300 villagers to include about 5,000 employees (its *huagong*, or painter-workers), selected through annual copying competitions. They work in about 800 workshops producing an amazing variety of copies of all oil paintings for office lobbies and hotel rooms world-wide. Today, Dafen is a renowned destination, earning itself a place at the 2010 Shanghai Expo Best Urban Practices Pavilion, partly through the determined promotion of the architectural practice of Urbanus in Shenzhen.

Further away from the urban centres and the urban fringes, there is something even more interesting taking place. This is the urbanization of the eastern half of rural China, where urbanization becomes more unique when compared with the experiences of Hong Kong and Singapore. While the urbanization of the western half of rural China was led by large industrial complexes and therefore cities and towns were built to support enterprises, the urbanization of the eastern half of rural China was driven by the clustering of small to medium-sized enterprises. The urban developments of the eastern half of rural China, particularly the provinces of Jiangsu and Zhejiang, surprised all observers. Traditionally, the Chinese imperial administration did not penetrate to the village level; the smallest administrative unit was the county, situated in the county capital city (*xiancheng*). The vast countryside was essentially regulated by family clans and kinship structure of many sizes and characters,[30] a social fact that was recognized by the first generation of Chinese sociologists such as Fei Xiaotong.[31] From the 1950s, a radical change took place under the communist leadership; all land was collectivized and all kinship structure was abolished. This traumatic and painful change transformed the Chinese countryside for good, and laid down the foundation for their urbanization from the 1980s. After decades of resistance to collectivization,[32] peasants in China finally achieved a legitimate status for their private business in the early 1980s. Combining the tradition of kinship organization and the heritage of communes, a spectacular explosion of enterprising energy swept through Jiangzu and Zhejiang provinces.

There are several types of self-organization that emerged from these developments; all of them seem to have relied on the principle of high concentration of enterprises as a way to gain competitive advantage. The first can be described as 'cluster type' (Wenzhou Model). In the city of Wenzhou in Zhejiang Province, for instance, there are more than 1,000 small and medium enterprises making lighters, producing 80 per cent of the lighters sold throughout the world.[33] In the town of Datang, part of Zhuji city in Zhejiang Province, 65 per cent of China's socks and one-third of the world's socks in 2010 were made by over 10,000 enterprises, employing 200,000 people.[34] There are more than 650 clusters of enterprises, each specializing in small amounts of commodities in enormous quantities, making up 70 per cent of the economic output of Zhejiang Province.[35] The advantages in logistics, distribution, technological transfer and quality of products are clear in this model, and it has been perhaps the most resilient and successful in the creation of production capacities and in urbanization.

The second model can be described as 'paternal type'. One of the most extraordinary examples of this organizational type is the city of Hengdian, which is perhaps better known as the Hollywood of China due to a lengthy story in the *Hollywood Reporter*. Hengdian's rise to fame owes a great deal to a curious mixture of kinship culture and the communist heritage, and under the strong personal leadership of a single man, Xu Wenrong. Xu founded Hengdian Group in 1990, a 'collectively owned' organization that encompasses a wide range of enterprises; it also took on the entire task of community development through its projects of schools, hospitals, urban infrastructure, and the inclusion of poor villages that were not part of the Hengdian Group.[36] In this sense, the development of Hengdian is that of the Hengdian Group, which began from a small silk factory in the 1980s and expanded to the high technology sectors such as hard and soft magnets and drugs manufacturing in the 1990s. In 1999 Hengdian Group invested in grass, cattle, and milk products, leasing 30,000 hectares of alkaline land in Shangdong Province; from 1996, it began an ambitious programme of building full-size replicas of many historical sites, both in existence (the Forbidden City of Beijing) and no longer existing (the Central area of Hong Kong in the late nineteenth century and the second-century imperial palace of the Qin dynasty) (Figure 2.10). Xu made these amazing reconstructions available free of charge to film crews, resulting in a dramatic increase in films and television dramas made in Hengdian, making it the unrivalled film and television production

Figure 2.10 Full-size replica of the Qin dynasty capital, Hengdian, Zhejiang Province

base. The food and lodging businesses of Hengdian profited from the influx of people, and the residents of Hengdian took part in the film production as extras. In many ways, Hengdian, in the form of the paternalistic Hengdian Group, has been more successful than Wenzhou in its policy of inclusion. Singapore, despite its colonial history and cosmopolitan outlook, is similar to the Hengdian Model in its heavy investment in infrastructure, health care, and education for all, high technological industries initiated by government-owned institutions (Jurong Corporation and Tamasek Holdings), and above all, in its paternalistic governance forged by one man, Lee Kwan Yew.

The third type of development is 'market type'. This seems to be uncommon as it requires a certain scale of economy for it to exist. As a city exclusively dedicated to the wholesale market, Yiwu is an astonishing result of the Zhejiang peasant industries and the enterprising skills of its people. Yiwu has over 62,000 stalls covering an area of 4.3 million square metres, selling over 1.7 million products across 43 industries, from 100,000 manufacturing enterprises. It is the largest commodity wholesale market in the world.[37] These stalls, in a way, are what Yiwu is all about: a *non-plus ultra* of

Figure 2.11 Shops at Yiwu, Zhejiang Province

commodities market for China and the world, gathering with great gusto products produced by village and town industries (Figure 2.11). Its population reflects the nature of this trading city: Yiwu has a population of 740,000, but non-Yiwu residents reached 1.43 million in 2010, with a daily movement of traders of 200,000 people. While having no particular history of Muslim influence, Yiwu now features many Middle Eastern restaurants and a mosque, reflecting the increasing importance of Muslim traders in the city. Yiwu's 2010 GDP is 61.4 billion Renminbi, an amazing feat for a place where merely thirty years ago villagers had great difficulty in securing basic food and shelter.

Through these three types of development and a mixture of them – the small enterprise cluster, the collective and paternalistic enterprise, and the commodities market – vast stretches of urbanization are taking place throughout eastern China. It has powerful influences in the rest of China. Xu Wenrong made his intention very clear: 'the future of peasants lies in urbanization';[38] rather than migrating to cities and taking on jobs no city dwellers are willing to do, Xu urges peasants to build cities in the countryside, living the lives of city people without leaving the countryside. To realize this, in 1995 Hengdian invited the Planning Department of Tongji University to carry out urban planning, and Yiwu proudly presents its urban planning by the Zhejiang Planning

Institute into the year 2020. These newly emerged rural cities have thrived because of their ability to offer, in the larger economy, products and services with maximum value at minimum cost through specialization and clustering. Together with the developments in the large cities, urban villages, and urban fringes, these self-grown cities bring substance and detail to the amazing urbanization processes centred on the four major areas in China: the Pearl River Delta, the Yangtze River Delta, the Beijing–Tianjin Axis, and the Chengdu–Chongqing Basin.

Notes

1. Li Shiqiao, 'Concealment and Exposure: Imagining London after the Great Fire', in Ryan Bishop, Greg Glancey and John Phillips, eds, *The City as Target* (London and New York: Routledge, 2012), pp.180–99.
2. Hugh Ferriss, *The Metropolis of Tomorrow* (New York: Ives Washburn, 1929).
3. Lewis Mumford, *The City in History: Its Origins, Its Transformations, and Its Prospects* (San Diego, New York and London: Harvest Books, 1961), pp.348, 392.
4. Laurent Gutierrez, Valérie Portefaix, and Ezio Manzini, eds, *HK Lab* (Hong Kong: Map Book Publishers, 2002).
5. www.heritage.org/index/ranking, accessed 2 September 2013.
6. Milton Friedman, 'Asian Values: Right …', *National Review* 49 (31 December 1997), pp.36–37.
7. www.hkcss.org.hk/cm/cc/press/documents/2010poverty.doc, accessed 29 June 2011.
8. B. Renaud, F. Pretorius and B. Pasadilla, *Markets at Work: Dynamics of the Residential Real Estate Market in Hong Kong* (Hong Kong: Hong Kong University Press, 1997), p.27.
9. Ibid.
10. Ibid. p.28; Stephen M. Rowlinson and Anthony Walker, *The Construction Industry in Hong Kong* (Hong Kong: Longman, 1995).
11. Alice Poon, *Land and the Ruling Class in Hong Kong*, second edition (Hong Kong: Enrich Professional Publishing, 2011).
12. B. Renaud et al., *Markets at Work*, p.28.
13. Julia Wilkinson, 'A Chinese Magistrate's Fort', in Greg Girard and Ian Lambot, *City of Darkness: Life in Kowloon Walled City* (Surrey: Watermark Publications, 1993), pp.60–71.
14. Ibid., p.67.
15. www.demographia.com/db-intlua-area2000.htm, accessed 13 July 2011.
16. Esther Lorenz, 'Real Image, Fake Estate', *The International Journal of Design in Society* 6:2 (2013), pp.11–26.
17. Rikkie Yeung, *Moving Millions: The Commercial Success and Political Controversies of Hong Kong's Railways* (Hong Kong: Hong Kong University Press, 2008), p.4.

18 Omega Centre, Bartlett School of Planning, and Hong Kong University of Hong Kong, *Hong Kong Airport Railway* (n.d.), p.77. Available at: www.omegacentre.bartlett.ucl.ac.uk/studies/cases/pdf/HK_AIRTRAIN_PROFILE_180511.pdf, accessed 26 April 2013.
19 Ibid., p.27.
20 Rikkie Yeung, *Moving Millions*, p.12.
21 Omega Centre, *Hong Kong Airport Railway*, pp.85–87.
22 Jean Baudrillard, *Selected Writings*, ed. Mark Poster (Stanford: Stanford University Press, 1988).
23 Alan Colquhoun, 'The Superblock', *Essays in Architectural Criticism, Modern Architecture and Historical Change* (Cambridge MA: The MIT Press, 1985), pp.83–103.
24 You-tien Hsing, *The Great Urban Transformation: Politics of Land and Property in China* (Oxford: Oxford University Press, 2010); Barry Naughton, *The Chinese Economy: Transition and Growth* (Cambridge MA: The MIT Press, 2007).
25 Niu Wenyuan, ed., *China's New Urbanization Report 2009* (Beijing: Science Press, 2009), pp.6–7.
26 You-tien Hsing, *The Great Urban Transformation*, p.45.
27 Ibid., chapter 4.
28 www.songjiang.gov.cn/view_0.aspx?cid=78&id=1835&navindex=0, accessed 15 July 2011.
29 You-tien Hsing, *The Great Urban Transformation*, p.129.
30 Maurice Freedman, *Chinese Lineage and Society: Fukien and Kwangtung* (London: The Athlone Press, 1966); Xiao Tangbiao, *Zongzu zhengzhi, cunzhi quanli wangluo de fenxi* (Clan Politics: An Analysis of the Web of Power in the Village Rule) (Beijing: Shangwu yinshuguan, 2010).
31 Hsiao-tung Fei (Fei Xiaotong), *Peasant Life in China: A Field Study of Country Life in the Yangtze Valley* (London: Routledge & Kegan Paul, 1939).
32 Ying Xiaoli, *Caogen zhengzhi, nongmin zizhu xingwei yu zhidu bianqian* (Grass Root Politics, the Autonomous Actions of Peasants and Systems Change) (Beijing: Zhongguo shehui kexue chubanshe, 2009).
33 Qiu Baoxing, *Duiying jiyu yu tiaozhan* (Response, Opportunity and Challenge) (Beijing: Zhongguo jianzhu gongye chubanshe, 2009), p.33.
34 www.zhuji.gov.cn/countrystreet.jsp?childcatalog_id=20040303000082, accessed 6 December 2012.
35 Qiu Baoxing, *Duiying jiyu yu tiaozhan*, p.33.
36 Xu Wenrong, *Puojie shiji nanti* (Solving the Difficult Problem of the Century) (private printing, 2003); Cheng Xiangge and Sun Shiyan, *Shichangxing gongyouzhi* (Market collective ownership) (Shanghai: Shanghai sanlian shudian, 1998).
37 http://english.yw.gov.cn/english_1/e_gyyw/e_hyc/, accessed 25 November 2013.
38 Xu Wenrong, *Puojie shiji nanti*, p.71.

3
The City of Labour

The city of maximum quantities cannot come into existence without a form of life that is grounded in a distinctive conception of labour. Labour is one of the most common features of human life; it is also an intellectually contested ground. The offerings of labour are intensely cultured activities, away from 'natural states of labour', perhaps because labour occupies a large proportion of our time and energy. The ways of labour shape the fruits of labour, leaving indelible marks on cities. The Marxist notion of labour, widely influential in the twentieth century, homogenizes labour by abstracting it from its cultural context; labour in this understanding appears as standardized and exchangeable units in value creation, serving the interest of the capital. Human lives, in this capitalist framework, are recast as quantities of labour, to be maintained, protected, divided, and harvested by the capital to fulfil its destiny of endless accumulation within a single world system.[1] The critical enterprise – that of the Frankfurt School, for instance – arising from Marxist analysis of the world capitalist economy hinges crucially on the isolated status of human labour, which is understood as having been alienated from a 'preferred condition' of human life. It is this preferred condition of human life that is a culturally formulated ideal state: it separates the good life of creative leisure and freedom from the bad life of tedious toil of subsistence. In the city of maximum quantities, however, this distinction between good and bad life is not so clearly visible; this blurred condition, as this chapter will argue, changes everything in the city, from the usage of the city to the design of architecture. Even though, since the 1980s, Hong Kong followed a familiar process of relocating its labour-intensive industries to China (spatial displacement of capital) and investing in infrastructure (temporal displacement of capital), it seems to have done so in a very different intellectual context.

Hong Kong's labour market seems to be underpinned not by the Marxist conception of labour, but by what may be described as the Chinese conception of labour. The investment pattern of Western capitalism, in slaves from other places, in cheap labour in other places, and in technology replacing both, does not seem to depict a fair picture of Hong Kong's economic activities. The employment of foreign domestic helpers from the Philippines and Indonesia in Hong Kong today may not have been modelled on the Western idea of slavery, but on a traditional Chinese conception of servitude. Instead of becoming a class of people, foreign domestic workers in Hong Kong become part of the family through the provision of a servitude that is an inherent part of the Confucianist family structure; in Hong Kong, they are often called 'sisters' (*jiejie*) by their Chinese employers as a symbolic gesture to place them within the family. Within this family structure, all are involved in the provision and reception of servitude based on hierarchies: sons to fathers, wives to husbands, sisters to brothers, and maids to mistresses. The bottom of this hierarchy is not a permanent and unchanging condition, unlike those in the caste system. Confucius exemplified this servitude by speaking to the officers of a lower grade at court freely and straightforwardly, and by speaking to officers of a higher grade with restraint and precision.[2] The Confucian formulation of the 'freedom' of the higher-ranking officials and the 'restraint' of lower-ranking officials does not seem to constitute a master and slave relationship; it defines freedom and restraint as conditional and relational. Understood in this way, labour is not seen as fragmented, repetitive and menial, which could be removed or relocated; it is by nature both free and not free, both pleasurable and laborious, a set of conditions that are naturally blended. In this sense, the accumulation of wealth through labouring activities does not lead to the transcendence of labour and class differentiations; it builds the idea of luxury to the very same layered conditions of labour. Here we find an opportunity to re-examine the meaning of labour in the Chinese city: the numerical and aesthetic sensibilities found in the city of maximum quantities are deeply bound up together with the Chinese conception of labour. If the Western city is invested in its social hierarchies formulated as class-based horizontal divisions, cultivation of manners and tastes that mark these horizontal divisions with behaviour characteristics, and spatial zonings of cities that accommodate collective practices of these behaviour characteristics, the Chinese city protects privileges in cities by physical compartmentalization, without fundamentally revising the existential meanings of labour. It is this interiorization of power in the Chinese city, rather than an outward public display of manners and tastes in the Western city, that gives rise in one important way to distinct characters of the Chinese city.

The Normative Status of Labour

The defining conception of labour in the Western cultural context is owed critically to that of the ancient Greeks, who considered one of the most crucial conditions of man – and not those of women and slaves – as 'freedom from labour'. This seems to have resulted in the production of leisure that not only defined the ancient citizenship against the backdrop of the institution of slavery, but also the contemporary bourgeoisie against the backdrop of mechanization of production. The ancient *otium ludens* (leisure and play), in recent centuries, became hobbies and pursuits unconnected to the labour of subsistence. Capitalism, through investment in means of production in the forms of slave labour, generated the wealth that enabled the divide between leisure and labour, between political life and biological subsistence, between freedom and slavery. Early Christian practices brought labour closer to spiritual life, as Lewis Mumford suggests, when manual labour was understood as possessing spiritual meaning: to labour is to pray (*ora et labora*);[3] it was a form of life that 'reduced the whole physical apparatus for bodily sustenance and ennobled work by making it a moral obligation'.[4] The Renaissance seems to have restored the divide between labour and work as it revived the intellectual conceptions of the ancient Greeks. Thorstein Veblen, in *The Theory of the Leisure Class*, described the performative realizations of bourgeois leisure through manners and estates,[5] which has featured prominently, since the Renaissance, in Western cities based on the division of labour and the definition of classes. Hannah Arendt thought that the widespread condition of labour in the twentieth century threatened to turn our contemporary society into 'the society of labourers'. In *The Human Condition*, Arendt distinguishes labour from work by tracing etymological differences between the meanings of these two words in many languages: a labourer (*animal laborans*) toils with his body to maintain the biological life in line with man's metabolism with nature; a worker (*homo faber*) creates products over and above the subsistence of life. The result of labour is ephemeral and that of work is lasting. This crucial distinction therefore constructs two quite different states of human existence, one liberal and noble, the other slavish and degrading. She criticizes Marx for failing to sustain the distinction between labour and work in his labour–value equation; this equation led to a 'glorification of labour' that threatens the quality of human life. She argued that the emancipation of labour for the first time in history, instead of attaining liberty for all, subjected all to the same conditions of labour. It is the consumer society that completely internalized the devouring character of biological life; with consumer products, the conditions of the labouring body are endlessly intensified through productivity and abundance: 'the spare time of the *animal laborans* is never spent in anything but consumption, and the more time left for him, the greedier and more craving his appetites'. This society of labourers alienated the nature of human work, and replaced it with indifferent labour.[6] Arendt's thesis is one of the most compelling, also one of the most indicative of an intellectual struggle to maintain a clear dividing line between labour and work in the West; it has a visible architectural consequence.[7]

Labour in the Chinese cultural context seems to be conceived intellectually as a condition among many, and not essentially as a lack. As a necessary and inescapable condition of human life, it is formulated as the Confucianist freedom/restraint hybrid. The Chinese language does not seem to have two separate words for labour and work: *laodong* or *laodongli* – the verb and noun forms of labour in contemporary Chinese – are relatively newly refreshed expressions from ancient texts to accommodate the ideas of Marxism as it entered into the Chinese intellectual life in the early twentieth century. *Laodong*, in a third-century biography of the renowned medicine man Hua Tuo, was used to mean 'physical exercise'.[8] In the fifth century BCE, Zuo Qiuming mentioned the notion of 'gentlemen labour with the mind, and little people labour with the body';[9] in the third century BCE, Mencius spoke of labour as being 'either mental labour or physical labour', and 'those who engage in mental labour rule, and those who engage in physical labour are ruled'.[10] Here, the distinction is one of hierarchical privilege based on power, not one of intellectual differentiation seen in the Greek divide between labour and work. 'Achievement' in the Chinese language is sometimes expressed as *gonglao*, labour's attainment; it does not seem to entertain the idea that only the kind of human activities leading to 'lasting monument' counts as 'good labour'. On the contrary, there is a highly valued sensibility among the literati that the ephemeral and the subsistential are equally significant intellectually. In the imperial imagination in China, labour sustained a legitimate position among those of hunt and games; after a century of the Mongol rule, the first Chinese emperor of the Ming dynasty (1368–1644), Hongwu (reigned 1368–98), put extraordinary emphasis on agricultural labour, instituting not only a moral code but also a set of physical restrictions on peasant mobility to ensure the exercise of daily agricultural labour.[11] Since the seventeenth century, emperors of the

Qing dynasty (1644–1912) performed their agricultural labour on a piece of ritual land of 1.3 *mu* (867 square metres) at the Xiannongtan Temple (The Temple of Agricultural Ancestors) in Beijing. Here, the symbolic toiling body engaged in agricultural labour went hand in hand with the brave body of hunt and games of the Manchu and Jurchen ancestors; the intellectual difficulty with labour found in the Greek thought seems to be largely absent here.

One of the most transformative events in twentieth-century China was Mao's great campaign in the late 1950s to introduce labour to all sectors of Chinese society; this included a 'cultural transformation' – the primary goals of the Cultural Revolution – based on peasant and folk art forms, a vision that he laid out in his policy on the arts first delivered in Yan'an in 1942. Instead of observing the Confucianist freedom/restraint hybrid in relation to labour, Mao believed in the boundless transformative power of labour, as he sent millions of Chinese government administrators and intellectuals to the countryside to engage in physical labour, requesting them to eat, live, and labour like peasants. This may have paralleled what Arendt called the 'glorification of labour' in the twentieth century, but it confirms the normative status of labour in China. This event certainly brought labour to the centre of Chinese life, blending the conditions of labour more deeply than before in Chinese cities. Behind the brutality in the execution of this campaign, which ruined countless promising intellectual careers of generations of Chinese scholars, there was a deeply held faith in the equality between mental and corporeal labour;[12] Mao's advocacy of the corrective power of labour as an existential form both responds critically to Mencius's hierarchy of labour, and runs counter to the Western instinct to denigrate labour. It perpetuates a Chinese conception: labour is both hardship and ingenuity, both tedious toil and energizing pleasure.

It may be argued, as Adam Smith's *The Wealth of Nations* did before Marx, that China's economy was driven traditionally not by the accumulation of capital, but by the production and proliferation of labour.[13] Smith thought that China's economy in the eighteenth century – by far the largest in the world in terms of gross domestic product – was a result of a 'natural course of things' in which human productive energy was first dedicated to agriculture, then to manufactures, and lastly to commerce.[14] This roughly corresponds to the social hierarchy in China that ranked people according to their importance from the highest to the lowest: scholars, peasants, craftsmen, traders. The Hongwu Emperor restricted the distance of travel for peasants to 100 *li* (58 kilometres) to discourage trade, although this was hardly enforceable and did not last very long. China regarded trade as profiting not from productivity, but from price differentiation, a form of economic life that was seen by Smith as 'unnatural and retrograde', best exemplified by Holland.[15] The seizure of 'extra-systemic resources' – spices, slaves, silver, oil – has been the foundation of capitalism in the West; Smith considered this as a form of 'capital accumulation' that cannot be sustained. The idea that China had always developed a market economy, not capitalism, is immensely important for an understanding of the Chinese society and the cities that accommodate that society. China's economic independence and rapid rise to a vibrant market economy, both in the past centuries and today, is rooted in its agricultural society, which is very different, in today's context, from the 'dependent economies' of Latin America, and the 'limited sovereignty' of Japan and Korea.[16] Through capitalism, Marx mapped the economic life of the West and critiqued the condition of labour as alienation from humanity, which echoes the Greek divide between meaningful work and subsistential labour. The Chinese conception of the normative status of labour not only points to a different form of economic life grounded in the market place, but also constructs a different city in which both the freedom and the constraint of the labouring body formulates its spaces of work, habitation, and pleasure.

The lack of a distinction between labour and work in the Chinese city is manifested by a different conception of social manners. Manners in the Western city, to think with Veblen, are the crystallization of leisure through performances that symbolically indicate class distinctions in our 'pecuniary culture'. To master and to control the subsistence-induced corporeal characteristics, as the ancient Greeks demonstrated through specific demands of standing, walking, and the control of body heat and speech, marked the distinction between free citizens and slaves and women.[17] These behaviour characteristics became increasingly codified in the Western culture, first in the courtly conducts during the Italian Renaissance, as Baldassare Castiglione's *The Book of the Courtier* (*Il Cortegiano*, 1561) and Henry Peacham's English translation *The Compleat Gentleman* (1622) demonstrated, and secondly in the cultivation of virtue and taste as the foundation for the culture of politeness in the eighteenth century. Manners, like modernity, can be seen as a product of purification: a human condition purified of animal features.[18] This framework both sustains a degree of equality among those who attained this cultivation, and justifies the use of violence against those who are judged to fall short of standards. In the Chinese city, behavioural codes are much more intensely nurtured as a hierarchical conduct instead of standard public performances. As exemplified by Confucius, people are more likely to show restraint and care in relation to those above their ranks, and freedom and friendliness among people of their own rank or below. It places tremendous strain on those at the lower end of the hierarchy to conform, and this is often construed as virtue. This rather fluid situation demands frequent shifting of behaviour modes in response to situations of interaction; often the hierarchical situations are not immediately clear. The Chinese sense of the comical, in one way, is derived from the misjudgement of behaviour codes in response to situations. Manners in this context, if there are any at all, are relational and not consistent. These very different 'manners' are crucially important to the construction and maintenance of 'connections' (*guanxi*) that are essential for an effective person to operate in the Chinese cultural context. Contrasting strongly with those found in the Western city, the conducts of people in Chinese cities appear to be most unformed among strangers where no hierarchy is perceivable; there is no *guanxi* to be established or maintained here. While the realm of strangers is constructed as public space in the Western city, it is seen to be a place with no hierarchical demands in the Chinese city. The dramatic increase of wealth in Chinese cities since the late twentieth century only intensified the relational behaviour codes of the newly rich, and did very little to establish a 'class distinction' in the line of the rise of the bourgeoisie in the West. Public conduct – from spitting to honking away pedestrians – in Chinese cities remains one of the most characteristic aspects of Chinese urban life. Relational conducts are increasingly burdened with gifts and favours to facilitate daily functions of life – from medical care to job opportunities – which demands a considerable amount of resources and cultivation as the wealth of the Chinese city increases.

The Chinese literati cultivated the hand through the arts (music, chess, calligraphy, and painting) and discernment through connoisseurship; these cannot be equated with the cultivation of manners in the West. The traditional social advancement was not through the accumulation of land and capital; these were often limited by imperial powers. Social advancement was made through imperial examinations that provided unparalleled access to imperial privilege and gentility. Connoisseurship was private and scholarly, manners are public and performative. Wealthy merchants in the Ming dynasty, unlike the European bourgeoisie, sought to take on a scholarly appearance rather than constructing and consolidating traits of a social class.[19] Social aspiration was not invested in manners, but in passing imperial examinations; successful candidates of imperial examinations became the prototype of social advancement for successful Chinese merchant families.[20] Through the demands of the examinations, the cultivated scholar would become a connoisseur of the arts. No text is more detailed and insistent on the delicate demands of connoisseurship in China than Wen Zhenheng's *A Treatise on Superfluous Things* (between 1615 and 1620), roughly the same time as Henry Peacham's influential book on manners in 1622. Wen Zhenheng (1585–1645) was the great-grandson of Wen Zhengming (1470–1559) – one of the greatest examples of the cultivated connoisseur in the Chinese cultural context – and was a member of one of the richest families in Suzhou. In his book of twelve chapters, Wen Zhenheng outlines the intricate art of distinguishing good from bad, elegant from vulgar, in relation to almost all aspects of material life – from clothing to gardening. However, Wen's *Treatise* was not a call for a reform of public manners and taste as one might find in Shaftesbury's *Characteristicks* (1711);[21] it was instead a document of private pursuits to be shared during elegant gatherings. Wen's descriptions of valuable things are much more detailed when compared to those of Castiglione, Peacham, and Shaftesbury;[22] perhaps the private and scholarly nature of Wen's connoisseurship, rather than the public and performative enterprises of his Western counterparts, allowed him to dwell at the level of details. The flourishing of literati gardens in the late Ming dynasty took place in the context of a surge of commercial culture; literati gardens, in this context, can indeed be seen as attempts to establish private spaces of connoisseurship outside a society that was increasingly dominated by the normative conditions of labour. The Ming scholar's studio, with its place in gardens and its display of the discerning taste of elegance in minute details, serves as one of the most enduring spatial achievements in China. The Chinese literati often regarded themselves as ineffective in the world of politics and administration; their writings frequently contain self-deprecating mockery and indifference to worldly affairs very different from the missionary energy of taste-building literature in the Western tradition. The elegant gatherings in the literati gardens are a form of opting out of the domination of labour rather than the denigration of labour.

Labour's Dependencies

There are two highly influential dependencies of labour that produce visible impact on the Chinese city: the normative status of labour in the Chinese city maintains the normative moral and aesthetic status of these dependencies. The first can perhaps be called identity dependency of labour. Identity dependency takes place in all cultures and cities, but it is its intensity and pervasiveness that give Chinese cities their unique features. The most effective way for those who engage in all-consuming labour to make sense of labour is by internalizing an identity narrative, a ready-made way of life that supplies an orientation of life. This often involves a placement and a reconstitution of subjectivity. Our consumer society has completely integrated this demand with strategies of commerce, making identity narratives available to everyone. Goods purchased with money become the visible proof of the meaning of labour; the illusion of possessing the meanings associated with the goods comes from the reality of owning them. While it is clearly seen to be a character of a much lower social status in Western societies – those who visit theme parks and emulate manners of higher classes are often sneered at by the cultivated and the intellectual – the Chinese society does not seem to have a parallel denigration. The moral status of 'being yourself' and that of being someone else are not distinctly different in Chinese cities. Cosplay is a form of creative identity dependency among the youth; it involves dressing up and behaving as manga characters with special powers. Although it began in Japan, like many other popular cultural trends in Asia, cosplay has a tremendous appeal to the Chinese youth

Figure 3.1 Cosplay at the Campus of the Chinese University of Hong Kong (photo by Esther Lorenz)

(Figure 3.1). It is only a matter of time before it becomes a major cultural feature in China. Getting married in China often involves the couple dressing up in at least two sets of costumes, Chinese and Western; but increasingly, the marrying couples put on thematic costumes, such as those from the traditional Chinese theatre and from the era of the Cultural Revolution. At this unique moment in life, the marrying couples engage in multiple reconstitutions of themselves, appearing in several cultural and intellectual identities. In the Chinese city, common with many other Asian cities, the youth today respond to different and often incongruous cultural demands simultaneously and equally. The ability to nimbly shift from one cultural setting to another, from one identity to another, is normal, accepted, and regarded as a source of aesthetic pleasure.

By far the most magnificent form of identity dependency is the act of purchasing a private residential unit in a themed development, undoubtedly the most costly purchase in the lives of most people. In Hong Kong, and increasingly in other Chinese cities, private residential developments are heavily themed. Valais, a low-rise residential area developed in 2010 by Sun Hung Kai Properties at Kwu Tung in the northern part of the New Territories, is an example of this literal theming. The development is made of three-storey townhouses with a total of 132 units, but it is designed and promoted as a generic Swiss village, with its surrounding low hills described as having an Alpine atmosphere and its internal circulation routes named accordingly as Interlaken Avenue and Rhein Avenue, etc. Most property developments take a rather blended approach to theming, often mixing different architectural features and not committed deeply to identifiable details of specific places. These developments, such as Lake Silver in Ma On Shan and The Palazzo in Shatin, have been very popular with buyers; they have been able to command much higher prices compared with older and more plain-looking residential developments nearby with similar apartment layouts and sizes. Theming is well practised and successful in Hong Kong, and it has become enormously popular in China. In Beijing, the property developer Zhang Yuchen built a loose replica of Château de Maisons-Laffitte; in Hangzhou, another developer, Huang Qiaoling, built a replica of the White House; in Shanghai, yet another developer, Li Qinfu, built a replica of the United States Capitol, topped by a three-ton statue of the developer himself.[23]

Theming took place in Shanghai in the form of new towns, under the One City, Nine Towns Development Plan adopted by Shanghai in 2001. This development inspired a nation-wide theme town movement that resulted in countless replicas – both amazingly thorough and shockingly loose – of almost all desirable locations in the world. For these developments in Shanghai, international competitions were held, with the foreign firms being told explicitly to build 'the spatial identity and quality of their own countries'.[24] In addition to cultural theming – English, Canadian, Italian, Dutch, Scandinavian, Spanish, and Chinese – there are also a number of functionally and ideologically themed towns such as port city and ecological city. Among all the themed towns, Thames Town stands out as perhaps the most committed effort to create a generic but distinctive English town by using a complete set of kitsch styles and objects, down to the fencing details and street furniture (Figure 3.2). On the other hand, the English appearance is only skin deep; inside these amazing-looking buildings, the spaces are rather similar to other Chinese residential and commercial developments. The British firm Atkins Design Studio designed Thames Town with 'terraced townhouses, detached villas, a town hall, a church (an almost exact replica of a church in Bristol, UK) and, most importantly, a "pub"'; Atkins claims that the Thames Town 'looks uncannily close to the original yet it is very different'.[25] Atkins justifies this obviously unusual project for an architectural firm in a Western city – a possible embarrassment to Western architects – by claiming that there was a demand and it was a pragmatic task to satisfy this demand in Shanghai. In 2010, the occupation rate of Thames Town was below 20 per cent, and most of the ground floor shops were empty; instead,

Figure 3.2 Thames Town, Songjiang, Shanghai

it became very popular as a setting for wedding photography, fulfilling a high demand for Western-style marriages. A small town in Guangdong Province, a residential project under construction in 2011 dressed up as a replica of Hallstatt, the UNESCO world heritage site in Austria, pushes this trend to a dramatic height. The apparent lack of any sense of irony and fantasy marks an important difference between these themed developments in China and the theme parks such as the Casinos in Las Vegas, Disneyland, and Universal Studios in America. Themed developments are not replacements of theme parks in China; between 1990 and 2005 there were about 2,500 theme parks opened in China.[26] Themed developments in China are for habitation rather than for entertainment; they fulfil a demand for identity dependency on a grand scale. It is perhaps inevitable that identity dependencies in the Chinese city will begin to manifest themselves in more sophisticated and creative ways in the future. These amazing cities in China stand as evidence of the wide-ranging urban consequences of the normative status of labour.

The second dependency may be called chance dependency of labour. The diligence and endurance of the labouring body forms a strong contrast with its passive belief in fate; perhaps the absence of self-determination as the primary condition of labour is internalized and inverted as a faith. A magnificent expression of this faith in chance can be found in the ancient canonical text *Book of Changes*, which laid out a set of chance-derived predictions through its sixty-four hexagrams. Perhaps the most common form of chance dependency of labour is seen through its daily use as what may be called 'chance narratives' – endless accounts of located forces capable of changing the course of life – which can be both conventional and creative. Often these narratives appear as 'micro chance narratives', such as those related to numbers; their most direct impact on a city like Hong Kong would be the missing floor numbers related to four (the pronunciation of four is similar to that of death) and the high values attached to eight (the pronunciation of eight is similar to that of prosperity). The number narratives are numerous and complex; they connect with the various numerical schemes in the Chinese cultural context discussed in Chapter 1. Common conventional chance narratives are also concerned with the presence of a large variety of gods influencing almost all aspects of life; often they have an architectural expression in the form of altars dotted around the city and in the interiors dedicated to these gods. Chief among these is the Earth God, an imaginary landlord who, if appeased appropriately, would ensure the proper and prosperous use of the land. The fate of the actions of the living therefore is often narrated as being in the hands of these gods. These gods are clearly not the same as those in what may be described as 'grand chance narratives' – those of major religions – which demand complete and exclusive devotion; chance narratives in the Chinese city are much more open and accommodating, devoid of demands of renouncements and incitement of violence. *Fengshui*, together with fortune-telling, may be seen as creative chance narratives. *Fengshui* has been a crucially important practice in all urban and building processes in traditional Chinese cities; it has maintained its importance consistently in cities such as Hong Kong and Singapore. *Fenghsui* declined in China in the era of the Cultural Revolution, and is regaining its status today. A creative combination of common sense, micro chance narratives, and the contents of the *Book of Changes*, *fengshui* brings chance dependency into architecture, influencing the decisions of directions of entry, partitions of spaces, uses of materials, schemes of decoration, placement of furniture, and so on. In Hong Kong, I. M. Pei's Bank of China building has been regarded as having bad *fengshui* as its dramatic angular forms – despite its great aesthetic potential in the creation of intense prisms and shadows – produce aggressive and destructive energy; Norman Foster's HSBC has its entry escalators angled in a particular direction to create the good flow of site energy; Wong and Ouyang's Hang Seng Bank ensures all its corners are rounded up smoothly to underpin the smoothness of its operations. Despite the use of contemporary building construction and management expertise in these buildings, the role of *fengshui* remains distinctive and powerful.

Nothing is more magnificent than the most amazing rise of casinos in Macau as the aesthetic outburst of the chance dependency of labour in the Chinese city. Gambling on horses, a highly popular activity in Hong Kong which made Hong Kong Jockey Club an extremely wealthy and influential organization, already provides an aesthetic expression of the chance dependency of labour; here, gamblers on the chances of horses winning races are less concerned with the aesthetics of the combatant origins of horsemanship associated with the chivalric tradition dating back to the medieval Europe, nor with the fascination with horsemanship in imperial courts of the Han and Tang dynasties. Culturally, the Chinese have always had an ambiguous sentiment towards horses which symbolized the alienating ways of life of nomadic tribes.[27] Casinos are different from horse racing; as Hong Kong makes casino gambling illegal, Macau has for many decades served as the destination of the gambling population in Hong Kong. Increasingly, Macau now serves the gambling populations in China; in 2010,

Macau's gross gaming and gambling revenue totalled 23.5 billion US dollars with its thirty-three casinos, and in 2006, with a revenue of 6.95 billion dollars, it had already surpassed that of Las Vegas, estimated at 6.5 billion US dollars. Although a common feature in many cities, casinos have a special importance in the city of labour. It is perhaps the highest aesthetic expression of the chance dependency of labour: devoid of economic purpose, the chance of winning is pure and the bet can be limitless. Most important of all, the reward of the casino is labour-free – a stylized speculation with instantaneous results – which commands perhaps the highest aesthetic value. This heightened aesthetic sense is certainly brought out by the architecture of Macau's casinos; it departs most wilfully from any recognizable connections of functions in its construction of illusions, indulgence in fantastic forms, and provision of pleasures (Figure 3.3). The theming strategies from Las Vegas have played important roles in Macau's fast rise to prominence in the gambling world and in the architecture of fantasy; it will no doubt combine with the Chinese gambling tradition to produce new generations of casinos in Macau. The Chinese city of labour, with its seemingly endless capacity to develop dependency-induced activities and architecture, is producing a spatially and visually distinctive environment on an enormous scale.

Figure 3.3 The Grand Lisboa, Macau

Uniformity in Abundance

If the Western city is dominated by the division of labour and the definition of class, the Chinese city can perhaps be characterized as resulting from a convergence of similar goals regardless of wealth and hierarchy. The differentiation in Chinese cities seems to be a matter of quantity, not of kind. This results in a seemingly contradicting condition: behind the abundance of things, there is an underlying uniformity. This is very strongly suggested by similar building features found in both subsidised housing and luxury apartments on the private market in the Chinese city; the dramatic differences in prices are often a function of the cost of materials and decorations, and not one of spatial quality. Apartments with a standard layout can either be sold as low-end apartments with low-cost decorative schemes, or as luxurious apartments with thematically decorated styles with high-end materials and hardware. Similarly, shopping malls are designed and managed in close resemblance to one another, populated by similar ranges of shops. In Hong Kong, primary and secondary schools are built from government templates developed by the Architectural Services Department. Parallel to this uniformity in architecture, behaviours and career paths tend to converge towards similar standards, taking advantage of the safety and wisdom embodied in group actions.

This is not proletariatization of the middle class; rather, it is the total convergence of behaviour codes in the Chinese cultural context. One of the most noticeable consequences of this lack of differentiation has been the ever-present practice of group activities. Group activities are found in all economic and social hierarchies. Perhaps the most spectacular is group marriages, with sometimes thousands of couples performing this ritual in unison. The most intriguing is perhaps the phenomenon of 'group design creativity', a term to describe the recent emergence of a large number of creative designers and architects contributing to different parts of one large development area. This trend in architecture perhaps began in 2002 in Beijing when the developer couple Pan Shiyi and Zhang Xin took advantage of the group design logic to create the Commune by the Great Wall. The 'commune' is a collection of eleven villas and one clubhouse designed by twelve Asian architects. It served no particular purpose: the villas had no clients, their designs promoted no particular architectural trend. It was a collection of Asian designer villas in the iconic setting of the Great Wall of China, much as a traditional Chinese connoisseur would have done with cultural artefacts. The programme of commercial resort villas was retrofitted onto the 'commune' by repeating some of more functional villas on the same site, and by converting other villas to function rooms, an awkward conversion that results in many nonsensical architectural consequences.

In the meantime, the company of Pan and Zhang, SOHO, is now ranked as the largest developer in China, overseeing a vast empire of developments across the country. Around the Foshou Lake outside the city of Nanjing, on a site of 21,000 square metres, twenty-four internationally well known architects – twice the number as for the Commune by the Great Wall – gathered together with twenty-four designs between 2003 and 2005, in an apparent attempt to repeat the success of the Commune by the Great Wall; except in this case, the government of Pukou District of Nanjing was involved with an initial investment of 300 million *yuan*. Like in the case of the Commune by the Great Wall, there was no particular urban and architectural context for these houses – no clients, no programmes, no community; the collection of twenty-four designs seems to be the primary motivation for the entire project, setting a scene perhaps for future property development opportunities around the site. The Jianchuan Museum Cluster, begun in 2009 by the collector Gong Jianchuan from Sichuan Province, gathered twenty leading Chinese architects who designed about twenty-five museums on a site of 33 hectares, supported by a range of accommodation and commercial facilities. The museum cluster is made up of buildings devoted to three broad themes: the anti-Japanese war museums, Cultural Revolution museums, and vernacular cultural museums.

One notable manifestation of group design creativity is the way in which state design institutes in the Chinese city organize their design capacities. The Beijing Institute of Architectural Design (BIAD), an 'aircraft carrier' of architectural design encompassing almost all design and construction functions under one single administrative and financial framework, contains its own internal version of group design creativity. The BIAD was one of the oldest architectural design institutes which were established in the 1950s to undertake designs of important state projects such as the Great Hall of the People and the Museum of Revolutionary History flanking Tiananmen Square in Beijing. A large state-run work unit (*danwei*) from the 1950s to 1980s, it has transformed itself from the purveyor of Chinese Beaux-Arts style into a powerhouse of contemporary architectural design since the 1980s. It now designs almost every kind of environmental project, offering reliable professional services from conception to construction, which are now eagerly sought by Chinese developers. In collaboration with international architects such as Paul Andreu and Norman Foster, the BIAD completed the National Theatre in Beijing and Beijing International Airport. It played an essential role in the design and development of the Olympic Village for the 2008 Beijing Olympic Games. The most extraordinary feature in its transformation from a drab state enterprise to a competitive design institute is related to its management of design talents within its institutional framework. Within its enormous constitution – with almost 1,500 professionals in 2009 – there is a system of 'design ateliers' (*suo*) which enjoy a semi-autonomous status, and the possibility of a 'free-market' of design talents between different 'ateliers'. This competition within the same institutional framework has worked wonderfully well, both financially and in terms of the improvement of quality of design. In 2010, the BIAD promoted an event called 'The Young People at the BIAD', exhibiting seven architects and their works as the creative forces of the BIAD. In an attempt to build its own creative content in order to emerge from the shadows of its more well-known international design partners in many of its high-profile projects, the BIAD taps into the idea of group design with great effectiveness; it is both confident and full of ambition to strengthen its design capabilities and its market share in the global context. The BIAD is one design institute among many in China with the heritage of state-owned enterprises; like the BIAD, many of them have achieved similar status in China.

The convergence towards similar goals, as a normative state of things, leads to visual and audio characteristics in Chinese cities. Here, the physical realities of the city of maximum quantities and the aesthetic and moral values of the normative status of labour are joined up through complementary forces. More is more: it is seen to be abundant fruits of labour, not as meaningless repetitions and disorderly clutters. There is uniformity in abundance. Things, spaces, and urban designs appear in profusion: great administrative centres, reconstituted traditional shopping streets, brand new board walks along waterfronts, fantastic new town developments, appear in multiple copies throughout China. This process can be both successful in its speed in reproducing proven development models, and brutal in its disregard towards environmental and design heritage of specific locations. The visual effect of this seemingly never-ending repetition is complemented by the audio effect of a cacophony of sounds. One of the most interesting features of Chinese cities is perhaps its aversion to silence; spiritual and mourning rituals are often not conducted in silence, but in sounds of repetition. For centuries, musical and theatrical performances competed with the loud chatter and shouting in the teahouses in China. In the literati gardens, it was not the silence of the monastic life and the library, but the chirping of birds, the flowing of water, the dripping of rain on leaves, and the blowing of wind through the leaves that set the acoustic backdrop for contemplation. Chinese parks today, open to all, tend to be filled with background music, routine announcements through loudspeakers, dance rhythms, and all kinds of sounds. In the Chinese cultural context, silence is often considered to possess the *qi* of death; a cacophony of sounds is much preferred as signs of vigour: the 'heat and noise' (*re'nao*) indicative of vibrancy. Perhaps the only legitimate place for silence is the body of restraint in front of superiors, in the Confucianist freedom/restraint formulation. The general aversion to silence is quite different compared with understandings of sounds in many other cultures, particularly in the Christian faith in which silence seems to be the precondition for an access to spirituality. As mental frameworks, transcendentality demands silence while immanence is situated in sounds. The spiritual, social, and intellectual use of silence in the Western city is extensive; as their preconditions, silence articulates preaching, speech, music, and thought in distinct ways. Silence and speech are controlled and have important roles in class differentiations in the Western city. In strong contrast, silence in Chinese cities seems to be something to be overcome, an undesirable void to be filled in with a cacophony of sounds. There is an anxiety of silence, a collective sedatephobia which responds quickly to fill all spaces with sounds: radios, televisions, loudspeakers, music are often used not as meaningful or aesthetic acoustic background, but as cacophonic space fillers. We must not understand these sounds as 'junk sounds' filling junk spaces, but as something fertile; they facilitate the convergence of similar goals, they bring together in one important way the normative status of labour with its dependencies within the city of maximum quantities. In the Chinese city, the normative spectrum of sounds does not span from the church and the library to the football match and the discotheque; it spans from the restrained body in front of superiors to the free body in front of peers, both most remarkably present during the ubiquitous eating rituals in Chinese restaurants.

In the city of maximum quantities, the acoustic abundance contributes to the material and visual abundance. In the urban context in which things and spaces appear in profusion, competitiveness of the market place tends to be brought to a cutting edge; the visual and audio abundance function crucially as ways of accessing instantaneous market and social information. Heat and noise depart from acoustic purification, but they are an important functional and aesthetic feature in relation to the city of labour. Perhaps the Chinese restaurant in contemporary Chinese cities captures the key characters of the city of labour more effectively than any other space: the ornate decorations and excessive quantities of food bring abundance to its most primary material form, the incessant chatter of the patrons and sounds from television screens initiate human relationships and business opportunities. If the Islamic city is symbolized acoustically by regular calls to prayers and the Christian city by the church bells dictating the ordered day, the Chinese city is distinguished by its perpetual amalgamations of cacophonic fluidity.

Notes

1 Immanuel Wallerstein, *The Modern World-system I: Capitalist Agriculture and the Origins of the European World-economy in the Sixteenth Century* (Los Angeles: University of California Press, 2011).
2 Confucius, *Lunyu*, Chapter 10, verse 2. Key words here follow the translation by James Legge, *The Chinese Classics*, in 7 volumes (Oxford: The Clarendon Press, 1893).
3 Lewis Mumford, *The City in History: Its Origins, Its Transformations, and Its Prospects* (San Diego, New York and London: Harvest Books, 1961), p.271.
4 Mumford, *The City in History*, p.246.
5 Thorstein Veblen, *The Theory of the Leisure Class*, ed. Martha Banta (Oxford: Oxford University Press, 2007, first published in 1899).
6 Hannah Arendt, *The Human Condition* (Chicago and London: University of Chicago Press, 1958). For quotation, see p.133.
7 Kenneth Frampton, 'The Status of Man and the Status of His Objects', *Labour, Work and Architecture* (London: Phaidon, 2002), pp.25–43.
8 Chen Shou (233–297), *San Guo Zhi, Huo Tuo Zhuan* (Records of the Three Kingdoms) (third century CE): '人体欲得劳动，但不当使极尔'.
9 Zuo Qiuming, *Zuo Zhuan* (Commentary of Zuo) (fifth century BCE): '君子劳心，小人劳力'.
10 Mencius, *Teng Wen Gong* (third century BCE), Part One: '或劳心，或劳力。劳心者治人，劳力者治于人'.
11 *The Ming Code*, trans. Jiang Yonglin (Seattle and London: University of Washington Press, 2005).
12 Mao Zedong, for instance, stressed that the goal of education is to mould 'a socialist and cultured labourer', *Maozedong xuanji* (Selected Writings of Mao Zedong) (Beijing: Remin chubanshe, 1991), Vol. 5, p.385.

13 Giovanni Arrighi, *Adam Smith in Beijing: Lineages of the Twenty-first Century* (London and New York: Verso, 2007).
14 Adam Smith, *An Enquiry into the Nature and Causes of the Wealth of Nations*, in 2 volumes (London: Methuen, 1961), pp.403–5; quoted in Arrighi, *Adam Smith in Beijing*, p.57.
15 Ibid.
16 Wang Hui, *Xiandai Zhongguo sixiang de xingqi* (The Rise of Modern Chinese Thought), in 4 volumes (Beijing: Sanlian shudian, 2008); Wang Hui, *The End of the Revolution: China and the Limits of Modernity* (London and New York: Verso, 2009).
17 Richard Sennett, *Flesh and Stone: The Body and the City in Western Civilization* (New York: W. W. Norton & Company, 1994).
18 Bruno Latour, *We Have Never Been Modern* (Cambridge MA: Harvard University Press, 1993).
19 Craig Clunas, *Elegant Debts: The Social Art of Wen Zhengming (1470–1559)* (Honolulu: University of Hawai'i Press, 2003).
20 Timothy Brook, *The Confusions of Pleasure: Commerce and Culture in Ming China* (Los Angeles and London: University of California Press, 1998), pp.210–15.
21 Li Shiqiao, *Power and Virtue: Architecture and Intellectual Change in England, 1660–1730* (London and New York: Routledge, 2006).
22 Craig Clunas, *Superfluous Things: Material Culture and Social Status in Early Modern China* (Honolulu: University of Washington Press, 2004), Chapter 2.
23 Thomas J. Campanella, *The Concrete Dragon: China's Urban Revolution and What It Means for the World* (New York: Princeton Architectural Press, 2008), p.22.
24 Harry den Hartog, 'Urbanization of the Countryside', *Shanghai New Towns: Searching for Community and Identity in a Sprawling Metropolis* (Rotterdam: 010 Publishers, 2010), p.34.
25 www.atkinsdesign.com/html/projects_masterplanning_thames.htm, accessed 9 August 2011.
26 Campanella, *The Concrete Dragon*, p.248.
27 Herrlee Glessner Creel, 'The Role of the Horse in Chinese History', *The American Historical Review* 70 (1965), pp.647–72.

謹慎

PART 2
Prudence

4
The Body in Safety and Danger

To this point, we have traced the interrelations between conceptions of quantities and their manifestations in architectural and urban forms. Instead of the master keys leading to the proportional just right, the Chinese conception of layered and distributed numerical schemes orders architecture and the city in unique ways; one of the most influential consequences of this conception of numerical schemes is that of the city of maximum quantities. Instead of the impulse to remove the conditions of labour through class differentiations, the Chinese understanding of labour as a normative human condition recasts the city of maximum quantities as the city of labour, formulating and disseminating the dependencies of labour as normative features of the Chinese city. In this part of the book, we focus on the human trait of foresight, and prudence as a resultant human behaviour. In the latter half of the twentieth century, the connections between the body and society received considerable attention in sociology in the Western intellectual context;[1] the bond between the body and the city seems equally strong.[2] If we see cities as enormous and elaborate systems to construct, maintain, and protect the body, the conceptions of potential threat and danger to the body become a critical force in the ways in which cities are shaped; in this sense, all cities materialize prudence. However, the use of threat and danger to the body is very different in different cultures; this, we argue here, leaves a large range of physical urban manifestations. In the following three chapters, these manifestations will be examined first as a corporeal condition, then as a spatial conception of degrees of care, and lastly as an antiseptic procedure in the contemporary bacterial and viral environment.

The Chinese way of life is often described as sedentary. In stressing the importance of agriculture and sericulture, it has moved along a path of civilization that presented a strong contrast with those in neighbouring territories, particularly the Eurasian steppe to the north and west of the central agricultural land. The Chinese imperial rulers seem to have demonstrated a consistent emphasis on stable social conditions for agricultural routines, such as the ideal of a peaceful empire of happy peasantry envisioned by the first Ming emperor, Hongwu (reigned 1368–98); the militant Han emperor Wudi (141–87 BCE) seems to be an exceptional case, a reaction to a long period of Han policy of appeasement. For the highly mobile and militarily powerful peoples symbolized by the archer on horseback, plunder and retreat had been weighed against agriculture and settlement;[3] to a greater or lesser extent, the Xianbeis, the Mongols, and the Manchus originating from the northern Eurasian steppe had chosen to settle on the central agricultural land after their military conquests. To take this step was not just a matter of relocation, but a matter of a far-reaching intellectual change; it is little wonder that all of them converged towards the existing Chinese culture which had been primed for a 'sedentary civilization'. At the heart of this Chinese culture was an all-consuming commitment to prudence; this is all the more remarkable when it is pitched against the notion of prudence in the Western civilization. Perhaps the most primary site for prudence is that of the body. The Western conception of prudence is characteristic of the proportional thought in the sense that prudence is only a positive human trait when it is just right, straddling, as Aristotle suggests in *Nicomachean Ethics*, between cowardice and rashness. Courage is understood as the proportional mean between cowardice and rashness.[4] From these deep and ancient roots, courage develops endless contemporary versions, such as those of the challenge of leaving one's comfort zone, and as fictional heroes and heroines teetering on the brink of failure in popular entertainment. Higher states of knowledge and human virtues are thought to have been attained in this process. Karl Popper framed the problem of scientific knowledge as one that conceives credible knowledge as possessing the potential of failure; this 'dangerous knowledge' is also the truth of knowledge.[5] 'Live dangerously!', Nietzsche exclaimed in *The Gay Science* (1882), 'Build your cities on the slopes of Vesuvius!' Nietzsche was a classicist; he was, in this seemingly enigmatic statement, expressing an ancient sensibility that was undermined by the age of industrialization. Nietzsche's city of industrialization, in his view, was perhaps too deeply engaged in the enterprise of protecting its precious labour force by removing dangers from cities. The removal of danger pacifies the body and makes it open to disciplinary regimes in the interest of efficient production. Danger is different from carelessness; it is cultivated and calculated. In contrast with those of Aristotle and Nietzsche, the Chinese conception of prudence tends to be more binary: danger is undesirable and should be completely removed. Prudence is pursued in accordance with its own inherent logic in the Chinese cultural context: to be safe to the greatest possible extent. Prudence is a primary virtue in agriculture, simply because cultivating land for a long period of time with almost no reward until harvest requires extraordinary endurance, sacrifice, and discipline. The harvest, furthermore, is never guaranteed. For two millennia, Chinese society was deeply grounded in this principle of endurance and an unknown future reward, manifested perhaps most clearly in the Confucianist notion of piety and its associated social norms.

The Body and Mind in Safety

The body in safety, in the Chinese cultural context, has a matter-of-course status. Ancient Romans delighted in watching the body of the gladiator in perilous danger and cheered for its courage in combat at the games. Considering the battle scenes and depictions of death so commonly found in Western art, it is astonishing that these themes are almost completely absent in traditional Chinese art. The depiction of violence in Chinese art is a phenomenon that began only in the twentieth century, an obvious result of Western artistic influence in China. If we seek an ideal body in Chinese paintings, it would be that of the literati in isolation, out of danger; this peaceful and unchallenged corporeal condition can perhaps be argued as an ideal state of civilization, in strong contrast with its utmost exertion in mortal combat. The depiction of the body in Wen Zhengming's representation of a literati garden (1531) is a good example of the Chinese ideal of the body in safety (Figure 4.1). The body is invariably located in landscape, under a tree, next to a rock, in a pavilion, appearing in isolation, or being attended by a boy, or in small elegant gatherings. Often depicted in crouched forms, these bodies engage in intellectual and contemplative activities. It seems to be slow, deliberate, and distant. It is, above all, safely concealed in landscape. Art loses its focus on the anatomical; the body, through its existence without strife, is often reduced to a figure in art. The chiselled bone structures and pronounced muscle groups so highly valued in Greek sculptures, in this context, would seem to be too suggestive of the forcefulness and exertion of the body, thus invoking the presence of danger and strife. It is perhaps this unsettled condition of the body – indicative of unsettled rather than harmonious life – that Chinese art avoided through softer features of the body. The literati art, in this sense, never valued the strong and agile body. The body in safety demands concealment, avoidance, detour, as François Jullien suggests in relation to the Chinese culture of the literati.[6] Martial art seems to have been excluded from this literati pursuit; it is a fascinating case of the strong and agile body engaged in combat without danger, and in attack without an opponent. In its resemblance to violence, martial art is much more ritualized than boxing matches; in its absence of *telos* of destruction, it can perhaps be understood as having had real corporeal danger removed in its elaborate fighting forms. Sunzi's *Art of War* (515–512 BCE) was entirely focused on waging successful wars through careful planning rather than actual combat; this differs considerably from the Greek focus on the courage, agility, and prowess of the fighter in phalanx. In these acts of danger exclusion in the Chinese cultural context, violence does not go away; when violence and representations of violence are excluded from moralization and aestheticization, they enter into a territory of their inherent logic: violence becomes cruel and unaccountable. An examination of the history of war and violence in China would reveal that, although there is an absence of representations of violence in Chinese art, for almost 40 per cent of the time during its 2,430 years of history China was under turmoil created by violent conflicts; the frequency of wars in China is comparable with that in the Western cultural context. The number of deaths and the depth of destruction in China – often involving slaughter of not only military personnel but their entire families – are 'rarely seen in the world'.[7]

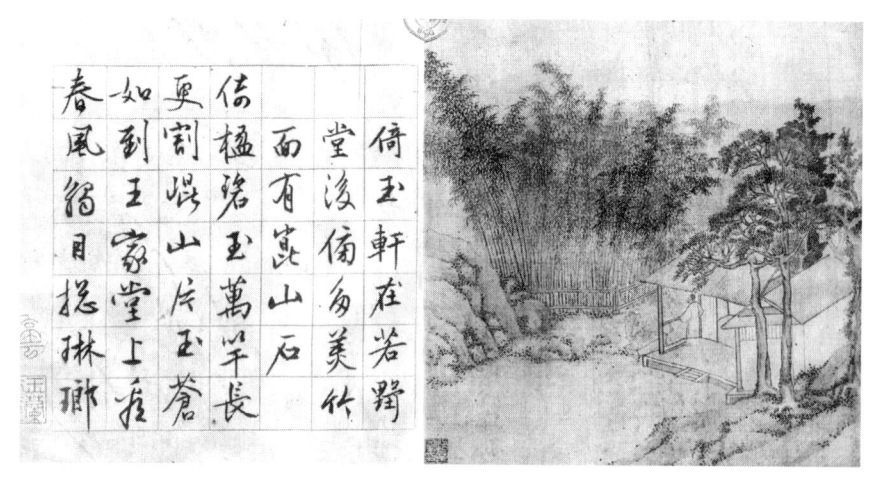

Figure 4.1 Leaning Jade Pavilion, the Humble Administrator's Garden (Zhuozheng Yuan), by Wen Zhengming, 1531

This desire to remove danger from the body completely has a large range of cultural consequences; the preservation of the body (*yangshen*) holds a supreme importance in the Chinese culture. The Western drug- and surgery-based medical practice isolates diet into a realm of sensual pleasures[8] and class differentiations, whereas the Chinese diet hybridizes food with health regimes. The conception of Chinese medicine is at the same time a conception of food, as the influential ancient Chinese text *The Inner Canon of Huangdi* (*Huangdi neijing*) already suggests. In *The Inner Canon*, the body maps closely the universe of the *Book of Changes*, analogously featuring *yin* and *yang* balance, the five elements, and the four seasons. Each season, *The Inner Canon* emphasizes, demands specific preservation regimes which are based on observations of the characteristics of the vegetation and animals in the season.[9] Over the centuries, this preservation imperative of the body developed a bewildering range of diet-based caring regimens; they are certainly central to the daily lives in Chinese cities today. *Weisheng*, or 'defending the body', has been largely focused on regimens of prevention through moderation, rather than cure.[10] Perhaps the most important consequence of the preservation of the body concerns the relationship between the body and its immediate environment. The natural environment is filled with danger; perhaps the most characteristic Chinese method of living with nature is to reconstitute the natural environment artificially, so that it is possible to live in nature without its inherent danger. This reconstitution of a 'safe nature' seems to be one of the most enduring principles in almost all aspects of Chinese cultural production; it seems to be at the heart of an interesting and intriguing Chinese condition: persistent claims to living with nature are made in relation to highly artificial and manipulated environmental features. The Chinese landscape painting is an example of this reconstitution of nature. As a pupil of traditional landscape painting, one does not paint, and endeavour to capture without prejudice, what is seen in the natural environment, but from a pattern book, the most well known of which is called *Manual of the Mustard Seed Garden*, an instruction book popular in the early eighteenth century and influential ever since. The manual can perhaps be considered as a form of pre-defined natural scenes – often with specific meanings associated with them – which can be created with specific brush stroke techniques (Figure 4.2). Through this process, natural environment is constantly internalized and appreciated through its reconstitution in painting. The long tradition of landscape painting in China produced an enormously sophisticated body of work highly admired worldwide;

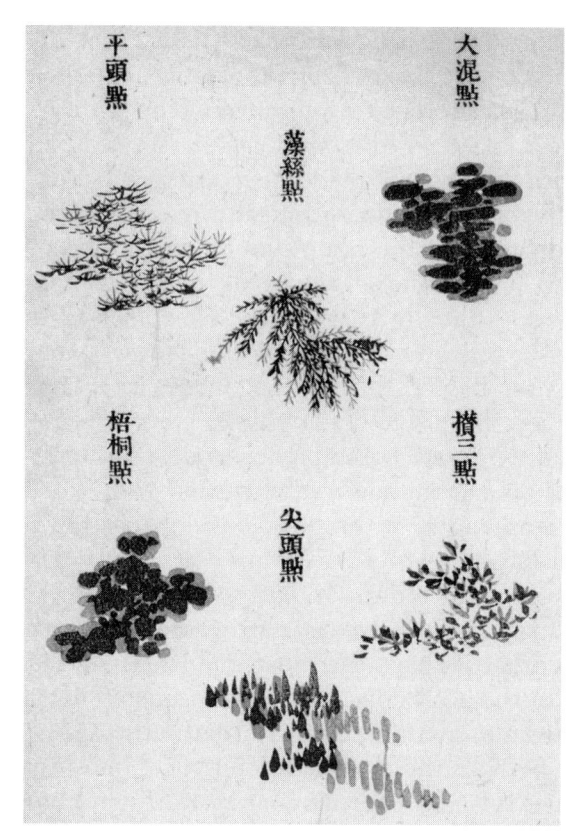

Figure 4.2 A page from *Manual of the Mustard Seed Garden* (1679)

the ability of this reconstituted and safe nature to enable intellectual contemplation is perhaps its most enduring attraction, while the difference between the painted landscape and the natural landscape may be regarded as its most provocative feature.

It is perhaps in the world of gardening that this danger-free reconstituted nature reaches its most magnificent form. Private gardens surviving from the Ming and Qing dynasties, particularly those in southern China, are often totally enclosed within walls. Through gardening techniques that create objects and vegetation approaching those found in landscape painting, these gardens provide safe locations for the body without losing the essential elements of nature. The iconic eighteenth-century Chinese novel *Dream of the Red Chamber* tells the story of the fortunes of a highly placed family; amazingly, both its detailed accounts of the Qing-dynasty social form and those of the mental states of its large cast of characters took place exclusively in a private garden, the Grand View Garden. This epitome of Chinese literary achievement is also a celebration of the triumph of the Chinese garden, an artificial construct that has entirely recreated the relationship between the body and nature, culture and society, enabling cultural and social events to take place within artificially constructed boundaries. It is tempting to see this as a metaphor for the Chinese civilization that reconstitutes all aspects of the human within its artificially created realms. As we will further elaborate in Part Three of the book, the Chinese gardens are made from abstracted and balanced forms of elements in nature, each fulfilling a place in a reconstituted natural order, within which actual dangers are removed and replaced with figurative dangers. A deep mountain range can now be found in rather ornately formed rocks and trees, and ferocious torrents in little falls simulating the rapid and sinuous movements of water. Ideal gardens would leave out nothing in nature; in their reconstitution, they also include nothing genuinely natural with all its inherent danger. This seems to be one of the most important foundations of the Chinese aesthetic experience, and it has, as we shall discuss in the next chapter, tremendous power in the formation of the Chinese city.

Freed from the burdens of self-defence in the face of danger, the body in safety in the Chinese cultural context is open to moral and disciplinary formulations. It is immediately subject to the notion of filial piety, the Confucianist demand for the son to pay respect and to provide unconditional servitude to parents. If we see prudence as a virtue of age, then filial piety taps into the importance of prudence in establishing the age-based hierarchical structure, and making it a moral code. Filial piety is not just a ritual between father and son, but also one between ministers and rulers; it is a full set of social and relational hierarchies that are constantly observed and performed, with the intensity of observation seemingly in direct proportion to the intensity of power and wealth. Piety, in this sense, can be seen to have formulated the form of social structure: Chinese social formations are fundamentally modelled on the family as an archetype. This web of social connections functions like a security system that protects the family and its derivatives, and excludes the stranger. The level of trust within this circle of family and its derivatives is high, while the tolerance of losing this social security system is low among the Chinese population.[11] The stranger, in this sense, does not really exist legitimately in Chinese cities. One is either inside or outside a multitude of social circles, and never independent from them. In China, a connection often begins with an association – a commonality reconstituted from a wide variety, including biological, clan-based, geographical, educational, and institutional ones – which is an embryonic form of a social circle. The morally disciplined body in safety foresees future disorder and compensates with a political conception of perpetual stability. All governments in China seem to appeal heavily to the notion of perpetual stability to legitimize intervention, and very rarely invoke notions such as unlimited rights; rights in the Chinese cultural context seem to be a layered and 'bundled' conception. The isolation and purification of rights in the Chinese context seems to be clearly effective only among certain intellectual circles influenced by Western liberalism. Prudence manifests itself in Chinese economic life: economic prudence is most clearly demonstrated through saving – or at least not borrowing – which can be understood as a distinctly agriculture-inspired behaviour. Prudence underlines a form of knowledge: scholarship in the traditional Chinese society was produced privately and kept safely within this private circle.[12] Knowledge was seen to be a form of family inheritance, a privilege not to be interfered with by people outside specific affiliations. Books were often kept isolated in places appropriately named 'mansions of hiding books' (*cangshulou*): to make them accessible to strangers is to expose scholarship to unacceptable levels of danger. Imperial collections of books, such as the Song-dynasty *Taiping yulan*, or *Imperial Inspected Encyclopedia of the Taiping Era* (977–983), the Ming-dynasty *Yongle dadian*, or *The Great Canon of the Yongle Era* (1403–08), and the Qing-dynasty *Siku quanshu*, or *The Complete Library in Four Branches of Literature* (1773–82), can indeed be seen to have been modelled on the knowledge of private circles.

The Body and Mind in Danger

Perhaps conceived in deliberate opposition against the natural tendency to be over prudent, as we observe in many civilizations, the ancient Greeks saw prudence as something to be overcome. Bertrand Russell spoke of this idea in relation to the Greek god Dionysus: 'The worshipper of Dionysus reacts against prudence. In intoxication, physical or spiritual, he recovers an intensity of feeling which prudence had destroyed; he finds the world full of delight and beauty, and his imagination is suddenly liberated from the prison of everyday preoccupations.'[13] Russell attempted to locate the primary urge against prudence at the centre of Western civilization; there is a clear and persistent faith in the Western city that prudence is destructive, which is very differently conceived from that in the Chinese way of life. One may attempt to explain this in terms of the frequent wars in ancient Greece, but there were also frequent wars in Chinese history, and indeed in the history of all civilizations. The ancient Greek conception of prudence and danger was a deliberate choice; the epics of Homer not only left us with records of certain details of this ancient civilization, but they also highlight the central importance of wars in moral and aesthetic formulations. This reality was perhaps reflected in the incessant conflicts between parents and children, brothers and sisters, in Greek mythology. Combat pushes the body to its physical limits; here lies a potential that was harvested for human virtue. In Sparta, boys at the age of seven were taken away from their parents and sent to military camps under gruelling training regimes until adulthood. Through this, they were transformed from dependent children to independent, strong, agile, self-disciplined soldiers. This tradition of cultivating the body has enormous influences; almost 2000 years later, the influential English scholar John Locke, in his *Some Thoughts Concerning Education*, stressed the essential conditions of hardship in the process of education of the body and the mind.[14] The height of ancient Greek civilization took place between the Persian Wars (499–450 BCE) and the Peloponnesian War (431–404 BCE), achieving an astonishing level of cultural production. At the heart of all these achievements is the culture of the combatant body.

The central meaning of combat is not violence; violence is always part of human nature, and it is present in all cultures. In ancient Greece, the central meaning of combat is about moralization and aestheticization of violence, attempting to separate acceptable violence from unacceptable violence. The Chinese civilization, in its avoidance of violence and its promotion of hierarchical harmony, chooses to leave violent and non-violent confrontations to a moral wasteland; the ancient Greeks moralized and aestheticized confrontation as the central path to knowledge and justice. Musing over the extraordinary cultural achievements of the ancient Greeks, Russell exclaimed that the sudden rise of Greek civilization is the most difficult historical event to account for;[15] perhaps this moralization and aestheticization of confrontation can provide a way to understand it. The divide between moral and immoral violence is hinged on the idea of 'moral laws', and not on despotic will or family hierarchy; on one side of the law, the ability to exercise violence is generally understood as courage, on the other side, cruelty. Herodotus, in his *Histories*, described the Persian surprise at the courage of Greek soldiers: just before the famed battle of Thermopylae, the Persian Emperor Xerxes asked Darmaratus, a Greek soldier in exile, how such a small number of Greek soldiers could have such courage to face the huge Persian army; Darmaratus replied, the courage of the Greek soldier comes from the fear of himself, not from that of the ruler.[16]

Competition is the peaceful expression of the combatant body; here, although life and death combat is surrogated by games and works judged by a jury, competition can be seen as a reminder of the combatant body and an exercise of its form. At the time of the ancient Olympics, combat and its surrogate in competitive sports seemed to be exchangeable; in both forms, it was the combatant body that occupied the centre of morality and aesthetics. In contrast, during civil service examinations, the Chinese scholars were disciplined in reproducing the Confucian classics flawlessly; the selected (presented) scholars (*jinshi*) were masters of a well-established literary style rather than winners of a competition. When Christian thought alienated the Greco-Roman view of the combatant body and inverted it through fasting, celibacy, and vegetarianism, their religious arts represented the body as possessing a minimal amount of vaguely articulated flesh. The Renaissance brought the body back to its combatant form with magnificence. The artistry of Leonardo Da Vinci and Michelangelo ensured a visual centrality of the combatant body in the Western conception of the body, and their influences cast a long shadow to our time. This was indeed a reassertion of sovereignty over the combatant body when it was taken over by religion. This detailed and precise gaze of the combatant body does not limit itself in the realm of the visual arts; it can indeed become a model for the world. Mary Douglas theorized this body consciousness as having played an essential role as the model for classification in the Western culture;[17] it certainly has a strong presence in theories of architecture, beginning with Vitruvius's speculation on the geometrical perfection of the male body and its relationship to architecture.[18]

Nietzsche's provocation to live in danger and to build a city on the slope of a volcano highlighted the fact that the combatant body cannot be separated from the form of the city. The danger in life is also the danger in the city. Nietzsche was perhaps reflecting on the urban reforms in the late nineteenth century when hygiene and safety were prominent issues in European cities that were focused on improving the quality of life of their labour class during the era of Industrial Revolution. The battleground for the body, to Nietzsche, seems to have been shifted from the country to the city, where a protective net had been formed to gradually transform the combatant body to the labouring body in the interest of the accumulation of capital. In this sense, Nietzsche's struggle was similar to that of the Renaissance artists: one wrestles the combatant body from the clutch of industrialism inherent in the capitalist economic development in the nineteenth century, the other wakens it from the grip of Christian faith.

The debating mind, in this sense, arose from the combatant body as its intellectual form; it is a formation of the mind in danger. In the Chinese context, debates would have been seen to be disruptive of the hierarchical scheme by foregrounding equality between debating parties, thereby presenting an inelegant intellectual form; the body in safety seeks simultaneously the mind in peace and concealment. In the Western cultural context, debate is perhaps the single most important method to gain knowledge. While Michelangelo painted the ceiling of the Sistine Chapel with combatant bodies, Raphael was imagining the production of knowledge in ancient Greece through his *School of Athens* in a different part of the Vatican City. Raphael's painting is one of intellects engaged in lively debates, with that between Plato and Aristotle occupying the centre stage. It would have appeared strange to a Chinese literati to see Plato's contemplative writings to be in the form of dialogues; it would seem to be more in tune with the peaceful order of things to appear in the form of instructions, as the *Analects* of Confucius are. But dialogues are the intellectual form of combat; in trading wisdoms backwards and forwards, a better state of knowledge is believed to emerge. In the medieval period, the logic of debate was distorted into disputation, and dialogues gave way to long theses as exemplified by those of Thomas Aquinas. Like the art that revived the combatant body during the Renaissance, the printing press and the emergence of the essay in the Renaissance reinvented debate with a much larger audience. For Renaissance intellectuals, Plato's debating mind in danger was the most fundamental model of intellectual life; the writings of Thomas Aquinas are contemplative but complex, heavily strategized on the image of scholarship rather than its substance in reason. Aquinas's use of complication as substance is not unlike the column of the Gothic cathedral compared with the Greek order; in the Gothic tradition, a column is often split into four or six smaller ones while functionally they serve as one.[19]

Dialectics provides the debate-based knowledge production with a structure that clearly articulates the emergence of a third state, a synthesis as Kant and Hegel describe it. Synthesis stems from the contradiction of thesis and antithesis, a mapping of debate as a central feature of the combatant body in the Greek conception. Through Kant, Hegel, and Marx, the progression of history and knowledge towards justice and truthfulness as being based on this triad of thesis, antithesis, and synthesis became widely accepted as the norm. The wrestling of the mind is here expanded and transformed as the wrestling of collective historical and epistemological forces. The combatant body and the debating mind, which are shaped critically by the presence of danger, influence almost all forms of social and political institutions. Parliamentary debates, courtroom expositions, and design critique sessions are modelled on the intellectual life of the combatant body. There is of course no guarantee that parliamentary debates will lead to fulfilment of common interests, courtroom expositions will arrive at justice, and critiques will lead to understanding of design; these are conventions of actions that are grounded in the idea of goodness, justice, and truth being attainable through a method. As Ulrich Beck explains in *Risk Society*, the possibility of failure and the production of risk have been essential to ensure the functioning of Western societies.[20]

Danger Aesthetics: Exposure

The combatant body and the debating mind lead us to aesthetics of danger. In ancient Greece, this aesthetics of danger was manifested as, first of all, nakedness of the male body; this is one of the most difficult aspects of Greek art to understand in the Christian era.[21] There were several important goals to be achieved through nakedness; the naked body is both vulnerable and a battleground to overcome weakness, the accomplishment of which becomes one of the most important foundations of aesthetics. Thucydides, writing about the Peloponnesian War, stressed that it was the Athenians and the Spartans who 'were the first to play games naked, to take off their clothes openly'; in ancient times 'even at the Olympic Games the athletes used to wear coverings for their loins, and indeed this practice was still in existence not very many years ago. Even today many foreigners, especially in Asia, wear these loincloths for boxing matches and wrestling bouts'.[22] According to Thucydides's recount of the Funeral Oration of Pericles mourning the deceased Greek soldiers, Pericles praised 'the way of life which has made us great'. Pericles spoke proudly that 'we, when we launch an attack abroad, do the job by ourselves', facing the possibility of death courageously.[23] The courage of the Athenians was a natural one, and not one that was inspired by the oppression; it was a state of being that could not be attained just by training long and hard, nor through the oppression of authority.[24] The exposure of the body – to the elements and to critical examinations – seems to have captured an important aesthetic expression of that way of life and gives the body its form; it is seen in the strength, posture, and deportation of the body.[25] The exposure of the body cultivates the value of openness of thought and social processes, and the value of a clear and penetrating view.

If the clear and penetrating view, a scopic regime, cultivates a crucial structure of knowledge in terms of its transparency,[26] and if that transparency is epitomized by the pure *logos* of mathematics, then the pure aesthetic expression of the clear and penetrating view would be proportion and perspective. As we have discussed in Chapter 1, Plato's *Timaeus* depicts a world of perfection as being composed of proportional relationships; harmony arises from proportional relationships of musical notes and geometric shapes. A building such as the Parthenon is crucially articulated by this proportional imagination; it demonstrates the transparency of beauty through its details and the whole just like the exposed male body. The Greek *polis* can be seen as a result of this scopic regime, which shaped its buildings and spaces, laying down some of the most enduring foundations of the Western city. Ernst Gombrich marvelled at the anatomical and perspectival innovations in Greek art, seeing them as something completely revolutionary in the history of human artistic abilities.[27] Perspective puts mathematics and geometry into the arts, allowing a visual and acoustic materialization of the clear and penetrating view to embody logical content. When the Jesuit Matteo Ricci visited China at the turn of the seventeenth century, one of the first things he observed of Chinese paintings was that 'They know nothing of the art of painting in oil or of the use of perspective in their pictures, with the result that their productions are lacking any vitality'.[28] While Ricci was confident of the perspectival abilities of European artists, the Chinese literati may have had very different ideas; by the tenth century (Song dynasty), the 'meticulous' (*gongbi*) painting style had already made use of bright colours and careful delineation of details often valued at the Chinese imperial court, but the literati generally regarded this form of painting as excessively laboured and preferred the enlightened and spontaneous flow of the brush. The Chinese literati would be more likely to agree with Qianlong (reigned 1735–96), who considered perspective as an unnecessary way to represent the imperfection of the human eye.[29] The painting of shadows, *chiaroscuro*, would also likely be seen in the same light, as Chinese paintings do not represent shadows; perception of shadows could indeed be seen as a flaw of the human eye. Various editions of Vitruvius and Palladio brought to seventeenth-century China by European missionaries produced little visible influence.[30] The seventeenth-century painter Wu Li

(1632–1718), who as a Christian convert was best known to have had exposure to Western painting tradition brought to China by the Jesuits, commented on Western painting:

> Our painting does not seek physical likeness, and does not depend on fixed patterns; we call it 'divine' and 'untrammelled'. Theirs concentrates entirely on the problem of dark and light, front and back, and the fixed patterns of physical likeness.[31]

He never seems to have adopted the Western focus on perspective and *chiaroscuro* in his own practice as an artist. The Chinese perception of perspective as something far less exalted and central to painting is fascinating. The Chinese painter seems to have adopted a distant and relational view; the extraordinary value placed on the artistic practice of capturing 'dark and light, front and back, and the fixed patterns of physical likeness' only makes sense when it is placed against the value of openness and exposure as a universal measure for justice, truth, and beauty, deeply intertwined with the physical characteristics of the combatant body.

One of the most extraordinary consequences of the clear and penetrating view, it may be argued, can be traced in the prevailing use of glass in the twentieth century. Scott Lash suggests that if we map the force of this view as one of the most distinctive measures of modernity, then it formulated itself through religion and painting in the fifteenth and sixteenth centuries, philosophy in the seventeenth century, the novel in the eighteenth and nineteenth centuries, and architecture in the twentieth century.[32] In its last formulation in architecture, it is glass as a building material that embodies most effectively the ancient clear and penetrating view. The use of glass is the danger aesthetic of our time. Almost appearing by accident as it was used in Joseph Paxton's Crystal Palace in 1851, glass has become one of the most commonly used building materials in the twentieth century. Brittle, and possessing little protective or insulating ability, glass has to be framed with other stronger materials, and the resultant interior spaces have to be regulated artificially in terms of temperature and lighting; it is perplexing that so much endeavour went into making glass a building material and a symbol of modernity. Nowhere does the use of glass in the late twentieth century reach its ironic height more so than in tropical Singapore; leaving aside its symbolism and expense, the Esplanade along the waterfront of Marina Bay in Singapore, designed by DP Architects and Michael Wilford & Partners, features its main public spaces under two large glass domes, which are shaded by metal panels from the intense heat and light of the tropical sun. The indigenous tropical wisdom in the built environment makes much more use of shade and flow of air in the creation of the built environment, while the Esplanade is obsessed with glass with a pathological compulsion. Today, the worldwide extensive use of glass as a building material is clearly visible; it pays tribute to transparency and to the exposed house – the Farnsworth House by Mies van der Rohe in 1945 and the glass house by Philip Johnson in 1949 – as possibly the last aesthetic expression of the clear and penetrating view. Here, the intellectual transparency of proportion is paralleled by the literal transparency of the glass. By the middle of the twentieth century, painters such as Picasso had long abandoned perspective and shadow and began to paint without their dominating influences. In both its exaltation and its denigration, the clear and penetrating view holds a unique place in the West, formulating art and architecture in influential ways.

Reconstituting the Body in Safety

The body in safety in the Chinese cultural context has undergone extensive changes in the twentieth century. They took place alongside a wide range of intellectual, social, and political changes that gripped early twentieth-century China, following a series of military defeats by Western and Japanese armed forces since the Opium War (1839–42). The Chinese reformers, in response to the Western military power that shocked the Chinese imperial court, first sought to acquire and utilize military capabilities following a traditional notion of 'self-strengthening', led by imperial officials such as Li Hongzhang (1823–1901). This was soon followed by an attempt to reform Chinese knowledge, led by the outstanding reformer Liang Qichao (1873–1929). It was the reform of the body that became one of the most significant changes in Chinese culture in the twentieth century; to change the traditional body in safety into a combatant body was the primary task of Ma Yuehan (1882–1966), the man who headed the Physical Education Department at Tsinghua College. Tsinghua College was founded in 1911 with a portion of the indemnity paid by China to the United States following the Boxer Rebellion (1898–1901), and was established as a preparation school for Chinese students to further study in the United States, supported by scholarships from the same fund. The College was determined to instil a sports culture where none existed. American college sports training was enthusiastically promoted, often by force, among Chinese students who were brought up with Chinese education and unfamiliar with the college sports culture; dormitories, libraries, laboratories, and classrooms were locked up at 4 pm so that students had nowhere to go except the sports fields, and tests in swimming, 100 metre and 400 metre runs, shot-put, and high jump had to be passed before graduation.[33] A biology major graduate of St John's University in Shanghai founded by the American Anglican Church in 1879, Ma Yuehan, joined Tsinghua College in 1914 and was in charge of physical education. Ma's influence in Tsinghua College (later Tsinghua University) and, through its reputation, the entire physical education in universities in China, is enormous: he maintained an unchallenged position for the soccer, basketball, and baseball teams of Tsinghua College, and his enthusiasm for physical exercise helped greatly change the perception of sports in the Chinese cultural context. Ma's exercise regime in Tsinghua College was remarkable when compared to Peking University, where the characteristics of the traditional Chinese scholar, albeit one that was enmeshed in reform, were much more apparent. The fragile scholar, in this new era exemplified by Tsinghua College, was no longer the only admired figure of the Chinese youth.[34]

Mao Zedong (1893–1976) was at Peking University, near Tsinghua College, from 1917 to 1919, working as a library assistant for the Marxist university librarian Li Dazhao and exposing himself to a lively intellectual scene greatly shaped by reforms and communist ideas. He would have known the reputation of physical education at Tsinghua College. Mao was later to call Ma Yuehan 'the healthiest person in the new China'; this clearly reflected Mao's deep fascination with Ma's enterprise to reshape the traditional Chinese body in safety. Well known for his physical exercise regimes, Mao was without doubt the greatest promoter of physical education in China in the twentieth century. Generations of children since the founding of the People's Republic were drilled in schools under Mao's ubiquitous slogan: 'develop sports, enhance people's physique', written in 1952. One of the most dramatic events in Mao's political career was the staged swimming across the Yangtze River in 1966, at the age of 73, to re-enact his first swim across the river ten years before in 1956. As both a political metaphor of a counter attack on his opposition unhappy with the Great Leap Forward campaign, and as a reaffirmation of the importance of sports, this historic swim continued to sustain a much changed notion of the body in China. The transformation of the female body in twentieth-century China is most extensive and remarkable; from the domesticated body with bound feet to the body that holds 'half of the sky', Chinese women changed beyond recognition within a century of revolutions. Mao's delight in combat – his 'endless pleasures in combating heaven, earth, and man' – was as far removed from the body of filial piety in the Confucianist tradition as it was an invocation of the Western combatant body. The propaganda posters of the Cultural Revolution certainly captured the spirit of the freshly minted combatant body in China by forging together various folk arts of China with some principles derived from a narrow strand of the Socialist Realism of Soviet propaganda art.[35] The literati painting was clearly ineffective in expressing this newfound theme of combat. One hundred years after these reforms, Chinese athletes demonstrated their achievements in competitive sports over a century, on a world stage, in the 2008 Beijing Olympics: while the first Chinese Olympic athlete, Liu Changchun – born almost exactly 100 years earlier – did not win any medals in Los Angeles in 1932, in 2008, Chinese athletes topped the medal count.

The body in safety, which resulted from centuries of prudent discipline and hierarchical demands, did not disappear after the dust of twentieth-century reform had settled; it has persisted and, in the post-Mao era, mutated into different forms and placed different demands on the design and construction of Chinese cities. While competitive sports in China become increasingly under the control of the elite system of selection and training, as well as being tightly interwoven with the project of nationalism, popular health regimens in China have reconnected with ancient wisdoms long described in classics such as *The Inner Canons*. Instead of competitive exertions simulating the body in danger, the Chinese ways of maintaining health are deeply focused on regimens of food, regularity, and exercise in moderation found in *Taiji Quan* (Tai Chi) and its contemporary derivatives such as the 'dance routines' as morning exercises. These activities on the streets, open spaces, and parks in Chinese cities give the Chinese city a unique spatial quality. If the combatant body found an aesthetic spatial expression in the form of the gym in the contemporary city, the reconstituted body in safety in Chinese cities locates itself in the 'idling centre', exerting a demand for a restoration of the legitimacy of the body in safety. The 'idling centre' (*xiuxian zhongxin*) – variously packaged commercially as saunas, massage parlours, water therapy centres, in Chinese cities – gives the body in safety its ultimate concealment. The body in passive reception of servitude and pleasure in the idling centre is deeply traditional, and contrasts starkly with the active exertion of the body in the gym, where the purposelessness of the exertion underpins its pure aesthetic nature. The exercise gym is an urban spectacle: elevated, bright, airy, full of motion; the idling centre is an urban hideout: enclosed, windowless, cellular, still. Both are entrenched in the contemporary Chinese city; they occupy two spatial extremes created by two very different conceptions of the body, allowing all to participate in hybrid forms in various degrees.

Notes

1 Peter Brown, *The Body and Society: Men, Women, and Sexual Renunciation in Early Christianity* (New York: Columbia University Press, 1988); Bryan S. Turner, *The Body and Society* (London: SAGE, 1996); Mike Featherstone, Mike Hepworth and Bryan S. Turner, eds, *The Body, Social Process and Cultural Theory* (London: SAGE, 1991).
2 Richard Sennett, *Flesh and Stone: The Body and the City in Western Civilization* (London and New York: W. W. Norton & Company, 1994).
3 Harold Peake and Herbert John Fleure, *The Steppe and the Sown* (New Haven: Yale University Press, 1928).
4 Aristotle, 'Nicomachean Ethics', in *The Basic Works of Aristotle*, ed. Richard McKeon (New York: The Modern Library, 2001), Book 3, Chapters 6–9.
5 Karl Popper, *The Logic of Scientific Discovery* (London: Hutchinson, 1968).
6 François Jullien, *Detour and Access: Strategies of Meaning in China and Greece* (New York: Zone Books, 2004).
7 Shi Gexin, *Zhongguo hongguanshi, luanshijuan* (The Macro-History of China: The Volume of Chaotic Eras) (Zhengzhou: Daxiang chubanshe, 2003), Preface.
8 'The principle change is that diet was originally aimed at a control of desire, whereas under modern forms of consumerism diet exists to promote and preserve desire', Turner, *The Body and Society* (London: SAGE, 1996), p.39.
9 'Basic Questions', *Huangdi neijing* (The Inner Cannon of Huangdi), ed. Yao Chunpeng (Beijing: Zhonghua shuju, 2009).
10 Ruth Rogaski, *Hygienic Modernity: Meanings of Health and Disease in Treaty-Port China* (Berkeley: University of California Press, 2004).
11 Elke Weber and Christopher Hsee, 'Culture and Individual Judgment and Decision Making', *Applied Psychology: An International Review* 49:1 (2000), pp.32–61. Quoted in Michael Keith, Scott Lash, Jakob Arnoldi and Tyler Rooker, *China Constructing Capitalism: Economic Life and Urban Change* (London and New York: Routlege, 2013).
12 Wen-hsin Yeh, *The Alienated Academy: Culture and Politics in Republican China, 1919–1937* (Cambridge MA: Harvard University Press, 1990).
13 Bertrand Russell, *History of Western Philosophy* (London: Routledge, 2000; originally published 1946), p.36.
14 John Locke, *Some Thoughts Concerning Education* (London, 1693).
15 Russell, *History of Western Philosophy*.

16 Herodotus, *The Histories*, trans. Aubrey de Sélincourt (London: Penguin Books, 1954/2003), Book 7, pp.448–50.
17 Mary Douglas, *Purity and Danger: An Analysis of Concepts of Pollution and Taboo* (Harmondsworth: Penguin Books, 1970); *Natural Symbols: Explorations in Cosmology* (Harmondsworth: Penguin Books, 1973).
18 Vitruvius, *Ten Books on Architecture*, trans. Ingrid D. Rowland and Thomas Noble Howe (Cambridge: Cambridge University Press, 1999), Book 3, Chapter 1.
19 Erwin Panofsky, *Gothic Architecture and Scholasticism* (Latrobe: Archabbey Press, 1951).
20 Ulrich Beck, *Risk Society: Towards a New Modernity* (London: SAGE, 1992).
21 Kenneth Clark, *The Nude: A Study in Ideal Form* (Princeton: Princeton University Press, 1972).
22 Thucydides, *History of the Peloponnesian War*, trans. Rex Warner (New York and London: Penguin Books, 1972), p.38.
23 Ibid., pp.145–46.
24 Ibid., p.146.
25 Sennett, *Flesh and Stone*, pp.31–67.
26 Martin Jay, *Downcast Eyes: The Denigration of Vision in Twentieth-century French Thought* (Berkeley and London: University of California Press, 1993).
27 Ernst H. Gombrich, *The Story of Art* (London: Phaidon, 1995), p.77.
28 Michael Sullivan, *The Meeting of Eastern and Western Art* (Berkeley and London: University of California Press, 1989), p.43. For Matteo Ricci, see Jonathan Spence, *The Memory Palace of Matteo Ricci* (London and Boston: Faber and Faber, 1984); Michela Fontana, *Matteo Ricci* (Lanham: Rowman & Littlefield, 2011).
29 See Chapter 9. Cécile and Michel Beurdeley, *Giuseppe Castiglione: A Jesuit Painter at the Court of the Chinese Emperors* (London: Lund Humphries, 1971), p.138. Nian Xiyao, a commissioner of customs, published a book on perspective (two editions, 1729 and 1735) adapted from Andrea Pozzo's *Perspectiva Pictorum et Architectorum* (1693), enlisting Castiglione's help.
30 Sullivan, *The Meeting of Eastern and Western Art*, p.46.
31 Ibid., p.58.
32 Scott Lash, *Another Modernity, A Different Rationality* (Oxford: Blackwell, 1999), p.19.
33 Yeh, *The Alienated Academy*, pp.213–15.
34 For a study of the fragile scholar prototype in the Chinese cultural context, see Song Geng, *The Fragile Scholar: Power and Masculinity in Chinese Culture* (Hong Kong: Hong Kong University Press, 2004).
35 Lincoln Cushing, 'Revolutionary Chinese Posters and Their Impact Abroad', Lincoln Cushing and Ann Tompkins, *Chinese Posters: Art from the Great Proletarian Cultural Revolution* (San Francisco: Chronicle Books, 2007), p.7.

5

Degrees of Care

The exercise gym and the idling centre, as spatial epitomes of intellectual conceptions of the body, exist in an urban context that may be described as having been constructed through degrees of care. Care giving, no doubt stemming from parental care, is fundamental to human communities; what is interesting is not the act of giving care, but the forms in which care is given. The 'care of strangers' in the city is perhaps the most important point of difference between the Western city and the Chinese city. The care of strangers – manifested as an Aristotelian loyalty to citizens of the *polis* above that to the family, as a Christian *caritas* providing care for all, and as the ideal of social welfare in our time – is inseparable from the care of public space in the Western city. In this equation of corporeal and spatial care, public space becomes an important measurement of other forms of care in the Western city. The care of strangers and common spaces in the Chinese city seem to be differently formulated; the Chinese city seems to have been conceived not with this 'universal care' emanating from those for citizens, strangers, and public space, but by the body in safety with 'ranked care' originating from corporeal preservation regimens, familial bonds, and concentrically cared spaces. The body in safety produces a far-reaching consequence in the city: it desires to barricade itself against a potentially hostile exterior instead of engaging with this potential danger through a moral and aesthetic framework that prescribes rules of engagement in peace and violence. The body in safety prefers concealment and the privileges and pleasures within that enclosure. This basic instinct, among myriad forces shaping the Chinese city, must be seen to be one of the most definitive in relation to the development of cities. If the notion of the public space mediates between homes and institutions in the Western city, this deep commitment to safety in the Chinese city applies degrees of care in cities; the resultant cities present a strong contrast of spatial care – from exquisite imperial and literati gardens to filthy common streets and water channels – which historically seems to be a persistent feature of the Chinese city. One of the greatest concerns in the governance of

Chinese cities has been in the area of urban sanitation; tremendous endeavours and resources were poured into public health improvement programmes in twentieth-century China under all political and cultural conditions.[1]

One of the clearest manifestations of the degrees of care in Chinese cities is the ubiquitous presence of walls. In the context of the combatant body in the Western city, walls are often conceived as military instruments. In ancient Greece and Rome, most cities were not walled;[2] this is consistent with the philosophical, moral, and aesthetic construct of the combatant body discussed in the previous chapter. Concealment through walls would have appeared to be cowardly, and the Spartans insisted on not building walls for their city state. Aristotle, while conceding that 'ordinary human valour' would not be sufficient for the increasing power of missiles and siege engines, also highlighted the notion that 'there is little courage shown in seeking for safety behind a rampart'.[3] Wall building in Europe experienced two rapid periods of development: the first was when the Roman 'frontier defences' broke down in the third century, and the second was the period of economic recovery in the twelfth and thirteenth centuries. From the second period, fortification became one of the most important features in urban design in European cities, as all major architectural treatises also contained chapters on fortification, and many skilled architects such as Leonardo Da Vinci and Christopher Wren were also skilled designers of fortifications. But, as Heinz Stoob's research suggests, the decision to build city walls was never a foregone conclusion in central Europe in the medieval period; only about 41 per cent of 2,309 cities in central Europe were fortified with walls.[4] Walls in the Chinese city seem to have transcended their defensive origin; they, as material forms of social-spatial degrees of care, play a far more important aesthetic role in the Chinese imagination. In traditional paintings, walls are often represented as imagined – painterly modifications of actual walls to approximate ideals of walls – which indicate much higher intellectual status of walls than those of defence.[5] Walls can be found in almost all civilizations and eras, but there are perhaps two important differences when we consider walls in China. The first is that walls tend to be greater in quantity in China; in the Ming dynasty (1368–1644), China's walled cities outnumbered European fortified towns;[6] they represented 'the largest constellation of walled cities on earth'.[7] The second difference is that walls are extensively built within the city walls in Chinese cities: those of imperial palaces, institutions, and private residences; in many

European cities, the spaces within the defensive city walls are relatively open. The pastoral Mongols of the Yuan dynasty (1279–1368) found the Chinese tradition of incessant wall building to be alien to their political goals and once forbade wall construction; in the century prior to 1368 few walled cities in China were constructed, and many city walls constructed before this period deteriorated.[8] Overthrowing the Mongol Empire in China, the first Ming emperor Hongwu took to heart the advice of his officials to build high walls, stock up grain, and postpone enthronement, which formulated the founding imperial policies and left an enduring heritage of wall building at the heart of the Chinese way of life.

The differences between the traditions of wall building in Europe and China seem to be those between 'frontier defence' and 'corporeal defence'. Frontier defence requires pushing of the 'safety zone' to the furthest edge; the ultimate goal – that of the perpetual peace – would be the disappearance of the frontier. This conception of frontier defence seems to be deeply rooted in Western civilization, from Roman military campaigns in the north and east to American wars in Iraq and Afghanistan, from understanding the American West as the frontier to the conception of the expansion into extra-terrestrial space as the frontier. The safety zone behind frontiers, in this conception, can be seen ideally as open, in the way in which the ancient Greeks imagined their *polis*. For as long as the frontier defence was solid, the Romans built their cities in relative openness and without walls. The Chinese corporeal defence begins with the guarding of the interior of the body in safety. The Chinese conception for this defence is *weisheng*, the guarding of life, which is materialized as a bewildering range of corporeal preservation regimens of diet and routine, which is very different from the dialectic functions of health and pleasure in the Western culture of diet and routine. The wearing of facial masks and the expulsion of 'toxic' phlegm, still practised in China outside hospitals, is instinctive and primary in this imagination of the defence of the corporeal interior. The mouth – as the metaphorical gate of the corporeal interior and the entry point of all illness (*bing cong kou ru*) – becomes a critical threshold of intake and expulsion. From this primary defensive post of the body, layers of safety zones unfold through an astonishing variety of mechanisms; among them the most visual and influential are those of architecture and urban design. In Hong Kong, for instance, urban edges – between the sea and the shore, the path and the ground, the road and the pavement – are heavily protected by defiant walls and robust handrails (Figure 5.1). These may indeed be exaggerated by the legal implications in the system of litigation in Hong Kong, but legal conceptions are grounded in cultural constructs, in this case, of internalization and externalization of danger in relation to the body. Hong Kong's heavy-handed protections contrast starkly with Italian and Dutch port cities where the sea and the shore exist without walls or railings between them. In this conception of corporeal defence for the body in safety, the interior and exterior of the body appear as a continuum. The Chinese city, in this sense, can be understood as complex layers of systematic corporeal defences that have undergone modifications through time; it is deeply committed to the spatial construction and reconstruction of the inside (*nei*) and the outside (*wai*) so that the social spheres can also be described in terms of the inside part (*neibu*) and the outside part (*waibu*). Degrees of care are then mapped onto these notions of inside and outside. This set of complex, layered, blended, and ever-changing social–spatial constructs of inside and outside leaves the city with a web of spaces in different degrees of care. Puzzling though it may be at first glance, it is nevertheless possible to understand the productive mechanisms behind the vastly different features and qualities of 'public spaces' in the Chinese city. The apparent confusing signs in Chinese 'public spaces' – treated by some as a rubbish dump and by others as the bedroom as they trod through the streets in pyjamas – would seem to be less perplexing when we see them as a set of outcomes of the spatial imaginations of the body in safety: the inside and the outside can be seen to have been defined not absolutely, but relative to personal perceptions. The sum total of all the individualized conceptions of the inside and the outside contributes to the seemingly incomprehensible features of the Chinese 'public spaces'. While the clarity and simplicity between the public and the private in the Western city cultivated highly visible and relatively consistent standards of public behaviour, in the Chinese city, it depends on the individual schemes of the degrees of care. Inside the work unit compounds (*danwei*) and walled residential communities (*xiaoqu*) the care of the ground and buildings are meticulous, dedicated, and exquisite. Outside these walled communities, the care of the ground and buildings is often absent: rubbish, phlegm, rudeness, and violence can, it seems, legitimately exist on the outside without moral predicament. Since the Opium War in the mid-nineteenth century, many cities in China such as Hong Kong, Guangzhou, Shanghai, and Tianjin had both been established and undergone significant transformations as they came under the control of European powers; in the twentieth century, the cleaning of streets and markets, the construction of sewage systems, the protection of rivers and lakes have all become routine urban issues,

Figure 5.1 Handrail, Hong Kong

revising many of the long-established concepts of diseases and hygiene in traditional medicine.[9] However, despite these changes in the twentieth century, Chinese cities have insisted on their deep-rooted conceptions of the inside and the outside, modifying the transformations of 'public spaces' in Chinese cities in most intriguing ways.

Intensive Care: The Protected Home and Its Derivatives

The protected home, instead of entering into a dialectic relationship with public space in the Western city, gravitates towards an absolute status as the space of intensive care in the Chinese city. The protected home captures the importance of the family as an archetype of society as formulated by Confucius; it is the first spatial defence beyond the corporeal defence of the body in safety. The family, as Fei Xiaotong's classic case study of a village in the Yangtze River region shows, is not only the focus of all social and economic life, but also the fountainhead of aesthetic experiences.[10] The family in Chinese society was founded on three important components: a book of family lineage, an ancestral hall at the centre, and the patrilineal inheritance. These components work together to uphold a strictly observed patrilineal hierarchy. The second century (Han dynasty), the tenth century (Song dynasty), and the fourteenth century (Ming dynasty) were crucial moments of canonization of Confucian values centred on the family as an archetype. Perhaps the greatest manifestation of this family archetype is the notion of the 'state family' (*guojia*) – Chinese for state – that expands the idea of the family to imagine a vast territory and a large amount of people; this is as different as it can be from the Western conception of the state. In *Politics*, Aristotle made a fundamental distinction between a great household and a small state;[11] he maintained that the state has a higher priority than the family just as the whole must exist prior to the constituent parts, and he emphasized that our natural loyalty is not to friends and family, but to truth.[12] Much is at stake in the Aristotelian conception: notions of truth, justice, and beauty can only begin to be formulated after this broad framework is set in place. One of the most interesting cultural manifestations of this basic instinct in the Western city is the act of 'leaving home', which recurs as a literary and dramatic theme in the arts. Sigmund Freud gave it a psychological form in his essay 'The Uncanny' (1919), in which the home is conceived to be both familiar and unfamiliar, both comforting and horrifying. The Chinese conception of the relationship between the family and the state begins at an entirely different end of the binary of the individual and the collective; once this is set in place, the entire spatial realm becomes distinctive.

The spatial archetype of the protected home in China – paralleling the social archetype of the family – is based on the courtyard house; this is the case for both rural and urban settings. Topography and climate make variations to this archetype of the protected home, but almost all traditional courtyard houses in China exhibit strong contrast between the interior and the exterior: while the interior is porous and richly layered, the exterior is inarticulate and forbidding. The exterior often shows little indication of what can be expected inside of a courtyard house, unlike Renaissance palaces with their imposing presence in the city that announces their interior magnificence from the outside. The protected home for the extended family, as variously exemplified by the Lu House in the southern city of Dongyang in Zhejiang Province (Figure 5.2) and the Round House in Fujian Province, is an expanded form of the archetype, proliferating with the same principle of the protected home. In imperial China, both government institutions such as ministries and courier stations, and religious institutions such as Buddhist monasteries and Islamic mosques, were imagined as derivatives of the protected home, most prominently defined with similar featureless walls enclosing these institutions. Among all the examples of the protected home and its derivatives, perhaps the most magnificent expression is

Figure 5.2 The Lu House, Dongyang, Zhejiang Province

that of the Forbidden City in Beijing; the seat of imperial power is the ultimate example of a massively expanded protected home, the most complex and richly decorated example consistent with the family archetype. Despite the differences in numbers, sizes, colours, degrees of ornamentations, the archetype of the protected home has been consistent in the use of walls, courtyards, and halls of varying degrees of importance. Perhaps the most sophisticated expression of this spatial archetype of the protected home is that of the interiorized literati gardens; here, the intricacies of designs inside the gardens are as astonishing as the starkness of their exterior appearances. The aesthetic potential of intensive care is rich and limitless, while the opaqueness of its interior is a common feature in Chinese cities.

It is perhaps this immense web of endless permutations of the protected home that twentieth-century Chinese writer Lu Xun (1881–1936) thought of as having spun an 'endless interior' from which it is impossible to escape. In the early twentieth century, Henrik Ibsen's play *A Doll's House* (1879) created a sensation among Chinese youths who were eager to remake their society and cities inspired by the Western model; their goals were to introduce a degree of exposure and transparency in Chinese culture, under the banner of 'democracy and science'. In this context, Nora Helmer, Ibsen's protagonist who left the oppressive bourgeois home and her husband, became a symbol of audacity during the May Fourth Movement in China. As one of the most determined reformers of Chinese culture, Lu Xun was nevertheless reprehensive of the aspirations of China's new youths. Lu Xun could not imagine, when speaking to the students of Beijing Women's Normal School in 1932, where a Chinese Nora Helmer could go were she to leave home. Lu Xun thought that she would either return home or fall; there would seem to be no space for her outside.

In contemporary Chinese cities one may find villas attempting to replicate those in the Western city, but examples are few; the villa, outside the painterly imagination of an isolated pavilion situated in nature, is almost completely absent from the repertoire of building forms in imperial China. The villa, with its aestheticized composure and exposure, would have appeared in the framework of intensive care to be too dangerously disposed; it is much more prudent to build barriers around the body in safety. In this cultural context, Mao's extraordinary experiment with the 'commune' between 1958 and 1984 in rural China was far less effective than Deng's 'family responsibility' system, starting from 1978, which captured the deep-rooted and organic force of family-based economic life. In China, the perfect state, such as Plato's Republic featuring state interests above family interests, or the existence of public institutions forming a dialectic relationship with the family, are subversive to the archetype of the family and the protected home.

One of the recent mass strategies to reinvent the protected home in the contemporary context of high-rise residential buildings is to build metal cages around the apartment (Figure 5.3). These defiant and robust metal cages in the air maintain some of the essential features of the defensive strategy: emphatic divide between the inside and the outside. The harshness of the metal cages seems to be a reincarnation of the ferocious dog and fierce gods guarding the peasant's courtyard home. The metal cages are certainly re-enactments of the featureless and forbidding exterior walls. As the protected home adapts to the condition of high-rise living – the traditional Chinese house never left the ground – it is the balcony that captures an intriguing moment of tension. The balcony – a feature of the high-rise living adapted from the Western house of openness – oscillates between a symbol of modernity and luxury and a source of potential danger in the Chinese city. More often than not, the Chinese 'balcony anxiety' overwhelms the body in safety, resulting in either enclosure with glass panels or encasement with metal bars. The balcony has turned against itself in the Chinese city, shifting from an access to air and view to a site of unacceptable risks; from the poor to the well-off, apartments and houses often have their balconies protected with enclosures. The caged home is perhaps a great source

Figure 5.3 Balconies behind metal cages, Changsha, Hunan Province

of comfort for the body in safety in the Chinese cultural context, while it is no doubt a clear trigger of anxiety for the body in danger in the Western cultural context. Between protection and imprisonment, the body in safety made a clear choice in the Chinese city. Few people can afford a plot of land in contemporary Chinese cities, when one can rely on traditional methods of wall-building to protect the home; for most residents in Chinese cities, the protected home becomes a state of mind brought into existence by a thin layer of metallic cage that is often gratuitous in relation to its function.

The grouping together of apartment blocks in contemporary Chinese cities is commonly known as 'micro-districts' (*xiaoqu* or *wuyuan*). Micro-districts are a result of the marketization of housing which, instead of a commodity, had been a form of standard state provision between the 1950s and 1980s. Since the 1980s, as more and more state-provided housing in Chinese cities disappears, new housing clusters emerge to respond to the new housing needs, and micro-districts are formed to accommodate a redistributed housing market. While similar in financial terms to real estate development elsewhere, these micro-districts are quickly conceived as 'expanded home' with strong protections. Beyond the apartment behind the metal cage, the micro-district is surrounded by solid walls with their gates guarded by security forces. Just as walls are conceived differently in China in relation to walls in the West, the micro-district is also understood distinctly in

China in relation to gated communities in the Western city and its global offspring.[13] While the Western gated communities often result from a strong desire to maintain class differentiation based on income levels – an issue of lifestyles, manners, moral values – the Chinese micro-districts emerge from a common pursuit of safety; between one micro-district and another it is not class differentiation, but the quantity of luxurious provisions that tells them apart. Beyond the material differences, lifestyles, manners, and moral values in all the micro-districts are surprisingly identical. Micro-districts are created and managed in Chinese cities in response to the model of the extended family; they are derivatives of the protected home. They are spaces of intensive care, with their fully manifested features represented in the exotic architectural styles, costly materials, and lavishly landscaped grounds announcing their status as spaces of the ultimate intensive care.

The 'state family' (*guojia*), in this context, is also constructed with the archetype of the protected home. Chinese nationalism appeals heavily to the family structure, imagining all Chinese to be the descendants of the same ancestral origin; historically, one of the most powerful expressions of the intensive care of the state would be the defensive wall built cross China's northern borders. In contemporary Chinese cities, this vast conception of intensive care of the state family can be featured in the form of 'prestige projects'; instead of the Great Wall, it is perhaps the great state projects – the Three Gorges Dam, the Olympic Games, the high-speed rail network – that are the key manifestations of the intensive care of the state family. The mobilization of resources and the sacrifices of ordinary people required for the speedy realization of these state projects – like the enormous labour and sacrifice that went into the construction of the Great Wall in different times – seem only accountable when we see them as part of this regime of intensive care. This intensive state care system is far from having realized its potential in China; in many ways, China's vast territories and sheer complexity have frustrated and prolonged the efforts to achieve a fuller extent of the state care capacity, something that a smaller state such as Singapore has been able to do effectively.

Regular Care: Units of Economic Interest

Moving down from the spaces of intensive care, we can probably describe a second group of spaces as those of regular care; these are often spaces with units of economic interest. Although never absolute, the divide between spaces of intensive care and those of regular care can perhaps be seen in the divide between family and kinship in the traditional sense. The walled village – as the space of kinship – can perhaps be seen as an archetype of the space of regular care, as the village was also a unit of economic interest. As units of economic interest transform with Chinese society and cities in the twentieth century, they seem to have maintained a few essential features of this kinship structure. Perhaps the most persistent feature in relation to the units of economic interest is that of the relational circle, or *guanxi*. Relational circles incorporate networks of people outside the family and create bonds that are modelled on the family relationships. If the family offers access to intensive care, the relational circle offers access to economic resources; just like care does not really exist outside the family, good economic resources are hard to find outside the relational circles. In this sense, there is essentially no place for strangers in Chinese cities; strangers must quickly identify relational circles and break into them so that they, like those who are in these circles, can have some access to resources. Relational circles can be created from a wide range of people; most readily-made relational circles are those formed early in life, such as those of kinship, clan, common place of origin, alumni circles, with the bond in these circles resembling closely that of the family. Relational circles must be cultivated and regularly cared for so that they maintain their reciprocal effectiveness; this is most commonly done through 'gift giving' in the Confucianist framework. Gift (*li*), in this context, is both social and material; it is both a tributary ritual (*limao*, the gift appearance) and an economic value (*liwu*, the gift thing).[14] In traditional Chinese cities, the cultivation of the relational circle took place primarily in the form of 'associations' (*huiguan*) which were made from either common trade (*shanghui*) or common place of origin (*tongxianghui*).[15] In contemporary Chinese cities, perhaps the most essential form of conducting this ritual of gift giving is around the table of an abundant meal.

The regular care of relational circles takes place in two enclosed rooms in contemporary Chinese cities, the dining room and the karaoke room. The enclosed room, or *baojian*, emerges from the late twentieth century as the epitome of Chinese social space. The enclosed room is a compartmentalized space separated from common spaces, and they often contain washing facilities; it is a minimum space that creates a complete enclosure. Windows seem to be incidental to these rooms, as they are neither rejected nor used appreciatively; many of these rooms are windowless. The enclosed dining room seems to be the most popular space of the relational circle; the extraordinary quantity and variety of these rooms in restaurants in Chinese cities are perhaps an indication of their vital importance of relational circles in need of regular care. The care of the dining room itself is expressed in two ways: it is highly decorated and it is named carefully. Many of them are themed along the narratives of significant places, flowers, historical figures, etc. Careful rituals – those based on the model of the family – are observed in this space: in a variety of ways the 'head position' is marked, usually facing the entrance, and people are often seated according to their importance in relation to the head position. The importance of this impromptu ranking exercise lies in its iteration of the hierarchies of the relational circles and their loose connections to the archetype of the patrilineal family hierarchy, even though this ancient origin may not immediately be comprehended in the contemporary context. Often food is offered from one person to another as a symbolic 'tributary' gesture; the taking of food is regularly interjected by regular 'tributary toasts', often originating from those of the lower rank to those of the higher rank, although, depending on the formality of the occasion, this may be only loosely observed. Nevertheless, the tributary gestures are regular and unmistakable; they are no doubt based on the familial and imperial tributary expectations so essential to the Chinese way of life throughout China's long history. Fulfilling a very different role, the karaoke room reverses and dissolves the hierarchy rehearsed so meticulously in the enclosed dining room, and compensates it with excessive relaxed animation. As important as the tributary etiquette in the enclosed dining room, the outbursts of spontaneous expressions and self-esteem – often sacrificed in the interest of hierarchical demands elsewhere – become acceptable in the karaoke room. In this equally important social space, the literary theming of spaces gives way to endless colourful sparkles; the karaoke room is a study of sensual stimulations in its most unmitigated form.

A ubiquitous space of regular care with a much longer lineage in contemporary Chinese cities is the work unit, or *danwei*. The work unit is a general term used to describe a wide variety of places of life and work established since the 1950s, ranging from government ministries, large industrial complexes, universities, and institutes of architectural design. Work units are hierarchical and not typological; their ranks are determined by their size and centrality to the government rather than by the type of work: they are either central (*zhongyang*), local (*difang*), or grass-root (*jiceng*). Being part of a work unit does not just mean having a job; its membership means a combined 'provision of housing, free medical care, child care centres, kindergartens, dining halls, bath houses, service companies, and collective enterprises to employ the children of staff – the *danwei* provides its members with a complete social guarantee and welfare services'.[16] The work unit is both a unit of production, a system of care, and a method of human management; for many decades since the establishment of the work unit in the mid-twentieth century, a person always belonged to a work unit and abided by the rules and regulations of that unit. All inter-work unit matters, official and personal, required 'introduction letters' from one's work unit. The work unit is an extraordinary crystallization of a wide range of demands in the Chinese city: cultural heritage, social welfare, ideological control, labour management, and economic viability.[17] Although not a direct derivative of the family, the work unit is parallel to the kinship structure as a unit of economic interest; it combines family-style protection, care, and control with the economic functions.

The work unit as a social imagination presents no distinct typological features; this is clearly reflected in the lack of architectural typological features in the design and layout of a work unit. Despite the various different functions of the work units – from production of useful things to the management of society – they are designed in strikingly similar ways. Usually a walled compound, it is dominated by a main building serving as the symbolic centre of that work unit, with less important buildings located around the centre, often organized through an axis. Appended to this main spine of important buildings, other functions such as canteen, apartments, kindergartens, schools, and sports grounds are placed based on the land resources. Differentiations, like the spaces of intensive care, are strategized on the basis of ranked quantities of sizes and degrees of ornamentation; a provincial government work unit would be much larger and more carefully landscaped than that of a county government. Although both enclosed within walls and guarded by security teams, the compound of the work unit is different from the compound of the micro-district. Micro-districts seem to be closely connected to the archetype of the protected home, and are cared for far more intensely whenever possible through theming and elaborate landscaping. Work units seem to be more analogous to the archetype of the village, an ingenious invention that blended the Chinese way of life with contemporary economic functions of the city. Like the enclosed dining room and the karaoke room, the work unit is a space of regular care. The absolute domination of the work unit perhaps ended in the late 1970s when the nascent market economy allowed private enterprises to employ people outside the framework of work units; however, private enterprises, instead of seeking their organizational and spatial features emanating from the logic of the market place, have become more like the work unit, simulating the management and architectural features of the work unit. With the emergence of a market economy in Chinese cities, the work unit does not seem to have been marginalized; it continues to play, in its original and modified forms, an important role in Chinese cities today.

Featuring prominently in spaces of intensive and regular care is the notion of what may be described as 'conspicuous safety'. Safety here appears as an over-compensated representation of care. It is both social and spatial. One common sign of conspicuous safety is to dress the security team in uniforms closely resembling those of the police and the army, a frequent sight in Chinese cities, with an abundance of security forces on display. Security teams are often drilled in open view, military style, as if to underline their protective capacity. In this context, the metal cages, the walls, the guarded gates are architectural elements of conspicuous safety, which result not from necessity but from representation. The body in safety lives in great comfort with endless representations of conspicuous safety in Chinese cities.

Carelessness: *Jianghu*

Within this immense and complex network of spaces of intensive and regular care, there is an equally immense and complex network of spaces without care. The incessant differentiations of spatial inside and outside in Chinese cities also map two distinct categories of people: the 'cooked people' (*shouren*) of the inside and the 'raw people' (*shengren*) of the outside. If the protected home is the archetype of intensive care and the village is the archetype of regular care, then *jianghu* – literally meaning 'rivers and lakes' but by analogy meaning an absolute outside – is the archetype of carelessness. Historically connoting both hermitage and opposition, *jianghu* is perhaps most deeply informed by the literary imagination found in the Ming dynasty (fourteenth-century) novel *Water Margin* (*Shuihu Zhuang*), which evolved over time and is now believed to have a collective authorship.[18] Set in the Southern Song dynasty (twelfth century), this highly popular novel is about 108 rebellious characters who gathered in Mount Liang Marsh, raised a powerful army, and were eventually granted amnesty by the government in order to defend China from foreign invaders. The meaning of *jianghu* elaborated in *Water Margin* is dependent on the double meaning of care – provision and control – in the sense that *jianghu*, through the absence of care, is a place of self-sufficiency and a place for the possibilities of justice. Instead of a Western triad of utopia, dystopia, and reality, it is a Chinese *terra non grata*. In its real and imagined forms, *jianghu* is on the one hand dangerous and filthy, and on the other rewarding and enticing. If the social ranking of the Ming dynasty put scholars, peasants, craftsmen, and merchants in their respective order, then *Water Margin* depicts a colourful range of characters – no high-ranking scholar officials and no peasants among them – outside the Ming social order; it is not surprising that, in 1642 shortly before its collapse, the troubled late Ming dynasty banned the book. It is also helpful to note that traditionally entertainers (*yiren*) were considered to operate within the realms of *jianghu* as entertainers perhaps did not fit into the Ming social order. Contemporary popular novelists and movie makers have made fruitful uses of the imaginary spaces of *jianghu* to accommodate gratuitous violence, unbelievable heroic deeds, and forbidden love. Hong Kong's movie makers, such as John Woo and Johnnie To, routinely use the dense and chaotic architecture of the city as scenes of triad gangs and police officers fighting out in the spaces of *jianghu*.[19] The features of self-sufficiency and possibilities of justice of *jianghu* do not make *jianghu* an Aristotelian state; *jianghu* is parasitic to spaces of care, and it is constructed as the place of the absence of care rather than that of potential institutions of universal truth and justice. The heroes of *Water Margin* did not establish a utopian state with alternative legislation; they returned to the state care of the imperial order. It may be possible to establish honour in *jianghu*; it is not conceivable to sustain trust. This Chinese social feature appeared to be astonishing to those coming from the context of faithful brethren among various Christian sects.[20] The immensity and complexity of *jianghu* in the Chinese cultural context is perhaps linked to the way in which each person could imagine a unique set of *jianghu* conditions; in some ways, politeness and rudeness exist side by side as one judges one's situations in fluidity in response to demands of intensive care and carelessness.

Understanding the spaces of *jianghu*, in place of public spaces, is crucial to an access to the spatial framework of shared territories in Chinese cities. 'Rivers and lakes' not only invoke analogous meanings of infinite free paths and forbidding natural barriers, but also bring forth literal meaning of water spaces. Water spaces are neither cultivatable nor inhabitable; in China, water spaces – rivers, lakes, the ocean – are often among the first to be carelessly treated with litter, sewage, and industrial discharge.[21] One common fate for rivers in Chinese cities is to be cleaned up and rebuilt like a sewer, with straight concrete channels and hard edges as if to anticipate and to fight future contamination. For similar reasons, beaches are particularly conducive places for careless behaviours; if water spaces are dangerous, beaches – as places where that danger begins – are unsuitable for cities. Imperial Chinese cities were historically not constructed next to water, unlike the cities founded by Western influences such as Singapore, Hong Kong, and Shanghai. Keeping shared water spaces from abuse has been one of the most difficult tasks to accomplish in Chinese cities; their literal connection with the spaces of carelessness can perhaps explain this urban feature which otherwise remains incomprehensible. It is the huge range of possible spaces that can be analogously regarded as *jianghu* that gives rise to some of the most potent forces shaping Chinese cities. Some would certainly consider the space immediately outside the windows and doors as *jianghu*, and feel comfortable to discard rubbish there in accordance with its status. Like the traditional alley ways (*hutongs*) outside the courtyard house in Beijing, the streets outside the contemporary micro-district can be regarded as a space of *jianghu*. Like rivers and lakes, streets in Chinese cities can often induce careless behaviours; their possible status as spaces of *jianghu* – as unclassified spaces linking spaces of various degrees of care – may have contributed towards their general neglect. The inside and the outside, in mapping spaces of intensive care and carelessness, is demarcated with physical boundaries and practised in everyday life. The regimes and nature of care in cities are visible through the demarcation of spaces, but they are also observable through the distribution of rubbish; in Chinese cities, rubbish distribution mimics their concentric regimes of spatial care to form, in the case of Beijing, a ring of rubbish mountains outside the perceived spatial boundary of the city.[22]

In countless attempts to wrestle the streets from the clutches of *jianghu*, many Chinese cities have run campaigns of public hygiene by requesting people to consider streets as home. The most effective strategy, even for colonial cities such as Hong Kong and Singapore, is to employ a large number of cleaners to keep up with endless elimination of litter. Otherwise, *jianghu* rules the streets. Hong Kong's experience with public space is an interesting example of adaptations of the Chinese sensibility of *jianghu* in the twentieth century. The pre-1997 colonial government legislated the standards of public space provision, but these are primarily dominated by prescribed 'uses' such as walking paths, children's playgrounds, and chess-playing tables. 'Public space' in Hong Kong was reimagined primarily through the provision of facilities. Managers of these spaces – often Chinese – were much removed from the lofty ideals of the legislators; they tended to manage the use of the spaces with a concept that may be seen to be closer to that of *jianghu*. Fences, restrictions, and controls are frequently applied to many public spaces, both to care for the space and to prevent it from abuse. A recent development in Hong Kong has been for the government to entrust the private sector to provide 'public space' – privately owned public spaces – in shopping malls and in the privately owned transportation infrastructure. While this strategy is both sensible in relation to the Chinese tradition of degrees of care and successful in relation to the city of maximum quantities in Hong Kong, it also places any possible realm of the public in the hands of the capital which reconstitute 'public spaces' through a range of visual and spatial manipulations. In Chinese cities, 'public spaces' tend to oscillate between those of intensive care, such as Tiananmen Square and Chang'an Avenue, and carelessness, such as countless open spaces and streets in Chinese cities with little care and with much filth and rudeness.

Between the 1950s and 1980s when the work unit dominated Chinese social and spatial reality, *jianghu* appeared to be an imagination of no great consequence; as the work unit loosens its grip from the 1980s, and as the massive migration of peasant labour into cities expands units of economic interests to an enormous degree, the notion of *jianghu* gains a critically important dimension in contemporary life. Migrant workers have not been absorbed into the work unit and will likely not be treated as 'strangers in the city'; instead, they exist on the margin of society and cities without normative provision of welfare that the members of a work unit enjoy. In the three decades since the 1980s, the migrant population in Chinese cities reached over 350 million; the conception of *jianghu*, in this age of mass and rapid movement of people, formulates urban conditions in Chinese cities. The ways in which *jianghu* reconstitutes itself in the twenty-first century in the Chinese city will lead to tremendous consequences for the physical and intellectual make-up of the Chinese city. In today's Chinese cities, the family, the work unit, and *jianghu* – three powerful archetypal social and spatial constructs being transformed by fast social and economic changes – define Chinese cities in important ways. Is it possible to make up a 'public realm' from a combination of these archetypal social and spatial constructs to ground a sufficient degree of equality, freedom, and justice? Spaces are cared for in their unique ways in the Chinese city, and the degrees of care are deeply rooted in the conception, valuation, and elimination of dangers that are so fundamental to the normative existence of the body in safety.

Notes

1. The greatest threat to public health improvement programmes was the worldwide spread of bubonic plague in the late nineteenth century; the conditions of Chinese cities were particularly susceptible to the spread of diseases. This caused a wide range of responses from both foreign and Chinese settlements in Chinese cities to contain the diseases and to sustain their urban life. See Carol Benedict, *Bubonic Plague in Nineteenth-Century China* (Stanford: Stanford University Press, 1996); Karrie MacPherson, *A Wilderness of Marshes: The Origins of Public Health in Shanghai, 1843–1893* (Maryland: Lexington Press, 2001); Yu Xinzhong, 'Night Soil and Waste in Modern China', in Angela Ki Che Leung and Charlotte Furth, eds, *Health and Hygiene in Chinese East Asia: Policies and Publics in the Long Twentieth Century* (Durham and London: Duke University Press, 2010), pp.51–72.
2. James D. Tracy, 'To Wall or Not to Wall: Evidence from Medieval Germany', in James D. Tracy, ed., *City Walls: The Urban Enceinte in Global Perspective* (Cambridge: Cambridge University Press, 2000), pp.72–73.
3. Aristotle, 'Politics', in *The Basic Works of Aristotle*, ed. Richard McKeon (New York: The Modern Library, 2001), 1330b, 1331a.
4. Tracy, 'To Wall or Not to Wall', p.79.
5. Nancy Steinhardt, 'Representations of Chinese Walled Cities in the Pictorial and Graphic Arts', in Tracy, ed., *City Walls*, pp.419–60.
6. James D. Tracy, 'Introduction', in Tracy, ed., *City Walls*, p.2.
7. Edward Farmer, 'The Hierarchy of Ming City Walls', in Tracy, ed., *City Walls*, p.486.
8. Sen-Cou Chang, 'Some Observations on the Morphology of Chinese Walled Cities', *Annals of the Association of American Geographers* 60 (1970), pp.63–91.
9. Ruth Rogaski, *Hygienic Modernity: Meanings of Health and Disease in Treaty-Port China* (Berkeley: University of California Press, 2004); Angela Ki Che Leung and Charlotte Furth, eds, *Health and Hygiene in Chinese East Asia: Policies and Publics in the Long Twentieth Century* (Durham and London: Duke University Press, 2010); Marta E. Hanson, *Speaking of Epidemics in Chinese Medicine* (London and New York: Routledge, 2011).
10. Hsiao-tung Fei (Fei Xiaotong), *Peasant Life in China: A Field Study of Country Life in the Yangtze Valley* (London: Routledge & Kegan Paul, 1939).
11. Aristotle, *Politics*, 1252a.

12 Ibid., 1253a.
13 Chris Webster, Georg Glasze and Klaus Frantz, 'The Global Spread of Gated Communities', Special Issue, *Environment and Planning B* 29:3 (2002), pp.315–20. Wu Fulong, 'Rediscovering the "Gate" Under Market Transition: From Work-Unit Compounds to Commodity Housing Enclaves', *Housing Studies* 20 (2005), pp.235–54.
14 Wang Hui, *Xiandai Zhongguo sixiang de xingqi* (The Rise of Modern Chinese Thought), in 4 volumes (Beijing: Sanlian shudian, 2008); Michael Keith, Scott Lash, Jakob Arnoldi and Tyler Rooker, *China Constructing Capitalism: Economic Life and Urban Change* (London and New York: Routledge, 2013).
15 Sun Dazhang, ed., *Zhongguo gudai jianzhu shi* (History of Ancient Chinese Architecture), Vol. 5 (Beijing: Zhongguo jiangong chubanshe, 2002), p.28.
16 Li Hanlin, 'China's *Danwei* Phenomenon and the Mechanisms of Conformity in Urban Communities', *Sociology Research* 5 (1993), pp.23–32, translated and quoted in David Bray, *Social Space and Governance in Urban China: The* Danwei *System from Origins to Reform* (Stanford: Stanford University Press, 2005), pp.3–4.
17 Bray, *Social Space and Governance in Urban China*; Lu Duanfang, *Remaking Chinese Urban Form: Modernity, Scarcity and Space, 1949–2005* (London and New York: Routledge, 2006).
18 Wang Xuetai, *Suihu, Jianghu* (Xian: Sha'anxi renmin chubanshe, 2011).
19 I am grateful to the observations of Esther Lorenz, who has studied the Hong Kong cinema in relation to the notion of *jianghu*. Also see Gina Marchetti, Esther M. K. Cheung and Tan See-kam, eds, *Hong Kong Screenscapes: From the New Wave to the Digital Frontier* (Hong Kong: Hong Kong University Press, 2010).
20 'The typical distrust of the Chinese for one another is confirmed by all observers. It stands in sharp contrast to the trust and honesty of the faithful brethren in the Puritan sects, a trust shared by outsiders as well', Max Weber, *The Religion of China: Confucianism and Taoism* (New York: The Free Press, 1951), p.232.
21 Yu, 'Night Soil and Waste in Modern China', p.57.
22 Wang Min'an, 'On Rubbish', trans. Li Shiqiao, *Theory, Culture & Society* 28 (2011), pp.340–53.

6

Antisepsis

At the turn of the twentieth century, Adolf Loos was deeply enthralled by the impact of plumbing in architecture. It was as if architecture was no longer driven by classical sensibilities of harmony and proportion perpetuated since the Renaissance, but by a deceptively simple technological scheme, the supply and drainage of water. For Loos, plumbing enabled daily washing, which had a great cultural significance: 'an increase in the use of water is one of our most critical cultural tasks'.[1] He called for a return to the love of water for the Austrians, who had been misled by a fear of water in the over-cultivated Latin culture epitomized by the French. The English and the Americans embraced the ancient Germanic love of water and had no fear of either dirt or water, which was the cultural root of their success: 'There would have been no nineteenth century without the plumber.'[2] Loos's sentiment was not entirely contrived; since the mid-nineteenth century, great advances in medical research have led to tremendous improvements in public hygiene in urban centres in Europe. Public health has been a crucial concern particularly for the 'labouring population' since the mid-nineteenth century. Edwin Chadwick's report on sanitary conditions in England (1842), and the subsequent Public Health Act 1848 and the establishment of the Board of Health, are well-known examples.[3] Central to these improvements were the design and construction of sewage systems, something that deeply impressed one of the earliest Japanese visitors to Europe, Nagayo Sensai, in 1872. In Berlin, he also witnessed, in amazement, the development of new hospitals and laboratories, and the beginning of a national public health bureaucracy.[4] Ancient attitudes towards dirt and washing seem to be confused – oscillating between holiness and defilement[5] – but the nineteenth century put forward a clear message: dirt and disease are inextricably connected. Loos was not alone in turning this long-standing nineteenth-century concern for public health into an architectural discourse; Le Corbusier brought a much more emphatic aesthetic and moral expression of public hygiene into architecture. The foyer sinks at Loos's Rufer House (1922) and

LeCorbusier's Villa Savoye (1929) are common attempts to aestheticize inevitable architectural consequences of the act of cleansing the body.[6]

Since Loos's pronouncements, hygiene in architecture has developed in two directions to become what might be described as the architecture of bacteria and virus control. The first direction is centred on whiteness in the early twentieth century; whiteness seems to have emerged from the visual act of bleaching, the physical and metaphorical removal of dirt as an antiseptic practice. The second appears to be rooted in the medical procedure of disinfection; the result of this in architecture is the homogenous surface. While plumbing reinvents the layout of habitable spaces through the creation of daily washing rituals for all, antisepsis impacts on surfaces, which disturbs and reorders traditional aesthetics of the surface – classical or modernist – in architecture. The antiseptic surface is thin and sealed, which deviates from the traditional 'thick surface' (*poché*) fundamental to texture and depth.[7] The thin surface is generating its own aesthetic realm and therefore can no longer be easily dismissed as 'untruthful' to the interior; it is combining the Baroque impulse for decorated surfaces with the logic of antiseptic procedures to create a new age of surface effects. Through a powerful alliance with the ubiquitous electronic screen that focuses tremendous intellectual energy on surface effects, the thin surface has acquired an extraordinary strength in contemporary design. Skin and wrapping, rather than depth and tectonics, are much more attractive architectural propositions today. This way of looking at architecture, in turn, points to its own pioneers and their manifestos – those of Florence Nightingale and the Centre for Disease Control and Prevention instead of Alberti and Le Corbusier – which present, without intellectual pretension and with starkness, some of the most important forces shaping a new hygienic architecture for our age.

How have Chinese cities responded to these developments in urban hygiene in the nineteenth century? Whiteness and disinfection have both taken root in Chinese cities and have done so in different ways from those in Western cities. Chinese cities were first linked to nineteenth-century movements in urban hygiene through the Chinese 'treaty-port cities' – Hong Kong, Shanghai, Tianjin are the most important among them – which were established as results of treaties signed between imperial China and Western powers to ensure the trading interests of the Western powers in China. They were also established in the context of a late nineteenth-century global spread of bubonic plague as they vigorously participated in global trade. Their concentrated urban environments – features of the city of maximum quantities and degrees of care – made these cities particularly vulnerable to infectious diseases. In various concessions in the late nineteenth century – zones of semi-independent administrations under various Western powers in China – urban hygiene became paramount if these places were to function at all. Their institutions and regulations of urban hygiene brought new practices to Chinese cities.[8] Chinese traditional strategies of health almost entirely focused on corporeal preservation regimens; urban hygiene, like public space, was dimly perceived as a regime of care until the New Policies period of the Qing imperial administration (1900–11). This cultural condition presented an enormous challenge to the treaty-port cities as they established municipal institutions taking charge of public space and urban hygiene. Urban hygiene was also high on the agenda of the Communist government after they took over the administration of cities in China in 1949. In dramatic and heavy-handed measures, Mao waged a civil war against diseases and pests; successive mass campaigns were launched to eliminate them. Urban hygiene was explicitly linked to the project of nationalism as the mass campaigns were called the 'patriotic hygiene movement'. From the 1980s, all Chinese cities began a system that requires all shops and institutions with street fronts to be responsible for the hygienic conditions of the 'front door' areas; it is always the space beyond the front door, rather than the space behind it, that seems to be a hygienic challenge.

It was perhaps the institutional infrastructure that contributed to the remarkable success of the treaty-port cities in establishing some degree of urban hygiene standards, although, then as now, urban hygiene in these cities requires constant external vigilance and enforcement. Among the first treaty-port cities, Hong Kong is the oldest and maintained an almost unbroken development under the British administration from its establishment in 1842; it is the most illustrative example of the city of maximum quantities, thus most 'hygienically challenged'. Hong Kong's urban transformation has been critically anchored by two key events: the 1894 outbreak of bubonic plague and the 2003 outbreak of SARS (Severe Acute Respiratory Syndrome), both clearly connected with the concentration of buildings and people in extreme proximity, something that has been internalized and aestheticized as its culture (Figure 6.1). Despite its colonial history which transformed many aspects of the Chinese culture in the city, Hong Kong remains unmistakably a Chinese city. Its urban hygiene practices had to respond and adapt to the conditions of the Chinese city; in many ways, Hong Kong is

Figure 6.1 Sai Yeung Choi Street, Mongkok, Hong Kong

Figure 6.2 Entrance door handle, foyer, Hong Kong Arts Centre (photo by Esther Lorenz)

an extraordinary experiment of the hygienic strategies of the Chinese city. Through Hong Kong, we can perhaps gain a glimpse into future cities in China: the roots of corporeal protection in ancient rites are now combined with modern medical knowledge to give rise to a new architecture that is yet to be described (Figure 6.2).

Whiteness

The twentieth century has imbued us with insensitivity towards whiteness in architecture such that it often escapes our thoughts; in both Western and Chinese cultures, whiteness is an unusual colour, if it is a colour at all. In the Chinese conception of colours, which is rooted in the *Book of Changes*, whiteness is understood as a state of 'depletion'; it plays an important role in the cyclical structure of five colours (*wuse*) – blue, red, yellow, white, black – which are parallel manifestations of the five elements of the universe. While white is the state of depletion, red is the state of full vitality. For this reason, red is used to celebrate life in its sanguine prosperity (weddings) while white is used to mark the depletion of life (funerals); in the ancient usage of colours, whiteness was carefully avoided generally unless it was used as a part of the set of five colours. With the introduction of Buddhism in China, whiteness has gained an association with the notion of 'pure land' within the Buddhist context. Whiteness, or more precisely emptiness, in the Chinese literati painting is regarded as the surface of the 'unexplained', which, when arranged skilfully, is highly valued. This whiteness in the visual arts is perhaps better understood as 'richness in nothingness', particularly in painting and calligraphy; it is always intentionally 'left blank' (*liubai*), and not 'painted white', as a way of sustaining artistic and philosophical space. The white walls in the private gardens in southern China should probably be seen in this context. The Western construction of whiteness, however, was perhaps first centred on its quality of potentiality rather than depletion; whiteness seems to present maximum potential in its purity (weddings), while blackness, one could argue, indicates its exhaustion (funerals). John Locke used the metaphor of blank slate (*tabula rasa*) to mean the maximum potential for new knowledge. The whiteness of the bedroom Loos designed for his nineteen-year-old wife in 1903 perhaps blended the potentiality of whiteness with that of the youthful female body. The second focus of the meaning of whiteness lies in its status as defiance of nature, which, unlike in Daoism, holds considerable prestige. The existence of the purity of whiteness is precarious; this fragility, like that of the body in combat and knowledge in contest, is pregnant with enormous intellectual and aesthetic content. The extraordinary struggle to sustain whiteness – as well as power, virtue, truth – seems to have become the ground for distinction: divinity, virginity, intellect, social and economic class. The potentiality of whiteness, in the Western intellectual context, could indeed be seen to be the 'mother and nurse' of all other architectural possibilities;[9] whiteness in architecture could be seen as 'the thin white line between architecture and decoration' which gives rise to the discipline of architecture.[10]

The moral and aesthetic potentiality became crucial in Le Corbusier's formulation of a theory of the superiority of whiteness in architecture, which contains three aspects. First, whiteness is honesty: 'Whitewash is extremely moral. Suppose there were a decree requiring all rooms in Paris to be given a coat of whitewash. I maintain that that would be a police task of real stature and a manifestation of high morality, the sign of a great people.'[11] Second, whiteness is a material form of equality: 'Whitewash is the wealth of the poor and of the rich – of everybody, just as bread, milk and water are the wealth of the slave and the king.'[12] Third, whiteness provides intellectual power, an 'unfailing imperative which is the sense of truth and which recognizes in the smoothness of ripolin and the white of whitewash an object of truth'.[13]

> The Stadium, like the Bank, demands precision and clarity, speed and correctness. Stadium and bank both provide conditions appropriate for action, conditions of clarity like that in a head that has to think. There may be people who think against a background of black. But the tasks of our age – so strenuous, so full of danger, so violent, so victorious – seem to demand of us that we think against a background of white.[14]

These arguments were powerful and became widely accepted by those who wished to depart from the mediocrity of Beaux-Arts architecture in the early twentieth century. Among the most extraordinary examples are the exhibition houses by sixteen architects built at Weissenhofsiedlung in 1927, which were constructed with a common directive of white exterior walls. Over a century, the white wall has become so common that one would generally associate 'modern architecture' with white walls.[15]

Whiteness in Hong Kong has a very different trajectory, which may explain the fact that the Hong Kong whiteness is more often 'off-white' – lightly coloured surfaces. There is an absence of policing the purity of whiteness, which perhaps resulted from the slightly uncomfortable association between whiteness in its purity and the depletion of life. In this sense, Hong Kong's use of whiteness may be seen perhaps to have been closely connected to a different architectural practice influenced by Florence Nightingale's *Notes on Hospitals* in 1863. Although generally ignored by architectural historians, perhaps for its lack of interest in architectural discourses, this 'architectural treatise' is extraordinarily precise because of its lack of interest in academic debates in architecture, and because of its tremendous influence in the construction of hospitals throughout the world. Nightingale's treatise resulted from her experience and achievement at the military camp hospital at Scutari during the Crimean War (1853–56). As a volunteer nurse, Nightingale arrived at the British military camp in 1854 to discover that ten times as many soldiers died of infections such as typhus and cholera than from battle wounds; there was an unacceptably high mortality rate there. After several improvements in drainage and ventilation instigated by her, mortality rate dropped dramatically. Reflecting on this and other experiences, she began her treatise on hospital design: 'It may seem a strange principle to enunciate as the very first requirement in a Hospital that it should do the sick no harm.'[16] The reality in hospitals at the time made it crucial for her to make the point that it was the architecture of the hospital that contributed to the high mortality rate. Nightingale shows that the mortality rate in twenty-four London hospitals in 1861 was over 90 per cent, while that in twenty-five county hospitals in country towns was just below 40 per cent.[17] She argued that this was due to the poor hygienic conditions in London, and cleaner air and better ventilation in county hospitals. Nightingale's campaign for hospital hygiene brought a new focus on the connection between health and hygiene; her highly influential principles of hospital design demonstrated dramatically the benefit of sensible designs, and these principles are equally applicable in the designs of other kinds of buildings in cities, particularly in the context of polluted nineteenth-century European urban centres.

Nightingale, like Chadwick, was a believer in the miasma theory of diseases, which departed from the traditional focus on the balance of humours and placed the root of diseases in the general lack of sanitary conditions in air and water, and on material surfaces. She believed that the sick exhaled substances that were 'highly morbid and dangerous', and this was 'one of nature's methods of eliminating noxious matter from the body, in order that it may recover health'.[18] The core belief of the miasma theory is the removal of poisonous substances from the living environment, which underlined the emphasis of ventilation and light. Miasma theory perhaps consolidated a long-standing search for methods of ventilation in hospital design. In 1777, King Louis XV of France appointed a commission of the Académie Royale des Sciences to look into the problem of building hospitals, in connection to the rebuilding of Hôtel-Dieu which was burned down in 1772, searching, over a decade, for the best and most hygienic plans for a 1,000-bed hospital. The hospital was seen to be a machine for ventilation, an architecture shaped by the movement of the air,[19] and perhaps not primarily understood as an architecture of surveillance in Michel Foucault's conception. More relevantly, miasma theory raised the importance of white and off-white surfaces as a way of making poisonous substances visible. Nightingale was highly critical of 'the gloom of a dark ward',[20] and recommended 'impervious material' with 'a white or tinted surface'.[21] Bathrooms should certainly be covered with white tiles.[22] It was important to use 'good colour, and not a dull dirty one' for the surfaces, Nightingale suggested, and 'a sufficiently good surface might be obtained by applying some of the better class of light-coloured paints'.[23] Nightingale's recommendation of white or off-white surfaces probably appeared to be strange at the time, when hospital interiors, let alone general architecture, were mostly covered with colours arising from aesthetic schemes. For instance, the 572-bed Poplar and Stepney Workhouse Infirmary (designed by A & C Harston in 1871) used mauve-grey coloured brick walls with their lower portions painted buff, with chocolate line and skirting.[24]

The philosophical and moral discussions of whiteness, over the twentieth century, have almost entirely eclipsed its hospital origins; this understanding of the ubiquitous white walls of modern architecture must be supplemented by a recovery of their practical roots in the promotion of health. The first great driving force for Hong Kong's urbanization came from the first wave of immigrants arriving following the Communist takeover of China in 1949, and from the disastrous fire at Shek Kip Mei in 1953 which left more than 50,000 people homeless. The housing crisis resulted in a pragmatic approach in architectural design which owed more to basic considerations of safety and hygiene than modernist theory; Hong Kong's public housing and community projects have always been designed with off-white surfaces. In the private sector, the use of off-white surfaces is equally prominent, particularly since the outbreak of SARS in 2003. New shopping malls such as the International Finance Centre in Central and renovation of older shopping malls such as New Town Plaza in Shatin are all dominated by the environment of off-white surfaces. In light of Nightingale's *Notes on Hospitals*, Hong Kong's extensive use of light-coloured material surfaces can be seen to have a much closer link with the implicit requirement of urban hygiene. The lightly coloured off-white surfaces in Hong Kong fulfil two seemingly conflicting demands: seeing the filth and avoiding the colour of the depletion of life. While traditional Chinese interiors – from domestic spaces to Buddhist temples – are intensely colourful, contemporary Chinese cities are pasted extensively with a layer of lightly coloured materials.

Shine

Another prominent feature of Hong Kong's interiors, particularly recently completed commercial and domestic interiors, is the surface shine. When this is combined with its off-white colour schemes, it produces an environment of off-white shine. An army of polishers, dressed in nurse-like uniforms, continuously mop and polish these surfaces with antiseptic solutions. It seems that it is important that these surfaces should shine constantly. This environment of off-white shine is a combined result of lightly coloured walls and ceilings, stainless steel surfaces, polished off-white floor tiles, glass and mirrors, and spotlights being bounced against these surfaces. The experience of this flickering environment can be visually disorientating and overwhelming, and it is very prevalent in commercial interiors. Leading examples of this type of interiors are shopping malls such as Pacific Place at Admiralty, Elements Mall at Kowloon Station, New Town

Figure 6.3 New Town Plaza, Shatin, Hong Kong

Plaza (Figure 6.3) and Grand Century Plaza in Shatin. Residential interiors, if show flats and clubhouses of prestigious developments in Hong Kong are indicative of a trend, are also moving towards a similar environment of off-white shine. Chinese cities in general, in the past decades, seem to have adopted the lightly coloured shiny material surfaces as an aspiring standard. In China, both the shopping malls built by Hong Kong and Singapore developers and those by local developers feature the ubiquitous off-white shiny environment. The aesthetic value of shine seems to be limited to objects in many cultures; it was never an environmental quality. The aesthetic and moral status of shine, unlike that of whiteness, seems to be uncertain. The Chinese tradition places shine in desirable individual objects – porcelain, precious metals, jade, and lacquered furniture – which sustain a sense of preciousness, cultivation, and refinement. The colours of shiny objects tend to be intense, which are in line with the demand for the fullness of colours – rooted in the nature of the objects – in the ancient conception of the five colours. Although imperial palaces and gardens used glazed yellow, green, and blue tiles to signify grandeur and hierarchy, their use was not universal outside the imperial context; the private gardens in southern China are generally free of environmental shine in their use of building materials. In the context of Western modern architecture, shine has a rather lowly aesthetic and intellectual status despite, or because of, its high capacity to delight the senses: for moralists, the shiny marbles in Roman interiors and the metallic and reflective shine of the French court taste point to a general moral decay. Western aesthetic theory seems to have made a crucial alliance between morality and a hierarchy of the pleasure of senses; in the ideas about beauty found in Plato, Shaftesbury, and Kant, physical senses must be restrained by the ideal 'moral sense' which originates from intellectual and rational principles away from sensual delight. The delight in shiny objects is seen to be indicative of bad taste and a general state of moral degradation.[25] While advocating whiteness for its moral and aesthetic superiority, Le Corbusier spoke disparagingly of shine; he was troubled by the 'most disturbing contrivance' of 'trees glitter, rocks shine, the sky glows, jade, jasper, onyx, agate, lapis, crystal' at the 1925 Exposition des Arts Décoratifs in Paris.[26]

Hong Kong's extensive adoption of the environment of off-white shine, like its vast stretches of off-white surfaces, possesses a similar moral and aesthetic indifference. If shine has little currency in moral and aesthetic constructs, it is essential to an environmental response to the understanding of the germ theory, firmly established since the discovery of bacteria by Louis Pasteur (1822–96) in the mid nineteenth century.

It changed fundamentally the way we live and transformed the ancient practice of antisepsis. The germ theory provided a scientific basis for the sanitarian theory and gave rise to vaccines and antibiotics, which dramatically reduced the infection and mortality rate in and out of hospitals. Pasteur's discovery is commonly acknowledged as the single most important medical event of all time; the period between 1879 and 1900 is known as the twenty-one 'golden years' of bacteriology, during which 'major diseases were being discovered at the phenomenal rate of one a year'.[27] It was in Hong Kong that Alexandre Yersin (1863–1943) – a Swiss scientist who was sent by the French Government and the Pasteur Institute – and Kitasato Shibasaburo (1853–1931) – a Japanese scientist who studied under Robert Koch (1843–1910) – simultaneously discovered the bacterium *Yersinia pestis* that caused the 1894 bubonic plague in Hong Kong, which was found to be transmitted through the rat.[28]

Bacteriology confirmed what Nightingale and many others suspected: diseases pass from human to human through poisonous effluvia, above and beyond contact; Nightingale thought the use of the term 'contagion' was a misconception. In addition to ventilation and light, Nightingale was very specific about the nature of surfaces in her recommendations for hospital design. 'The amount of organic matter given off by respiration and in other ways from the sick is such that the floors, walls, and ceilings of hospital wards – if not of impervious materials – become dangerous absorbents.'[29] She objected to the use of 'common plaster' because of its absorbent quality,[30] and recommended 'impervious material capable of receiving a polish'.[31] The Italian non-absorbent cement was a good choice for the warm climate, and polished oak floor saturated with beeswax would be a good choice for the English climate; however, 'the means of producing a really good impervious polished surface, with little labour, have yet to be discovered'.[32] Today, Nightingale's heritage can perhaps be seen in the *Guideline for Disinfection and Sterilization in Healthcare Facilities* (continuously updated) published by the Centers for Disease Control and Prevention; here, through a division of critical, semicritical, and noncritical areas (the Spaulding scheme), domestic interiors are readily understood as a noncritical area that is subject to a rigorous regime of disinfection. In Hong Kong, guidelines for infection control are prepared jointly by the Infection Control Branch of the Centre for Health Protection under the Department of Health and the Hospital Authority, divided over three categories of general public, institutions and businesses, and health professionals.[33] Under this classification of degrees of disinfection, washable walls and cleanable floors, free of fissures, open joints, and crevices, continue to be understood as the standard hygienic architecture.[34]

As if answering the call of Nightingale to discover 'a really good impervious polished surface', the variety of contemporary building materials is bewildering today; there are countless choices of impervious materials – natural and artificial – that fulfil Nightingale's criteria. Industrial standards are being established on antiseptic materials with extraordinary speed.[35] Hong Kong is deeply influenced by these developments in building material science; the anti-bacterial properties of building materials have a tremendous appeal in Hong Kong. Over much of the twentieth century, the surfaces of Hong Kong's architecture – from its Art Centre to general public amenities – have been dominated by the use of off-white ceramic tiles, which have created affordable impervious surfaces capable of receiving regular washing and wiping. While tiles are still extensively used in government projects, projects in the private sector in Hong Kong make use of more refined impervious materials such as polished stone, stainless steel, plastic, and glass, expanding their building coverage at a high speed. The fast-improving technologies of cladding have made these expansions desirable and affordable.

In the indifference towards the intellectual debate on the nature of materials, roughness and ruin is more readily associated with dilapidation, aged materials with the lack of hygiene. Hong Kong's urban renewal, which has resulted in the regrettable violent renovations and demolitions of many old buildings, was partly grounded in the argument of old buildings being unhygienic and unsafe in the city; the development pressure and high land prices perhaps also deliberately cultivated the association of the old with the unhealthy. Roughness and age in building materials have served fundamentally important intellectual purposes in the academic discourse of architecture: Greek and Roman ruins played critical roles in various constructions of architecture as an academic discipline. Like whiteness, roughness suggests potentiality.[36] Roughness and age possess a capacity to indicate time (ageing process of materials) and space (sitedness of materials), which underpins a broad urban environmental framework that supports much of our intellectual and cultural activities. Hong Kong's environment of off-white shine moves away from this traditional scheme of meaning in the urban environment, and seeks other methods of spatial and temporal location. Like industrial buildings in the context of the Beaux-Arts architecture in the nineteenth century, Hong Kong is an unintentional avant-garde city; it signals, often in visually unpretentious ways, the emerging sensibilities and aesthetic potentials in future cities in Asia. Like washing the body, cleaning buildings inside and outside has become

Figure 6.4   Zhan Wang, *Urban Landscape*, 2006 (courtesy of the artist)

essential and desirable in our continuously renewed relationship with bacteria and viruses; our aesthetic sensibilities may have to internalize these critical requirements.

The ubiquitous environment of off-white shine, represented in one way by Hong Kong's urban reality, perhaps inspired the Chinese artist Zhan Wang in his installations *Urban Landscape* (from 2003) with shiny stainless steel cooking utensils (Figure 6.4). Zhan Wang began his artistic career with a performance piece *Clean Ruins* (1994), in which he painted some of the ruinous surfaces of traditional courtyard houses in Beijing just hours before they were demolished to make way for a shiny building constructed with investment from Hong Kong. In his *Urban Landscape*, Zhan Wang's initial protest has turned into deeper reflection; the polished stainless steel represents one of the most enduring and effective antiseptic materials that transformed our urban landscape. He presented his vision through reconstituting both Chinese and Western cities. Zhan Wang commented that his installations were driven by a sensibility that is 'forced on him' in Asian cities, like a never-ending storm on the senses. Similar to his shiny stainless steel versions of the ornamental rocks in traditional Chinese gardens, the cities with off-white shine in stainless steel are 'a reinterpretation of our urban life through a change of materials, a reluctant acceptance of a new fact of life imposed on us by a new material'.³⁷ Zhan Wang's metallic shine is a tremendous challenge to architects; 'reluctant acceptance' has been a recurring feature in the history of architecture, and this particular version we are facing today is no exception.

The Chinese City as Infection Barriers

Among all the varied conceptions of the city, barriers remain a constant feature. The city as barriers is a paradox: an act of creating a community engaged in ceaseless struggles for isolation, urban barriers have been erected in defence against enemy invasions, class struggles, trade wars, and now bacterial and viral infection. The Chinese city, as we have discussed, is conceived as a set of concentric corporeal defences of the body, the family, the village, the work unit, and the state family. If walls are the preferred method of defence in traditional cities in China, infection barriers will become the defence of the future, which will take on some of the characteristics of the traditional walls in their concentric forms. High density produces high infection rates; this was was brought into a painful realization during the outbreak of SARS in 2003 in Hong Kong, where almost 300 people died from 1,755 infections within a few months, recording one of the highest mortality rates in a major infected area in the world. Unlike city walls, gated communities, and trade regulations, infection barriers in cities are taking place in line with the principles of antibiotics, fighting bacteria and viruses from within the tissues of architecture. Beyond ventilation and light, it is the environment of off-white shine that best fulfils the requirement of antisepsis, and that provide the conditions for a new urbanism of infection barriers. Whiteness and shine have their roles in traditional moral and aesthetic formulations, but the necessity for bacterial and viral control in cities is reconstituting their roles, fundamentally regulated by a determination to keep bacteria and viruses at bay.

Unlike other barriers, infection barriers have to be constantly refreshed in order to be effective; normal disinfection procedures are effective for a few hours only.³⁸ To establish effective infection barriers, the city has first to educate its inhabitants regarding bacterial and viral environments. In Hong Kong, the entire urban structure is now mobilized as a giant behaviour reform machine; posters, audio announcements, and television broadcasts on public transportation, as well as television broadcasts, orchestrate mass campaigns of hygienic habits. Schools frequently incorporate regular and mandatory hand-washing, mask-wearing, and temperature-measuring into their daily routines. One of the most visible rituals of disinfection takes place at meal tables, where eating utensils are ritually washed in tepid tea; there is no evidence to show that lukewarm tea can be used as an effective antiseptic solution, but the purpose of this ritual, like the nature of many other rituals, is to instil and reinforce a commonly shared infection anxiety. This is perhaps in line with the accident-focused news reporting in Hong Kong – one of the liveliest and most sensationalist in the world – which instils and reinforces a danger anxiety. The need for constant behaviour reform and surface disinfection creates a distinct kind of space for the city of maximum quantities, a space that looks, smells, and sounds distinctively. In Hong Kong, the hospital is poised to take over the entire city, spreading its standard practices of hand-washing, mask-wearing, and temperature-taking; through its standard disinfection procedures, the hospital is transforming the city through the use of whiteness and shine as bacterial and viral defence from within the architecture of the city.

Perhaps the deepest impact of the city as infection barrier is the consequence of what may be described as 'disposable architecture'. The relative disconnection between the off-white shiny surfaces and moral and aesthetic discourses enables a much faster cycle of reconstruction, much like the disposable plastic gloves and table cloths. Discarding possibly infected items by-passes disinfection and sterilization, and is very effective as an antiseptic procedure. Discarding a building or an interior can be seen in the same light as an antiseptic procedure. In Hong Kong, demolition and renovation are frequent and unsentimental; this is perhaps both a consequence of linking old buildings with the lack of hygiene and safety, and a result of economizing in construction. Some of the demolition and renovation is rooted in the short life span of many buildings in Hong Kong. Almost all concrete residential buildings constructed in the 1950s and 1960s, when Hong Kong was under tremendous pressure to house a large amount of immigrants from China, were built to last no more than fifty years; this amounts to 4,000 buildings in 2012 and 16,000 by 2030 which could collapse.[39] Under the management of the Urban Renewal Authority, a proportion of these deteriorating structures have been replaced by new developments, either through its partnership with private sectors or through 'demand-led' developments. Development pressure at prime locations in Hong Kong results in a short life span of buildings that were constructed to last much longer, such as the Hilton Hotel in 1963 and Furama Hotel in 1977; they were demolished and replaced, despite being sites of cultural memory, by more profitable office towers in 1999 and 2005 respectively. In parallel to these high profile redevelopment projects, there are numerous residential and small business interiors – in an attempt to refresh simultaneously property value, aesthetic sensibility, and hygienic properties of architecture – that contribute crucially to a fast-changing urban environment in Hong Kong. 'The Town is Ever New', exclaims the current marketing tagline of New Town Plaza in Shatin. The 'disposable architecture' in Hong Kong seems to have its equally remarkable counterpart in China; in 2010, Deputy Minister of Housing and Urban–Rural Development, Qiu Baoxing, a noted scholar on urbanization in China, commented that the 'average life expectancy of China's buildings' was twenty-five to thirty years, while those in Britain and United States are 132 years and seventy-four years respectively.[40] 'Architecture aims at Eternity': Christopher Wren began his treatise of architecture in the seventeenth century with this often repeated statement,[41] echoing and anticipating long lists of architectural treatises assuming the essential importance of permanence of architecture. Permanence gives architecture a unique power. Between Wren's eternity and China's thirty years, how long should buildings last in cities? The Western city and the Chinese city seem to have made their distinctive choices; in Chinese cities, the

Figure 6.5 Self-help disinfection station at New Town Plaza, Shatin, Hong Kong

quality of construction – often rightly identified as the reason for the short life span of buildings in China – seems to be a function inextricably linked to the need to refresh property value, aesthetic sensibility, and hygienic properties of architecture regularly. The Chinese city, as we shall discuss next, does not rely to a great extent on locating cultural memories in the authenticity of architecture as does the Western city; this memory strategy works hand in hand with the disposable urban strategy of a relatively short life span of buildings.

One of the most intriguing signs of our time is that the foyer sinks at Villa Savoye and Rufer House have already been replaced by stations of antiseptic hand gel dispensers throughout the entrance lobbies in Hong Kong (Figure 6.5). From the removal of dirt through washing to the eradication of bacteria through disinfection, the city has been transformed in one important way, through its concentration of buildings and people, by antisepsis. In the context of Chinese cities, the hygienic architectural features of whiteness and shine anticipated by Florence Nightingale in her *Notes on Hospitals* in the nineteenth century have been transformed in Hong Kong as architecturally assisted antiseptic procedures. Through their immense scale and astonishing speed of development, Chinese cities have brought an ancient sensibility of prudence to bear on the form of cities; this is a complex matrix of layered forces that influence the conception and management of quantities, the understanding and accommodation of the conditions of labour, the strategies of placing concentric defensive spaces in the city, and the contemporary battle against bacterial and viral infections.

Notes

1 Adolf Loos, 'Plumbers', *Spoken into the Void*, trans. Jane O. Newman and John H. Smith (Cambridge MA: The MIT Press, 1987), p.49.
2 Ibid., p.45.
3 Anthony Ley, *A History of Building Control in England and Wales, 1840–1990* (Coventry: RICS Books, 2000), pp.20–32.
4 Ruth Rogaski, *Hygienic Modernity: Meanings of Health and Disease in Treaty-Port China* (Berkeley: University of California Press, 2004), p.141.
5 On the relationship between religion and dirt, see Mary Douglas, *Purity and Danger: An Analysis of Concepts of Pollution and Taboo* (London: Routledge, 1966/2002).
6 Nadir Lahiji and D. S. Friedman, eds, 'At the Sink: Architecture in Abjection', *Plumbing: Sounding Modern Architecture* (New York: Princeton University Press, 1997), pp.35–60.

7 For instance, as discussed by Mohsen Mostafavi and David Leatherbarrow in *On Weathering: The Life of Buildings in Time* (Cambridge MA: The MIT Press, 1993), and in David Leatherbarrow and Mohsen Mostafavi, *Surface Architecture* (Cambridge MA: The MIT Press, 2005).

8 Extensive scholarship in this area includes Carol Benedict, *Bubonic Plague in Nineteenth-century China* (Stanford: Stanford University Press, 1996); Karrie MacPherson, *A Wilderness of Marshes: The Origins of Public Health in Shanghai, 1843–1893* (Maryland: Lexington Press, 2001); Angela Ki Che Leung and Charlotte Furth, eds, *Health and Hygiene in Chinese East Asia: Policies and Publics in the Long Twentieth Century* (Durham and London: Duke University Press, 2010).

9 Mark Wigley likens this aspect to Xenophon's description of husbandry as a woman, 'the mother and nurse of all other arts', as well as Alberti's characterization of architecture as a virtuous woman, in 'Untitled: The Housing of Gender', *Sexuality and Space*, ed. Beatrice Colomina (New York: Princeton Architectural Press, 1992), p.361.

10 Ibid., p.360.

11 Le Corbusier, 'A Coat of Whitewash, the Law of Ripolin', *The Decorative Art of Today*, trans. James I. Dunnett (Cambridge MA: The MIT Press, 1987), p.192.

12 Ibid.

13 Ibid.

14 Ibid.

15 Mark Wigley, 'Introduction', *White Walls, Designer Dresses* (Cambridge MA: The MIT Press, 1995).

16 Florence Nightingale, *Notes on Hospitals* (London: Longman, 1863), p.iii.

17 Ibid., p.4.

18 Ibid., p.17.

19 John D. Thompson and Grace Goldin, *The Hospital: A Social and Architectural History* (New Haven and London: Yale University Press, 1975), pp.125–26.

20 Nightingale, *Notes on Hospitals*, p.19.

21 Ibid., p.68.

22 Ibid., p.72.

23 Ibid., p.69.

24 Jeremy Taylor, *Hospital and Asylum Architecture in England, 1840–1914* (London and New York: Mansell, 1991), p.18.

25 Shaftesbury, *Characteristicks of Men, Manners, Opinions, Times* (London, 1714).

26 Le Corbusier, *The Decorative Art of Today*, p.4.

27 Roy Porter, *The Greatest Benefit to Mankind: A Medical History of Humanity from Antiquity to the Present* (London: HarperCollins, 1997), p.442.

28 Ibid., pp.443–44.

29 Nightingale, *Notes on Hospitals*, p.44.
30 Ibid., p.45.
31 Ibid., p.68.
32 Ibid., p.70.
33 I am grateful to Professors Jean Hee Kim and Kristal Lee of the School of Public Health, the Chinese University of Hong Kong, for sharing their knowledge of public hygiene practices in Asian cultures and for guiding me through the extraordinary maze of infection control guidelines in Hong Kong.
34 The American Institute of Architects Academy of Architecture for Health, *Guidelines for Design and Construction of Hospital and Health Care Facilities* (Washington DC: The American Institute of Architects Press, 1998), p.46.
35 For instance, the Japanese Industrial Standard JIS Z 2801:2000 measures the antibacterial activity in hydrophobic materials, which has influenced the formation of a draft ISO standard, and a host of industrial standards of building materials in other countries. This includes those relating to antiseptic plastic and glass coatings specified by the Building Material Industry Standard of China currently being established.
36 David Leatherbarrow, *Architecture Orientated Otherwise* (New York: Princeton Architectural Press, 2009).
37 Zhan Wang, http://www.zhanwangart.com, accessed November 26, 2013, in texts explaining the motivation for the installation. My translation.
38 Centers for Disease Control and Prevention, *Guideline for Disinfection and Sterilization in Healthcare Facilities* (Atlanta: CDC, 2008), pp.29–30.
39 Urban Renewal Authority, *Urban Renewal: New Horizons, Annual Report 2011–2012* (Hong Kong: Urban Renewal Authority, 2012), p.6.
40 Wang Qian, 'Short-lived Buildings Create Huge Waste', *China Daily*, 6 April, 2010, www.chinadaily.com.cn/china/2010-04/06/content_9687545.htm, accessed 5 December 2012. Qiu Baoxing's books on urbanization in China include *Duiying jiyu yu tiaozhan* (Response, Opportunity and Challenge) (Beijing: Zhongguo jiangong chubanshe, 2009); *Zhongguo chengshihua jincheng zhongde chengshi guihua biange* (Urban planning and reform in the process of China's urbanization) (Shanghai: Tongji daxue chubanshe, 2005).
41 Christopher Wren, 'Tract I', collected in *Parentalia* (London, 1750), p.351.

造象

PART 3
Figuration

7

The Empire of Figures

Abundance and prudence, while functioning in some capacities as organizing principles of things in cities, impose relatively loose degrees of selection; the first is accumulative and the second, preventative. What eventually emerges as the supreme ordering force in the Chinese city can perhaps be described as figuration, a process through which all accumulated and allowable quantities in cities transform to take specific meaningful physical forms. This process is subtle and complex, particularly in the context of global exchange of ideas and services today; but working beneath various hybridized conditions, it is distinctive in making Chinese cities recognizable as Chinese cities. What is figuration? In China, figuration is usually only described poetically, as that which captures a spirit or energy (*shen* or *qi*) inherent in a social, political, or artistic act; often it is also described obliquely through exemplary actions. It is not *veritas* in that it does not operate according to the Greek mimetic principle, it is not *logos* as it does not formulate cause and effect as being distinctly different states, and it is not *telos* as it deals with a situation rather than the projected end result of that situation.[1] Marcel Granet placed a power of immanence in figures (emblems) in Chinese thought; this has been very influential in subsequent scholarship on Chinese culture. I propose here to begin, like Granet, with the principal surrogate of figuration: the Chinese writing system. As a major character-based language today, the Chinese writing system invents a set of forms that are always already bonded with all meanings, blending them at the very foundation of making sense and making form. The process of blending form and meaning at the inception of language is here understood as figuration in its most elementary state, its first defining act. While the more abstract alphabets allow a temporary suspension of form and therefore a relative purity of meaning, the Chinese square words clearly place form before meaning. This is something that troubled considerably such early modern thinkers as Francis Bacon, who considered this reversal of form of meaning as primitive and unsophisticated; it burdened thoughts with preconceptions inherent in forms that could potentially confuse thinking. It is also something that delighted Enlightenment thinkers such as Gottfried Leibniz, who longed for a language of characters that could convey things and thoughts directly rather than through signifiers of things and thoughts. However, both pronounced their judgements without extensive experience of using the writing system as language. The way of making form and meaning inherent in the Chinese writing system is far more than just a linguistic strategy; it is one that frames to a greater or lesser degree all post-linguistic mental and physical activities. In the Chinese cultural context, figuration gives rise to the final philosophical and aesthetic forms of things and spaces; ultimately, it shapes the resulting quantities from acts of producing abundance and prudence, in a way that could be seen to be comparable to the effect of truth in the Western conception.

The Empire of Figures

A Chinese character, or a square word, is made of a graphic unit (morpheme) and meanings associated with that unit; what is crucially different from alphabet-based languages is that the graphic unit is not made from a relatively small set of abstract symbols, but with a large range of unique graphic components. The authoritative eighteenth-century imperial dictionary of Chinese characters, the *Kangxi zidian* (1716), contains about 49,000 characters; about 6,000 characters are generally in use today. A literate Chinese uses between 4,000 and 5,000 characters, while the Japanese and the Koreans use about half of this number. These large quantities of characters are made from 214 semantic components known as radicals, and 800 semi-phonetic indicators; but there are no consistent rules for making a character with these components.[2] The argument that these radicals and semi-phonetic indicators are components of a phonetically-based language is fraught with difficulties for the same absence of consistent rules. The Chinese writing system, because of the disassociation of graphic and phonetic conventions, has the ability to hold different dialects together, turning what would have been considered as different languages into varieties of the same writing system. The phonetic differences between the Hunan dialect and the Beijing dialect are probably as extensive as those between Spanish and Italian, but what are spoken in Hunan and Beijing are dialects of the same language, while Spanish and Italian are considered to be two different languages. There has been a long-standing debate in Western scholarship between those who argue that the Chinese language is largely an under-developed phonetic system and those who argue that it is a character-based writing system. For the 'phoneticists', such as John DeFrancis and William Hannas,[3] the Chinese language is fundamentally flawed as a phonetic system. They often delight in romanticization of the Chinese characters, but at the same time complain that the Chinese language displays a 'high degree of graphic redundancy', and its insistence on one sound for one character resulted in 'high incidence of homophony'.[4] What is at stake, in their view, is that this rigidly repetitive 'endless procession of monosyllabic morphemes'[5] is in fact a 'failure to transcend the concrete world of perceived phenomena',[6] forming an obstacle to creativity. According to Hannas, the creativity of Chinese civilization – and that of East Asia as a whole – under the influence of this writing system suffers critically from the restrictive and oppressive social, political, and artistic mechanisms necessary to sustain its writing system in all its unreasonable complexities.

While these conclusions may be startling,[7] they certainly draw our attention to the deep psycho-linguistic territories within which actions concerning city-making decisions are also shaped. The question here is perhaps not so much about the way the character-based language is, but about why it is the case despite the inherent difficulties in mastering it. A Chinese square word works in a different way from the Greek alphabet; it is invested heavily with a figure and a one-syllable sound, and this investment comes at a high cost. As DeFrancis and Hannas pointed out, this high cost takes the form of high memory demand and high incidence of homophony, making speech communication difficult. Historically, the written language (*wenyan*), the form of Chinese writing most commonly used by the educated in China before the adoption of contemporary Chinese (*baihua*) in the twentieth century, defended with great determination the purity of the square word against the insertion of grammatical and phonetic indicators; the pronunciations of the square words are by no means certain even for the most cultivated. Written Chinese today, with its adoption of punctuation and grammatical symbols, is a result of Western influence in the twentieth century; even after this 'improvement', it still does not carry consistent phonetic information. The distinction between writing (*wen*) and speech (*yu*) in Chinese works differently from that in the alphabetic languages; instead of the primary importance of speech in language advocated by Ferdinand de Saussure, writing claims an absolute priority in Chinese, often at the expense of speech. The Chinese expression of civilization is not etymologically connected with *civitas* and its inherent demand for speech-based communication; it is rooted in 'textualization' (*wenhua*) which insists on transforming all things – including, I argue, cities – into the writing system and its derivatives. Chapter 9 provides a more detailed elaboration on this point. As a result, speech in Chinese, particularly when it is imbued with social and political importance, is slow and deliberate, perhaps both as a way of emphasizing the importance of the written square words and as a way to avoid potential confusion due to its high incidence of homophony. Speech in Chinese pays homage to the writing system.

The return of this investment is apparent; the standard square form and single syllable sound, resulting in the staccato phonetic quality of the language, places an ordered visual and phonetic grid regardless of the number of components (number of strokes) of each square word. This can be seen as an extraordinary cultivation of standardization, highly valued by a corresponding social and political form. Based on this standard square form, each square word is then designed as a figure. This sets off a strategy of meaning that is both familiar and very unfamiliar in the Greek mimetic tradition. The square word may begin as a visual representation of a thing, but it is also quite far-removed from the thing to become something else: a character of a second degree. Herrlee Glessner Creel, the outstanding American sinologist, attributes this second-degree development of the Chinese square word to its extraordinary longevity compared with other graphically-based languages, such as Egyptian hieroglyphics.[8] It is, ultimately, not a copy of something, but an original form at the moment of inception. The capacity to create figures is common to all cultures, as Philippe Lacoue-Labarthe recognizes in the form-producing facility of the mind (Gestalt capacity); the figure, like truth, has 'an ontological status' of its own.[9] The tendency to copy natural and artificial forms, a condition so vividly described by Jean Baudrillard's simulacrum as a copy without an original, is also widely practised in different cultures.[10] The Chinese figuration, here examined through its writing system, is neither Gestalt nor simulacrum; it is not contingent on the notion of authenticity. The Chinese writing system is an empire of figures that attains an existence in its own right; its inherent system of formulation does not enter into a bonding dialectic relationship with 'the real'. If we consider the flow of *mimesis* as being from the external to the intellect, we can perhaps construe the flow of figuration as being from the intellect to the external. It is very important that figuration has to be conceived outside the familiar dichotomy of idealism and empiricism in the Western tradition; figuration is not dialectical and it does not construct the idealism/empiricism distinction. In fact, through its own ontological status, the empire of figures does not conceive a definitive realm of reality beyond its own essentialized blend of form/meaning combination.

One consequence of this much freer association between the empire of figures and 'reality' is that it is already a classification system; the visual character of the square words constructs orders of assembly that are concrete and not abstract. Bees and wasps are both written as '*feng*', which serves as the primary group of flying insects that have stings; a second square word preceding that of the primary group indicates further division, those that produce honey are 'honey *feng*' while those that look yellow are 'yellow *feng*'. *Yu*, abstracted from the form of fish, is more telling; while most fish are described as *yu*, whale is also described as *yu*, despite the fact that the whale belongs to a species far removed from fish. Here quantities are always already associated with the formal characters of things being quantified, the power of immanence in Granet's conception; a street is always described as 'one string of street', and a board is always described as 'one square of board', and so on. In architecture, this 'morphological classification' inherent in the writing system can perhaps also be observed, for instance, in the term *guan*, which means perhaps a place that offers family functions but is not itself family nor located within the family. *Guan* includes *can guan* (restaurant), *lü guan* (hotel), *hui guan* (clubhouse), *cha guan* (teahouse), *tiyu guan* (gymnasium), *tushu guan* (library), *meishu guan* (art gallery), a single spatial category containing typologically very different spaces. It is significant that classification here does not seem to be a separate mental activity, but one that has already been integrated into the structure of the square words. *Guan* (舘), in it is graphic form, features, on the right side, a roof and two rooms underneath the roof.

The Chinese writing system is a shared medium of spiritual and political power, and this ranges from the spiritual powers of Daoist or Buddhist scriptures to the political significance of Mao's calligraphy.[11] It is the primary source of aesthetic pleasure. Instead of constructing multiple aesthetic realms outside language as we find in the Western tradition, the empire of figures is already aestheticized and defends the primacy of this aesthetic realm with great determination. The highest form of beauty, it may be argued, is the writing of the square words themselves: calligraphy. Again, the empire of figures does not signify beauty; it is beauty, immanently. Other forms of beauty measure themselves against this first criterion, constructing their aesthetic qualities, it may be argued, as derivatives of this primary form. This is extraordinarily influential and productive.

There are several distinct principles in which figuration operates as a productive force. Figuration first relies on the principle of singularity and distinctiveness – a fundamental aesthetic trait of the square words. Compared with alphabetic words, which are responsive to contexts through declensions and conjugations, the square words have an extraordinary stability: although they can be calligraphed in different styles, they do not change their components according to circumstances of quantity, possession, time, or delivery. Instead, they maintain the integrity of their form despite the changes of linguistic contexts. The figure is insistent. The stability of the figure, it may be argued here, cultivates a centrality of form that is both an intellectual habit and an aesthetic force. The creative act, under this condition, seems to be primarily concerned with the integrity of the created thing, and only secondarily (if at all) concerned with its context. When this deeply rooted aesthetic sensibility is manifested in the built environment, the result is a distinctive coming together of forms and colours, an amalgamation of separate acts of sustaining the centrality and stability of form. In addition to the Chinese numerical schemes that provide distributional principles in relation to an order of prominence and relationality, the figurative sensibility places aesthetic consideration on objects rather than context. We can perhaps understand this as a cultivated sensibility to imagine the building, like a square word, to achieve an internal aesthetic balance in relation to itself; the relationality here is based not on contextually formulated proportioned quantities, but on figuratively and hierarchically formulated centrality. The parade of quantities is accompanied by a parade of figures; each demands its internal singularity and distinctness. The traditional way of creating a set of large and complex spaces through an amalgamation of singular buildings linked by corridors, to some extent, can be seen to match the combined demand of numerical schemes and figuration. In today's context, this demand is perhaps more prominently captured by the endless appetite for distinctive buildings that are – again like the square words – simultaneously form and image, meaning and thing: Shanghai Television Tower as the oriental pearl, the National Grand Theatre in Beijing as heaven above earth, the Beijing International Airport as flying dragon, the Jinmao Tower as a pagoda, Guangzhou Opera House pebble stones washed smooth by Pearl

River, the Olympic National Stadium as a bird's nest and heavenly circle, the National Swimming Centre as a water cube and earthly square. As meanings and things are inseparable in the Chinese writing system, we also find that importance and size are not distinguished; the legitimacy of the figure can be recognized in relation to its size. The figure relies on largeness to attain the figurative power: importance as *shown* rather than as *demonstrated*, and greatness as largeness often blended in the same word (*da*). Largeness of scale in construction projects in China, often exceeding necessity, acquires unique significance in the context of figuration. This is perhaps similar to the phenomenon of 'big character posters' (*dazibao*) during the Cultural Revolution; here, the largeness of the square words was seen to have the potential of an increased polemic persuasiveness. Largeness as content can be seen as an indication of the 'thickness' in the figuration of each square word as a signifier, a representation, a visual creation: a distinct, balanced, and stable figure. Both the consumer society and the avant-garde art in China have made use of this strategy of persuasion. While distinct and large architectural shapes are common in all cultural contexts, the Chinese use of these forms seems to feature a parallel trait with its writing system, which brings a way of thinking and an aesthetic sensibility to bear on the production of architecture. This is, in one important way, what gives rise to the character of the Chinese city.

The second principle of figuration is that function follows figure. One of the most common experiences of the Chinese city, when the initial sensations become moderated by longer exposure, is that the relationships between form and use, between form and materials, and between form and structure are often not causal. The seeming disconnect between form and function, material, and structure can be seen as a consequence of figuration; it results from a formal concern that was never primarily focused on typological, material, and structural formulations. The Forbidden City in Beijing, for instance, shows a very different understanding and use of form from that in the Western architectural tradition. The Forbidden City is an extraordinary complex of 170,000 square metres of space that accommodated a rich court life. However, the architecture that housed these courtly activities was derived from one single type – that of the courtyard and a primary building form made of a slightly curved and tiled roof, columns, and a podium. What created the distinctions in this vast maze of courtyards was size, number, and colour; here, largeness as content is manifested architecturally as the imperial throne, the Hall of

Supreme Harmony (*Taihe Dian*) (Figure 7.1), the largest timber building of the Forbidden City. Unlike Brunelleschi's dome in Florence which traces gravitational forces in their most direct ways, the timber columns of the Hall of Supreme Harmony are partly disguised behind systems of timber bracket sets (*dougong*) (Figure 7.2). The timber structures of the Forbidden City do not seem to have resulted directly from material properties; instead, there seem to be other important reasons for their forms. The decorative use of the bracket sets in the Ming and Qing dynasties (fourteenth to nineteenth century) had much earlier structural origins, as Liang Sicheng, one of the founders of twentieth-century Chinese architectural education, demonstrated through his studies of Tang and Song dynasties (ninth to eleventh century) buildings. However, despite this knowledge, it is difficult to explain the ninety-degree bend in the bracket sets structurally. There seems to be a lack of a body of knowledge that articulates the causal relationship between the material properties of timber and structural forms in Chinese architecture. On the whole, this lack of interest in typological, material, and structural properties has been a prominent character in the Chinese building tradition. The structural logic of the bracket sets – made from horizontal and vertical members only – seems to be difficult to understand at first glance, particularly when diagonals, as used in the *Fachwerk*, would be the simplest way to achieve stability. It is perhaps possible to suggest that the figure of a building, rather than the material tectonics, had been more important in the determination of form; the diagonals may have been avoided here because it is figuratively unacceptable as it may carry a risk of the unstraight. The concepts of authority, correctness, centrality, and moral uprightness are signified by an important square word, *zheng* (正), a form that is composed of five bracket-like straight lines; the concepts of evil, crookedness, and moral degradation are signified by the square word formed by two components to mean 'unstraight' (歪). If the material properties of timber justified the diagonals in *Fachwerk*, the figurative properties of *zheng* could have demanded the removal of all diagonals from timber structures. The 'uprightness of the upper beam', in the Chinese language, gives rise to many linguistic metaphors for moral uprightness in daily conversations; a diagonal beam, in this context, would seem to be rather difficult to fathom even when structure demands it. Chinese architecture before the twentieth century never deviated from the archetypal roof–column–podium timber building; this can perhaps be seen as the power of the figure over that of material tectonics. Emperor Qianlong (reigned

Figure 7.1 Hall of Supreme Harmony, The Forbidden City, Beijing, 1407–1421

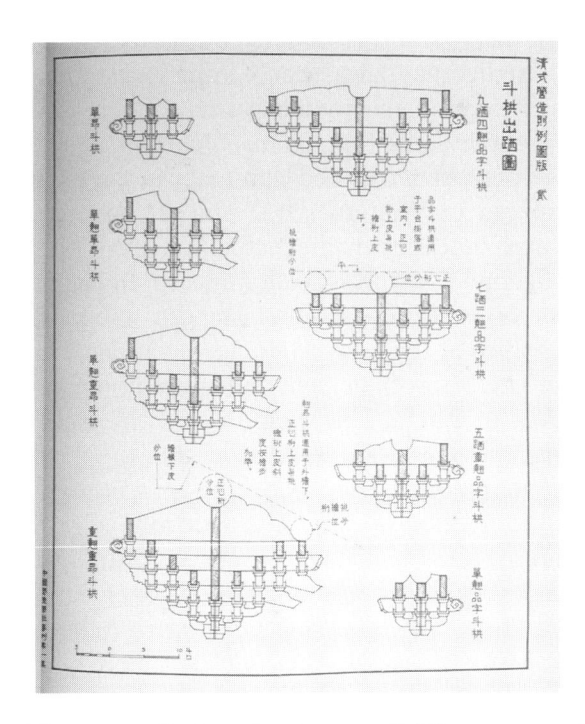

Figure 7.2 Illustration 2, *Qingshi yingzao zeli* (The construction principles of the Qing dynasty) (Beijing: Zhongguo yingzao xueshe, 1934)

1735–96), for instance, disliked staircases when he first encountered the idea brought to him by Jesuit missionaries. He thought it strange 'to live in the air'; for him, perhaps the staircase, while functionally understandable, alienated the figure of the archetypal building as the most primary form of human habitation.[12]

The third principle of figuration is that of completeness (*wanzheng*). The completeness of each square word – unlike the alphabets – endlessly reinforces the completeness of other intellectual conceptions; this works hand in hand with the numerical completeness discussed in Chapter 1. When Emperor Qianlong first learned the practice of foreshortening in painting in the West, he disliked it; he remarked that 'the imperfections of the eye were no reason to represent the objects of nature as imperfect'.[13] Giuseppe Castiglione (1688–1766), an Italian Jesuit missionary and painter trained in the late Baroque culture but working at Qianlong's court as a painter in the hope of gaining imperial approval of Christian missions in China, used Chinese parallel lines rather than perspectives. Distant from a mimetic act, figuration is not technically committed to mimicking a reality; instead, it acts to capture a condition with visual compensation through several points of view. The measuring standard of figuration, therefore, is grounded in how completely one can represent a situation or a conception from a number of views. If perspective is understood as technical mappings of biological and intellectual flaws, then completeness is considered as a demanding and more valuable mental capacity. There is a much greater emphasis on completeness (*quanmian*) than perspective (*jiaodu*) in China; although perspective gained legitimacy in the twentieth century through the spread of Western scholarship, it has not replaced the demand for completeness. Each intellectual activity – conceptualization, innovation, judgement, action – is often measured against the ideal of completeness. From the presentation of food to the planning of cities, from the conception of the body to the imagination of knowledge, the idea of completeness is both ancient and contemporary, both intellectual and material in China. This desire for completeness – the *yin* as well as the *yang*, the dense as well as the sparse, the delicate as well as the strong – is often equated with eclecticism, a notion that misreads the poetic centre of Chinese cultural productions.

The enormous intellectual and aesthetic investment in the empire of figures is protected by profound anxieties over figurelessness and disfigurement. These anxieties are, not surprisingly, rooted in the integrity of the square words themselves. The Chinese artist Xu Bing, through his elegant work *Book from the Sky* (1987–1991), effected a powerful moment of figurelessness which deeply disturbed many of the Chinese politicians and intellectuals (Figure 7.3).

Figure 7.3 Xu Bing, title block, *Book from the Sky*, 1987 (courtesy of Xu Bing Studio)

Described as 'the most important Chinese art work of the twentieth century',[14] Xu Bing's work consisted of 4,000 unrecognizable Chinese-looking square words, beautifully hand-carved into woodblocks in fifteenth-century Ming dynasty imitation of tenth-century Song dynasty font (*fangsongti*). Prints were made from these woodblocks into scrolls, as well as a set of four bound volumes that resembled traditional canonical texts in literature, medicine, and law. The exceptional skills with which Xu Bing created these woodblocks and prints brought a moment of disbelief for those who were compelled to read the text; the familiarity of the form and the profound meaninglessness of the 'text' played against each other in high drama. By maintaining the form and suspending meanings at the same moment, one is made to experience a possibility of seeing the empire of figures as its ghost. Xu Bing describes this condition through the phrase 'image as text', which he used to correct the misconceived notion of the Chinese square words being 'text as image' as it was described in the exhibition catalogue by Western art connoisseurs and collectors in an exhibition of his work at Princeton University in 2003.[15] In Xu Bing's mind this distinction is much more profound and influential than his Western audience realized. Xu Bing's work caused considerable criticism from many sectors of Chinese society when it was first exhibited in 1987; it highlighted the Chinese anxiety over figurelessness through a spectacular experience. The anxiety over disfigurement is no less powerful; perhaps the most vivid example is that when sentenced to death, a person is visually condemned to death by the use of a large red cross over the square words of the name of the condemned person. There seems to be an equation between the ultimate form of destruction and the disfigurement of square words; the ruined square words seem to be equivalent to ruined bodies. In imperial China, square words used in the names of emperors were completely taken out from general use, and replaced by the same square words with missing strokes; it is such a consistent practice that editors and historians make use of the practice as a dating technique. Putting the square words of imperial names on paper perhaps represented an unacceptable risk, exposing the square words to potential disfigurement.

From Falsehood to Figuration

Figuration is most effectively understood in relation to *mimesis*, a method of thinking and making that the ancient Greeks established and the contemporary Western cities inherited. E. H. Gombrich highlighted a moment of the emergence of Greek *mimesis* through two ancient vases, Achilles and Ajax Playing Draughts (*c.*540 BCE) and The Warrior's Leave-Taking (*c.*510–500 BCE) (Figure 7.4).[16] On these vases, we find foreshortening perhaps for the first time in the depiction of toes. A more developed version of foreshortening is perspective, a supreme achievement of the Italian Renaissance in the mimetic tradition. Erich Auerbach explained this mimetic tradition through a comparison between Homer's *Odyssey* and the Bible. In *Odyssey*, the discovery of Odysseus's scar, in Book 19, by the old housekeeper Euryclea was narrated with rich and complete details in episodes and memories, despite the fact that this discovery marked a dramatic turn of events in the epic. Technically, this key dramatic turn was implied in the narration, not in abstraction, while in the Bible, God's command to Abraham (Genesis 22:1) was given without definite time, place, or context.

On the one hand, externalized, uniformly illuminated phenomena, at a definite time and in a definite place, connected together without lacunae in a perpetual foreground . . . On the other hand, the externalization of only so much of the phenomena as is necessary for the purpose of the narrative, all else left in obscurity; the decisive points of the narrative alone are emphasized, what lies between is nonexistent ...'[17] So remarkable was the achievement of the Greek civilization that Bertrand Russell, in his survey of Western philosophy, exclaimed that 'In all history, nothing is so surprising or so difficult to account for as the sudden rise of civilization in Greece.[18]

This extraordinary desire to represent reality as 'external truths' has a remarkable impact on culture; it is certainly at the core of Greek *techné*. As Gombrich observed, the five little circles which are the representations of the toes of the departing soldier being attended by his parents are evidence of an artistic revolution; they are both a 'truthful' representation and an innovation. While foreshortening and contextual narration sustain the tradition of *mimesis* in art and

Figure 7.4 The Warrior's Leave-Taking, *c.*510–500 BCE

literature, typological analyses, material properties, and gravitational forces may be seen to be the 'external truths' that are at the heart of a mimetic conception of architecture. For a long time, science was held as the epitome of mimetic *techné*, as it was developed with great energy in seventeenth-century Europe. At the outset of this scientific enterprise, the boundaries between 'external truths' and 'internal distortions' were clearly policed, as we can see them demonstrated in the writings of Francis Bacon. In his *Advancement of Learning* (1605), Bacon argued that the hieroglyphic appeared before the alphabetic as a distinct stage of the development of the human intellect, a stage when thoughts were only present in figural forms. The goal of knowledge is to purge the hieroglyphic from its domain. Bacon identified three kinds of hieroglyphic thinking, three vanities of thought: the fantastic, the contentious, and the delicate, exemplifying different ways of the form of thinking substituting the substance of thought. As a follower of Bacon, Robert Hook made important contributions to the rise of modern science and to the practice of architecture. In his *Micrographia* (1665), a collection of surprising images of very small things and insects drawn from his observations through the microscope he invented, Hooke paraded the triumphs of science and its suppression of the figure. The first image of the book was a drawing of three common things: the tip of a needle, a printed period mark, and the edge of a razor (Figure 7.5). Hooke shows them to be different from what we normally thought: the sharp needle point is seen to have a '*broad, blunt,* and very *irregular* end', the printed period mark looks like a 'great splatch of *London* dirt', and the edge of a razor appears to be 'almost like a plow'd field'.[19] The figural thoughts would repeat comfortably statements such as 'as sharp as a needle's point' or 'as sharp as a razor's edge', but there is, in Hooke's mind, no truth in them. These are, essentially, figures of the mind. If we see *Micrographia* as an aesthetic adventure, much of the twentieth-century modern art moved along the road of this adventure by progressively removing physical and intellectual conceptions such as those of landscape (Monet, Seurat, Cézanne) and the body (Picasso, Matisse, Bacon), often resulting in nothingness (Rothko, Creed). To put all these acts of suppression of the figure in the context of Chinese figuration, the Chinese artist Qiu Anxiong, in his work *New Book of Mountains and Seas* (2004–08), reverses the mimetic tradition and creates a range of mythological creatures figurated from the objects of modern science; the entire piece of work traces the format of one of the earliest and most well-known mythologies, *Book of Mountains and Seas* (Warring States *c.*450 BCE to Han *c.*200 BCE).

The Empire of Figures

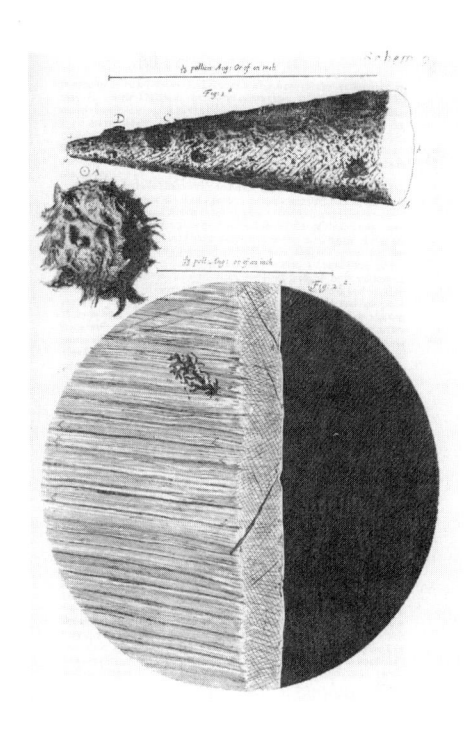

Figure 7.5 Robert Hooke, Scheme 1, in *Micrographia*, London, 1665

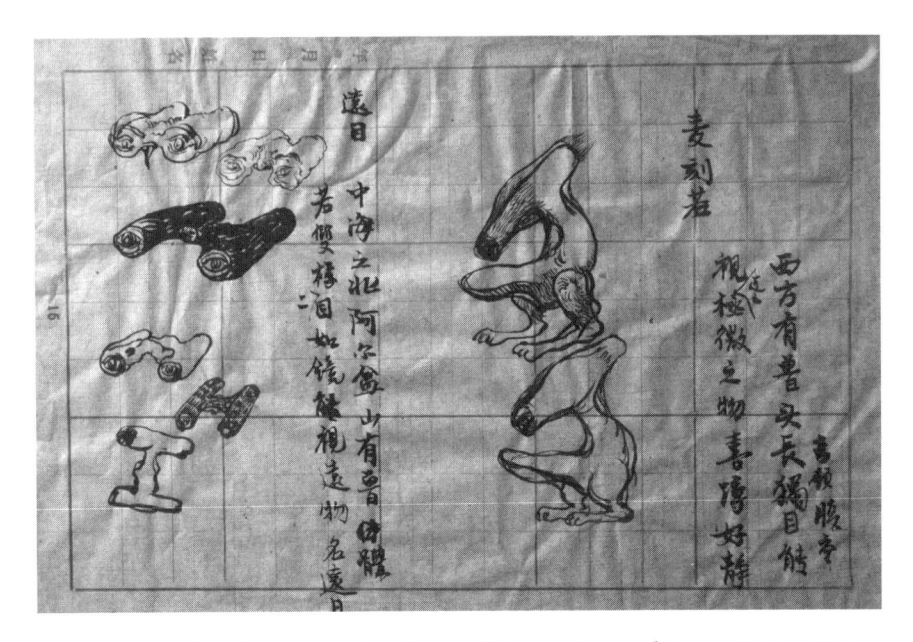

Figure 7.6 Qiu Anxiong, *New Book of Mountains and Seas*, 2004–2008: (*right*) *maikenuo*, sketch detail (courtesy of the artist)

In a contrived world where the Chinese figurative practice encounters Western science for the first time, Qiu Anxiong's objects mythologized scientific objects as exotic creatures like the mythological animals in China's past. They reinvent moments of figuration. Among many exotic creatures created to figurate modern machines, Hooke's ingenious invention of the microscope became Qiu's *maikenuo* (microscope) (Figure 7.6), which is described as a long-headed and one-eyed beast from the West (itself a mythical notion) who can see very small things, and who has a quiet disposition.

Perhaps the most easily anticipated consequence of the Western tradition of *mimesis* is a distrust of image; if knowledge lies in 'reality' from which form emerges, then image is only a truth of the second degree. Image is falsehood. This is central to Plato's writing; he suggested that the image makers – poets, playwrights, musicians, painters – should be excluded or controlled in his ideal republic for ideal citizens. For Plato, one of his most powerful philosophical impulses was to conceive the separation of the real from its shadows, and to safeguard the real from distorting images. The Platonic influence on the early Christian thinkers brought the concern dialectic of image and truth to a new context; imaging the divine in the Christian faith was for a long time ardently contested by Iconoclasts and Puritans. The desire for 'truth', rather than the image of truth, from God had given rise to a great deal of intellectual and violent dispute in the past. Image was heresy. Immanuel Kant maintained the Platonic divide between the material and the ideal at the centre of his philosophical scheme, shaping philosophical debates decisively for centuries. His distinction between noumena and phenomena, between appearances and things-in-themselves, reconstitutes this tradition of conceiving image as falsehood. William Hannas's criticism of the Chinese square words as endless processions of images with tenuous connections to the real world was, in some ways, grounded in this perceived failure of image to capture truth.

Image as falsehood is at the heart of Marxist critique of culture: the sum total of images constitutes a false consciousness created by the capital, an ideology of the capitalist society. Whether it is the characterization of image as an 'industry' by Horkheimer and Adorno,[20] or as a 'hyperreality' by Debord,[21] or as a critical blow to the spirit of art by Benjamin,[22] or as simulacra by Baudrillard,[23] these critical insights reaffirm the primacy of the original and denigrate the use of image. Electronic media present a complex dimension to the critique of image; media theories accordingly are more reflexive, working with the assumption that media – and thus image – are unavoidable and inescapable.[24] Media need to be accepted as one of the fundamental things in life,²⁵ and demand their own cultural heroes, as Friedrich Kittler proposes, such as Edison in place of Nietzsche and Goethe.²⁶ The rise of media theories perhaps spurred on an extraordinary period of media-inspired cultural production; fragmentation and congestion, perhaps some of the results of the instantaneous over-supply of information typical of the electronic media, gained some form of legitimate status at least in art and architecture, as evidenced by Rem Koolhaas's *S,M,L,XL* (1995). The book itself is essentially an image of the book. As a book, *S,M,L,XL* subverts reading (too bulky to hold, too digressive to contemplate with, too provocative for the coffee table); instead, it reinforces the image of the sacred book in an over-compensated form without actually becoming one. *S,M,L,XL* contains an image of research in the forms of observation (stark photography), documentation (statistics), and analyses (maps of lines) – the appearances of the hallmarks of conventional science.

This entire enterprise of the critique of the capital, image, spectacle, simulacra hinges on a notion of authenticity, the idea that humanity possesses original and naturalist life-forms that have been alienated by icon, image, media, fame, consumption. It is often surprising how little these aestheticized and moralized discourses of the image mean in China beyond intellectual circles. The Chinese word for 'image' is in one way represented by painterly and photographic image (*xiang* 像) and in another way by the figure (*xiang* 象); neither term contains any moral or aesthetic judgement; they carry nothing that could resemble the enormous moral forces easily detectable in Western critical theory. The Chinese word for 'copy' (*chao*) was traditionally an operational word also devoid of obvious moral connotations; the Chinese word for 'emulation' (*fang*) had perhaps greater moral approval than disapproval; it speaks of respect instead of moral degradation. Emulations were not false and empty, but carried something substantial, albeit less substantial than its first appearance. The imperial civil service examinations were almost entirely conceived as, and assessed by, the skills and completeness of emulation of classics. In contrast with the critique of image, those who deviated from emulation often encountered considerable resistance. The notion of intellectual property – commodification of idea predicated on the crucial notion of the authenticity of the original – could not begin to be substantially formulated in this context. The very different fates of the Four Wangs and the Four Monks in the seventeenth century are perhaps indicative of the social and moral status of emulation. The Four Wangs – Wang Shimin, Wang Jian, Wang Hui, and Wang Yuanqi – were painters renowned for their emulations of masterpieces of earlier eras, and they commanded high social status and imperial recognition, while their contemporaries the Four Monks – Zhu Da, Shi Tao, Kun Can, and Hong Ren – played a marginal role at the time for their more innovative spirit in their arts. The fact that we value the Four Monks today above the Four Wangs only reflects how the world of art criticism changed in the twentieth century. The Four Wangs marshalled the primary cultural forces in the tradition of emulation, built up an extraordinary artistic enterprise that appealed to a wide audience, and upheld a tradition of painting established by their master Dong Qichang (1555–1636). What perhaps legitimized emulation is a process, demanded by figuration, of approaching gradually the stabilized and essentialized poetic centre of artistic productions. This is perhaps the same process found in the tradition of evidential scholarship (*kaozheng*) which aimed to restore classics to their status of *orthos* (*zheng*) by purging impurities accumulated through countless copies through time.

The Perpetual Homecoming

The empire of figures produces a deep consequence in thinking which returns to the city with powerful influences; it establishes a parallel between the figure and home, and a home-like thinking space where the Western strategies to suppress the figure no longer exists. The figure and home, here, are both understood as locations of final emotional and intellectual retreat, as places where their inherent forms stemming from that of the womb outweigh the strength of logic in instrumental reason. Extending from this parallel, the figure assumes its ontological status against the plane of truth, and home constructs a realm in contrast with the sphere of the public.

Sigmund Freud's 1919 essay 'The Uncanny' placed in psychology a fundamental principle of what may be described as 'the Western social-spatial form': the city is only possible when one leaves home. An early version of this proposition can perhaps be found in Aristotle's *Politics*, in which he stressed that home is where emotional and hierarchical authority dwells, while the city – housing, so to speak, a political life (*bios politikos*) – is where equality and freedom becomes possible. The *polis* – the assemblage of spaces that physically manifest the notion of a political and public life – became the embryonic form for the Western city; the language of urbanism couched in terms of natural rights to free open space and community-based life in the West still reach all the way back to those of the *polis*. Neither the imperial imaginations of ancient Rome nor the missionary ambitions of the Christian Church had deviated from the urban goals of the *polis*; the public realm, together with its urban-based institutions such as squares, city halls, museums, cultural centres, libraries, universities, remained the most important site to construct a public life. This is an extraordinary conception, particularly when we consider that our natural loyalty tends to gravitate toward the family, and towards institutions modelled on the family as an archetype. If we postulate that the urge to build a public life runs against a biological intuition to strengthen and protect the family, then what force has been at work to effect such a rebellion of nature? This question perhaps highlights the importance of Freud's work, not that it pointed towards a universal truth, but that it captured an intellectual construct that seems to be so puzzling to the Chinese reader and yet so reassuring to the Western reader. The force that worked to incite an act of leaving home in the Western cultural context is constructed by Freud in the notion of the uncanny, the feeling that there is something familiar yet strange about home, both as a real space and as a signifier for the womb and for thought. The desire to leave home and to sustain the public realm is cultivated so intensely that it seems to have produced a feeling of repulsion for the familiar, a strangeness in the well-known. Freud explained that the uncanny is nothing new or foreign, but something familiar and old; what created the feeling of uncanny is rooted in the process of repression that transforms the familiar into the uncanny. This repression of homeliness in the psyche parallels the suppression of the figure in epistemology.

While the psychologized uncanny incites the act of leaving home, the forces of figuration ensure a perpetual homecoming. One may suggest that in traditional China philosophy and aesthetics never left home; furthermore, there was nothing significant outside the home. The power of the figure in securing its own homeliness lies in the way in which it constructs – through analogy rather than *mimesis* – an entire realm that replicates external references and replaces them altogether. Under this condition, what is outside home can only be perceived philosophically as a 'not-home', the *jianghu*, a tremendously important notion with great consequences in the production of the built environment discussed in Chapter 5. A novel such as Cao Xueqing's *Dream of the Red Chamber* (1791) would take place entirely within the garden compound of a socially and economically well-off family, as if to highlight the fact that all human affairs have already been reconstituted in the Grand View Garden. During the May Fourth Movement in 1919, China's first effective introduction to Western cultural concepts, many intellectuals began to experiment with different scenarios of home. Ba Jin's novel *Family* (*Jia*), a story of the different fates of members of an upper-class family caught up in the upheavals of the May Fourth Movement in the 1920s, explored the crisis of this deep-rooted social form in China. Its main protagonists showed tendencies of both staying at home and leaving home, highlighting a transitional condition of the Chinese society. Here, to go through again an example discussed in Chapter 5 in the context of the figure and home, Henrik Ibsen's play *A Doll's House* (premiered in 1879 in Europe) created a sensation among Chinese youth who were eager to remake their society and cities inspired by the Western model; the notion that a women (Nora Helmer) of a bourgeois family would choose to leave her husband stirred deep emotions in the Chinese youth seeking to change their society. Lu Xun, however, paused to ask the question: What happens to Nora after she leaves home? Here, Lu Xun's anxiety can be seen to be about the merging of the figure and home, about the inherent formlessness of *jianghu*, which would leave the Chinese Nora Helmer with few prospects. Lu Xun's note of caution speaks of a deep perception of a social form in which home is never made uncanny or unhomely; instead, this social form cultivates the force of the perpetual homecoming. Immensely agitated by the urge to reform the Chinese culture to respond to the enormous social and political crisis in early twentieth-century China, Lu Xun proposed the abandonment of the Chinese square words and the adoption of alphabetic and phonetic notation systems. Echoing a common sentiment of the time which was expressed by prominent intellectuals and reformers such Cai Yuanpei, Qu Qiubai, Qian Xuantong, and Mao Zedong, Lu Xun claimed that China would perish if it did not abandon the square words. The fact that the Chinese square words were seen by them as the critical barrier between the traditional China and a new China modelled on the Western precedent highlights the depth of power of the Chinese writing system. The alliance between the figure and home, I argue, is critically important to the formation of the Chinese social-spatial imagination. Language is both a tool of communication and a way of thought. If the alliance between the figure and home produces endless permutations of derivatives of the family, it creates degrees of care that trace the spatial orders of the protected home. The early Chinese reformers were deeply agitated by the absence of 'society' outside the family, and by the absence of an equal and free 'public space' outside those of the various degrees of care; the issue of public space in China can indeed be linked, in some senses, to the issue of the Chinese writing system, although on the surface they may seem to operate on very different intellectual planes.

Like many intellectual conceptions in China, homecoming is both intellectual and material; each year, during the Chinese New Year, homecoming is a huge emotional and aesthetic affair in China, particularly in relation to the migration of workers and immigrant Chinese abroad. During the ten days between 7 and 17 January 2012, the peak travel period of the Chinese New Year, there were more than 56 million people travelling on the railway system in China, returning home.[27] This, probably the world's greatest annual migration of people, is grounded in the psychological power of the intensive care of home rather than its alienation. *Huijia*, or returning home, has an unquestioned high importance in Chinese society. The alliance between the figure and home foregrounds every action in China; it is not possible to understand the Chinese city without first understanding this crucial alliance. The figure and home alliance puts a strong intellectual foundation to spaces that approximate homeliness rather than unhomeliness, giving a much more rooted meaning to degrees of care. It is the culmination of a cultural force that saturates the Chinese society with intellectual, social, and spatial degrees of care. Prudence as a preventative strategy ultimately acquires an intellectual agenda through this alliance: the security of the home becomes its intellectual space. If unhomeliness, so exquisitely described by Freud, indicates an important intellectual force of rebellion, what could sustain a comparable condition in the Chinese cultural context? Does the empire of figures cultivate only stability and distaste for rebellion, and allow nothing that subverts its grip? I would like to argue that the empire of figures formulates its own criticality; it is one that does not always follow the logic of critique – a process of establishing contexts, tracing origins, and building a history of authenticity – as the substance of a critical act. It certainly does not hinge on a visual display of critique – open speech-based debate – as an effective way to convey a different opinion. Dissent, in the endless home of the empire of figures, either takes up an appearance of an uncomfortable agreement or that of a disruptive figuration. The primary critical strategy here is not to articulate an analytical framework that places both the canon and dissent into 'objects of criticism', but to act within the canon. Xu Bing's *Book from the Sky* and Qiu Anxiong's *New Book of Mountains and Seas*, as critical acts, worked within this laconic criticality, and with the primary media of the empire of figures. They are examples of what may be described as 'the figurative criticality' in the Chinese cultural context, an indigenous dissent with meaningful strategies of engagement. The figurative dissent is a critical propensity that engages and modifies as it proceeds; it subverts the figure through the figure, and opens up new necessities of figuration that may approximate economy, function, and life with new strategies of figuration.

Notes

1 François Jullien, *The Propensity of Things: Towards a History of Efficacy in China* (New York: Zone Books, 1995); *Detour and Access: Strategies of Meaning in China and Greece* (New York: Zone Books, 2004).
2 William Hannas, *The Writing on the Wall: How Asian Orthography Curbs Creativity* (Philadelphia: University of Pennsylvania Press, 2003), p.246.
3 John DeFrancis, *The Chinese Language: Fact and Fantasy* (Honolulu: University of Hawai'i Press, 1984); William Hannas, *Asia's Orthographic Dilemma* (Honolulu: University of Hawai'i Press, 1997).
4 Hannas, *The Writing on the Wall*, p.172.
5 Ibid., p.316, note 2.
6 Ibid., p.198.
7 The proposition that creativity only begins when linguistic signs become separate from meanings is not necessarily a conclusive one; the relationship between language and thinking, as in cases of animals and children, do not have a distinct causality. The Chinese thing-based thinking process, enabled by its thing-based linguistic structure, leads to a kind of thing-based creativity that is not abstract but phenomenological.
8 Herrlee Glessner Creel, 'On the Nature of Chinese Ideography', *T'oung Pao* (second series) 32:2/3 (1936), pp.85–161.
9 Philippe Lacoue-Labarthe, 'Oedipus as Figure', *Radical Philosophy* 118 (March/April 2003), pp.7–17.
10 Jean Baudrillard, *Simulacra and Simulation* (Ann Arbor: University of Michigan Press, 1994).
11 Shawn Eichman, 'The Art of Taoist Scriptures', *Orientations* 31 (Hong Kong: December 2000), pp.36–44; Robert E. Harrist, Jr., *The Landscape of Words: Stone Inscriptions from Early and Medieval China* (Seattle and London: University of Washington Press, 2008), Chapter 3; Richard Curt Klaus, *Brushes with Power: Modern Politics and the Chinese Art of Calligraphy* (Berkeley: University of California Press, 1991).
12 Cécile and Michel Beurdeley, *Giuseppe Castiglione: A Jesuit Painter at the Court of the Chinese Emperors* (London: Lund Humphries, 1971), p.73.
13 Ibid., p.138.
14 Jerome Silbergeld and Dora C. Y. Ching, eds, *Persistence/Transformation: Text as Image in the Art of Xu Bing* (Princeton: Princeton University Press, 2006), p.19.
15 'Image as Text' was the title of Xu Bing's lecture given at Princeton University in 2003, see Silbergeld and Ching, *Persistence/Transformation*.
16 E. H. Gombrich, *The Story of Art* (London: Phaidon, 1995), pp.80–81.

17 Erich Auerbach, *Mimesis: The Representation of Reality in Western Literature*, trans. Willard R. Trask (Princeton: Princeton University Press, 1953), p.11.
18 Bertrand Russell, *History of Western Philosophy* (London: Routledge, 2000; originally published 1946).
19 Robert Hooke, *Micrographia* (London: 1665), pp.3–4.
20 Max Horkheimer and Theodor W. Adorno, 'The Culture Industry: Enlightenment as Mass Deception', in *Dialectics of Enlightenment* (Stanford: Stanford University Press, 2002).
21 Guy Debord, *The Society of the Spectacle* (New York: Zone Books, 1995).
22 Walter Benjamin, 'The Work of Art in the Age of Mechanical Reproduction', in Hannah Arendt (ed.), *Illuminations* (New York: Harcourt, Brace & World, 1968), pp.217–52.
23 Jean Baudrillard, *Simulacra and Simulation* (Chicago: University of Michigan Press, 1995).
24 Scott Lash, 'Critique of Representation: Henri Lefebvre's Spatial Materialism', in *Critique of Information* (London: SAGE, 2002), pp.114–28.
25 Bernard Stiegler, *Technics and Time 1: The Fault of Epimetheus* (Stanford: Stanford University Press, 1998).
26 Friedrich A. Kittler, *Gramophone, Film, Typewriter* (Stanford: Stanford University Press, 1999), p.xxxiii.
27 www.gov.cn/gzdt/2012-01/19/content_2048691.htm, accessed 9 December 2012.

8

Memory without Location

One of the most profound paradoxes of China, the great Chinese reformer Liang Qichao (1873–1929) mused at the start of the new century in 1902, is that it recorded so much of its past yet it did not have a history.[1] Ancient Chinese records such as the *Spring and Autumn Annals* (*Chunqui*) by Confucius (551–497 BCE), Liang Qichao complained, were far too brief and lacked factual precision. They recorded events but neglected the connections between them, and they focused on individuals but failed to account for collectivity. His comments came after he encountered the Western notion of history for the first time while in exile in Japan following his unsuccessful reform attempts in 1898 known as the One Hundred Days Reform. He began in the late 1890s with an attempt to reform imperial institutions, but realized that it was knowledge in China that required a major rethinking. He was convinced that only a new knowledge could give China a new century; at the heart of his knowledge reform was the enterprise of history. The idea of history he was attracted to, through Japanese translations, was one that relied on the crucial notion of 'the historical fact' and the meaningful connections between those facts. The historical fact, in turn, is grounded in the central notion of its authenticity, which could be seen to be nested in authentic locations.

Many years later, in 1927, Liang Qichao attempted a history of Chinese cities as part of a larger history of Chinese culture;[2] this time, the paradox appeared in a more explicit way: there was an amazing richness in textual descriptions of ancient Chinese cities, yet there were few verifiable facts that could be located in original sites. All the great cities in history, despite their central cultural significance, had failed to leave sufficient material traces to ground a history of Chinese cities. To Liang Qichao, this paradox could not be more clearly demonstrated than in the very different fates of two ancient cities following their discoveries: the discovery of Pompeii and its preservation secured a renewal of our understanding of the Roman Empire, while the discovery of the Song dynasty Jülu City (built in 1108) in China was met with little preservation efforts and the ruins of the city were soon looted.[3]

Father Ricci's Memory Methods of Western Countries

Liang Qichao was not the first person who encountered what could be seen as a distinct character of memory in the Chinese cultural context. In the sixteenth century, Father Matteo Ricci (1552–1610), an Italian Jesuit who travelled to China as part of the Counter Reformation drive of the Catholic Church, appears to have also recognized the nature of memory in China. Ricci studied classics in his native town Macerata, and became a novice at the Society of Jesus in Rome in 1571. In 1577 he embarked on a journey to the Far East and spent the rest of his life in China. Unlike many of his contemporaries, Ricci was proficient in classical Chinese and had great appreciation for the Chinese culture; this unique knowledge allowed him to adopt an approach of speaking of European innovations in knowledge, such as those in astronomy and mathematics, through the Chinese language as testimonies to the power of his faith. In this context, Ricci wrote a small treatise on mnemonic arts in Chinese, *Xiguo jifa*, or *Memory Methods of Western Countries*, in 1596, as a present to the Governor of Jiangxi Province Lu Wan'gai for his three sons who were about to take the civil service examinations.[4] At first glance, this intellectual labour seems to be entirely unnecessary; over a thousand years, the Chinese culture had been grounded in the central practice of memorizing canonical Confucian texts and reproducing them perfectly, particularly at the civil service examinations. This great emphasis on memory, as we have discussed, appears to have been rooted in the very structure of the Chinese writing system. However, Ricci perhaps thought that he could offer something new. He recognized two opportunities in writing this treatise: the Chinese square words being a set of ready-made images for memory (*xiang*), and the need to place them in sites (*chusuo*). Ricci used four examples of the Chinese square words – *wu* (war), *yao* (want), *li* (profit), and *hao* (good) – to demonstrate the mnemonic potentials of the Chinese square words. More importantly, Ricci stressed the importance of placing images of memories in places, which was different from the Chinese traditional methods of repetition, recitation aided by mnemonic poems and rhyming jingles.[5] To reinforce his point about the place of memory, Ricci told the story of Simonides, the inventor of the art of memory, who invited close friends and family to a banquet where the roof had suddenly collapsed onto the guests and their bodies had become unrecognizable. Simonides, at the moment of the collapse, was called temporarily outside the house, and, upon return, was able to recall each person from their sitting locations. Deriving from this story, Ricci told his Chinese readers, places can hold memories, and there are three grades of places of memory – large, medium and small – each being able to hold as many images as necessary for what is to be remembered. A large place could be a bureau, a palace, a temple, a courtyard house, or a multitude of them up to a few hundred; a medium place could be a hall, a pavilion, a room; and a small place could be a corner of a room, a shrine, a cabinet or a chair.[6]

In writing this treatise on the art of memory, Ricci drew extensively on a tradition of mnemonic arts which stressed the locations of memories. The story of Simonides was made well known by Cicero, who, through this story, described the mnemonics of places and images in his *De oratore*.[7] The anonymous *Ad Herennium* (written approximately between 86 and 82 BCE), believed to be a work of Cicero for most of the medieval period and thus highly influential, contained a detailed explanation of the art of memory grounded in locations; Quintilian's treatise on rhetoric (*Institutio Oratoria*, 95 CE) also offers a clear explanation of the locations of memory through the architectural type. One highlight of this tradition was perhaps Guilio Camillo's Memory Theatre conceived in the 1530s, where a complex set of storage spaces was arranged in seven rising sections (marked as the seven pillars of Solomon's House of Wisdom). Camillo's Theatre was well known in the early sixteenth century; his *Complete Works* (*Tutte le opera*), followed by nine other editions, was first published in 1552, the year Matteo Ricci was born.[8]

Ricci's *Memory Methods* contained an essential proposition that memories reside in locations. The fundamental importance of this conception of memory could perhaps be indicated in one way by the usage of places – topics, *topoi* – to signify meanings. Ricci's discovery of the Chinese square words as ready-made images for memories did not change this essential proposition; his Christian faith reconstituted and reinforced the central importance of the locations of memory through the idea of 'relics' and the pilgrimages that continue to sustain the meaning of authentic objects in original locations.

All these are not just cultural peculiarities; there are two important notions at stake in the art of memory. When memories have locations, they substantiate specific spatial and temporal ideas; this is perhaps clearly seen in two outcomes of Ricci's memory techniques which were appreciated highly by his Chinese hosts – the world map and the Western calendar. Ricci's world map with place names translated into Chinese – amalgamated from several published maps of the world he brought with him to China – had been reproduced many times, the grandest version of which was presented in six separate panels, each over six feet wide, in the inner chambers of the Palace of Emperor Wanli (reigned 1572–1620).[9] The value of the Ricci maps is perhaps understandable when we consider the contemporary Chinese map making, such as those depicting Zheng He's voyages in Mao Yuanyi's (1594–1641) *Treatise on Military Preparations* (*Wu bei zhi*) in 1621. In section 240 of this enormous and well-illustrated treatise on warfare, Mao's 'maps' contained essential navigational information such as place names, precise compass directions, depth of water, star positions, and sailing time, but these descriptions are placed on the pages as textual information. They are closer to the landscape scrolls rooted in literary narratives than spatial maps with scale and orientation. Together with other Jesuit missionaries such as Adam Schall (1592–1666), Ricci contributed crucially to the calendar reform of Xu Guanqi (1562–1633) known as the *Astronomical Treatises of the Chongzhen Reign* (*Chongzhen Lishu*, 1629–34), which was commissioned by Emperor Chongzhen (reigned 1627–44) with, among other features, calculations to predict precisely solar and lunar eclipses.

It is these spatial and temporal frameworks of knowledge that were recognized by Liang Qichao in his reform agenda in the early twentieth century. To develop a new knowledge in China, Liang Qichao insisted, the Chinese must learn to establish two central branches of knowledge: geography and history. The establishment of history in China, Liang Qichao stressed, was the most difficult task for China. Liang Qichao composed three treatises expounding the central concepts of history and historiography: *New Historiography* (1902), *Research Method for Chinese History* (1922), and *Compendium to the Research Method for Chinese History* (1926–27). They have had significant influences in the formation of the academic discipline of history – very different from its traditional conceptions of past events – in twentieth-century China. His son, Liang Sicheng (1901–72), one of the founders of modern architectural education and profession in China, was deeply influenced by the historiographical imagination of Liang Qichao; Liang Sicheng's early intellectual development was in one way shaped through his participation in the Chinese translation of H. G. Wells's *Outline of History* in 1921, a task assigned by his father. Liang Sicheng's pioneering history of Chinese architecture, grounded in surveys of buildings with authentic locations, could be seen as an example of Liang Qichao's new history in which the significance of Chinese architecture is articulated in relation to the authentic locations of architecture and their connections to global frameworks of space and time.[10]

In the Western conception, a city can be seen to be the *locus* of memories; it provides an immediate materiality in the construction of located memories and in the establishment of the frameworks of space and time. Preservation of the original locations under original conditions – in conjunction with the archiving of documents – therefore serves an important intellectual purpose in cities far beyond that of collective nostalgia. We may describe cities that serve this important intellectual function as 'archive cities'.[11] A city as an archive does not mean a city of perpetual preservation; on the contrary, it describes the profound power of the archive in its ability to effect new content. In archive cities, memories are precisely located in urban archives, and the preservation of locations is deeply meaningful in sustaining systems of values, processes of legitimation, and centres of power. The word archive is derived from the Greek word for town hall (*arkheion*). An archive city functions like an archaeological site, with located and authentic fragments at its foundation of knowledge; here, knowledge is modelled on archaeology. The sum total of knowledge is continuously revised by the discovery of new fragments which may insist on alternative and more advantageous narratives. This metaphor of the archaeological site has underpinned Michel Foucault's radical re-ordering of knowledge in humanities; Sigmund Freud, in one of his influential books, *Civilization and Its Discontents* (1930), imagined the unconscious as an archive city where memories are rooted in ruins:

> Now let us, by a flight of imagination, suppose that Rome is not a human habitation but a psychical entity with a similarly long and copious past – an entity, that is to say, in which nothing that has once come into existence will have passed away and all the earlier phases of development continue to exist alongside the latest one. . . . In the place occupied by the Palazzo Caffarelli would once more stand – without the Palazzo having to be removed – the Temple of Jupiter Capitalinus, and this is not only in its latest shape, as the Romans of the Empire saw it, but also in its earliest one, when it still showed Etruscan forms and was ornamented with terracotta antefixes.[12]

The archive city invests enormous resources in the institutions of archiving: authentic fragments are preserved and presented in its 'cathedrals of authenticity' – museums and libraries – sustained by well-rehearsed rituals of viewing and authentication. The architecture of museums and libraries in traditional archive cities acquired a *gravitas* much like that of the cathedral. The archive city also cultivates intellectual and social prestige of its archivists – historians, curators, heritage architects – as high priests of authenticity. The enormous scholarship sustaining these institutions places great emphasis on dating and attribution as dedicated intellectual labours to locate artefacts. In a commemorative publication by the International Council on Monuments and Sites (ICOMOS) in 1994, the *Magna Carta* of the archive city, the Venice Charter (1964), is revealingly printed as a hand-written document at the start of the publication as an image of its own authenticity. In their expressive and psychologized forms, these investments constitute a 'fetish of the ruin' which is visible in many Western cities. One interesting result from this fetish would be John Soane's representation of his own architectural works as ruins.

Inevitably, such intense cultivation of the value of authenticity as locations of memories and meanings is perpetually accompanied by deep anxieties over the loss of the archive. Walter Benjamin's characterization of the modern condition of homelessness is both a rehearsal of Freud's notion of unhomeliness and a display of an archive anxiety – memories and meanings in search of authentic locations when mechanical reproduction removes authenticity from objects. Jacques Derrida described this deep anxiety over the loss of the archive as a Freudian 'death drive', an 'archive fever': an act of archiving that erases as much as it imprints, and produces as much as it records. If a general archiviology were to exist, it would have been plagued by this psychoanalytic anxiety.[13] The fetish of the ruin and the anxieties over the loss of the archive, as in many other cultural conditions, lends an incredible strength to the archive city as an antithetical mode of legitimation; its influence throughout the world is very significant. Father Ricci's *Memory Methods of Western Countries* was much more than just exotic memory tricks to impress his Chinese hosts.

Spatial and Temporal Relocation

Astonished as they were by Father Ricci's ability to remember Chinese square words, the Chinese hosts did not seem, ultimately, to be convinced by Father Ricci's memory treatise; as it turned out, it did not contribute too much to the success of the three sons of Governor Lu, who did extremely well in their civil service examinations due to their reliance on traditional memory techniques.[14] This is perhaps an indication of the fact that the entire memory strategy works differently in China; it is deeply intertwined with the Chinese writing system, and with many associated social and political features. At the heart of this distinct character of memory in the Chinese cultural context, in contrast with Western conceptions of a universal space and time, seems to be a spatial and temporal relocation. This is perhaps best seen in several examples in Chinese cities. In 1985, the city of Wuhan reconstructed the Yellow Crane Tower (Huanghe Lou), a building that probably began as a military observation tower in the Three Kingdoms Period (third century), but it also commemorated the legend of the yellow crane painted on the wall of a teahouse which danced at the sound of a flute. The flute was given to the owner of the teahouse, Widow Zhang, by a fairy – in the appearance of a weak old man – as the reward for her kindness towards the old man. From the Tang dynasty (seventh century), a succession of poets – from Cui Hao and Li Bai to Mao Zedong – had been inspired by its spectacular view of the Yangtze River and written popular poems on or about this place. Mao's 'Huanghe Lou' in 1927 – a Song-dynasty-style poem – combined the Chinese literary tradition with twentieth-century revolutionary sentiments, thus enjoying enormous popularity and contributing crucially to the fame of the Yellow Crane Tower. It is highly significant that the Yellow Crane Tower, as one of the most significant places in the Chinese imagination, does not possess an authentic materiality; it had been reconstructed many times over the centuries. The 1985 reconstruction was an approximation of a Qing-dynasty reconstruction (burned down in 1884) of an earlier tower (Figure 8.1). In contrast to the Qing-dynasty version, the new tower in 1985 was not built in timber, but in reinforced concrete with an air-conditioned reception room and mechanical lifts, and it has five instead of three stories. The new tower is also built about 1,000 metres away from the previous location, which was occupied by the current bridge crossing the Yangtze River. In the current form, the Yellow Crane Tower remains, as before, a hugely popular destination; for many who visit this partially air-conditioned tower framed in reinforced concrete, its antiquity is beyond doubt and taken for granted. The antiquity of the tower is both material and immaterial. In 2004, in a volume commemorating the construction of the new Yellow Crane Tower, Guan Yonghe, the Vice President of the Writers Association of Wuhan, wrote in the Preface joyfully: 'the newly constructed *Huanghe Lou* is five stories high, much more magnificent, much more glorious than before'.[15] A painting of the new Yellow Crane Tower in traditional style features on the cover of this commemorating volume, thus completing the act of reconstituting locations from memories by re-inscribing the new tower into the Chinese traditional memory.

Figure 8.1 Yellow Crane Tower (Huanghe Lou), Wuhan, Hubei Province: (*left*) after 1985 (photo by Zhang Tianjie); (*right*) before 1884

In 2006, the city of Hong Kong reconstructed its Edinburgh Ferry Pier in Central, a building that recreated an Edwardian pier building of 1912. The Edwardian building was demolished in 1957 to make way for a new modernist pier, which in turn was demolished in 2006 due to the construction of a new highway along the waterfront of Hong Kong Island. The new Central Pier, constructed with reinforced concrete rather than with iron, bricks, and stone, bears some resemblance to the 1912 Edwardian pier, but in every detail it differs from the original building (Figure 8.2). In addition, it is located about 350 metres north of the original site. In the twentieth century, Hong Kong had not put the preservation of the built heritage high on its economic agenda; many old buildings were demolished under intense pressure from financial imperatives. In recent decades there has been a rising awareness in Hong Kong of the loss of its architectural heritage, and the city has begun to make greater efforts to preserve its urban memory; the 2006 Central Pier perhaps reflected the growing collective anxiety over that loss. The significance of Hong Kong's endeavour to redress its loss of memories lies in its approach to authenticity; instead of excavating and preserving material remains of Edinburgh Pier and the modernist pier, it invests in a new, similar-looking, and differently located building. In this sense, the new 2006 Central Pier shares a common intellectual framework of antiquity with the Yellow Crane Tower in Wuhan; here, the 2006 Central Pier supplies the memory of the 1912 Edinburgh Ferry Pier

Figure 8.2 Central Pier, Hong Kong, after 2006

by supplanting the original building with a new building, reconstituting the location of memory through the act of remembering.

We must distinguish these examples of reconstructions in Wuhan and Hong Kong from simulated fantasies (such as those of Disneyland); simulation is clearly defined against binary realms of fantasy and reality, representation and authenticity. The status of their confusion as a simulacrum does not change this basic binary structure. In Wuhan and Hong Kong, the central conceptions of memory are not results of a confusion of the real and the imitated; instead, they are clearly not troubled by any notion of material reality or authenticity. If we can describe the strategy of memory preservation of the archive city as having a dual existence of located and authenticated ruins and as licensed replicas displayed in museums, then in the Chinese tradition memory reconstitutions do not have a separable status from that of antiquity. The reconstituted new old buildings in China possess some degree of 'immaterial authenticity' in the collective memories of people, which is maintained through their spatial and temporal relocation. In 2003, the United Nations Educational, Scientific, and Cultural Organization (UNESCO) met to establish the notion of 'intangible heritage' to be preserved in conjunction with monuments and sites. While intangible heritage (cultures and customs) was conceived as an expansion of location-based heritage preservation (monuments and sites) by UNESCO, in China, it is more likely to be understood as memory without location. This recent directive from UNESCO has been warmly welcomed in China, although it may be interpreted and practised very differently. The 1985 Yellow Crane Tower and the 2006 Central Pier are not isolated examples; they reflect a widespread and prevalent practice in Chinese cities despite the official promotions of a different ideal – derived from the intellectual conceptions of the archive city – by the academic elite in China who often lament the absence of the archive city in China.

The historical awareness in Chinese cities can arguably be traced back to Liang Qichao's historical writings, while Liang Sicheng was certainly one of the important intellectual pioneers of a history of Chinese architecture. They propagated a considerable critical force against this Chinese tradition of spatial and temporal relocation. In 'Architecture and the Restoration Plan for the Temple of Confucius', Liang Sicheng remarked as early as in 1935 that 'the only objective of past repairs was to replace the old building with a glorious and sturdy new building; if this meant the demolition of the old building, it would be all the more praise-worthy as virtuous achievements of an high order'.[16] Liang Sicheng was conscious of the deep-rooted tradition of reconstitution of antiquity; the two examples in Wuhan and Hong Kong do not speak of a twentieth-century phenomenon, they are two of countless recent examples of an ancient tradition. At the same time, Liang Sicheng heralded a new era of heritage conservation in China. The state legislation in China – its Venice Charter inspired heritage conservation law established in 1982 – demands authentic locations to be preserved without alteration or relocation. However, this statutory enforcement to preserve monuments and sites, recently formulated and put in practice, has always been challenged by the Chinese memory strategy. Like the fate of Father Ricci's treatise on memory, the conservation efforts of Liang Sicheng were often met with suspicion; his proposal in the 1950s to locate the administrative centre of the new Chinese government to the west of the city in order to preserve the imperial palace of Beijing was highly criticized and was one of the main causes of persecution that contributed to his demise in the 1970s. The political power, at least at that time, was not ready to abandon the opportunity to reconstitute the traditional axis of power; it tapped into the tradition of representing power through the central axis in the creation of Tiananmen Square. Despite the introduction of the heritage conservation law in China which calls for systematic conservation of locations of memories, the Chinese city continues to trace its profound cultural tradition in the memory strategy of spatial and temporal relocation.

Memory without location is more pervasive than buildings; we can perhaps observe this spatial and temporal relocation as a practice that permeated many other aspects of Chinese cultural and social life. As much as Chinese art connoisseurship respected past masterpieces, collectors of precious art often alter the original art by printing stamps on paintings and calligraphies; this was a conventional practice and it perhaps represents a mild form of temporal relocation. The strength of temporal relocation is perhaps best illustrated by the practice of setting the year to zero at the start of each imperial reign, indicating a collective shift in temporal conceptions. Scholars in China make extensive use of rubbings of stone steles – bound into volumes – which, while serving as sources of authority, dislocate the stone carvings spatially.[17] The fate of the twelfth-century construction manual the *Yingzao fashi* in twentieth-century China is an exceptional example of this spatial and temporal relocation. First published in 1103, the *Yingzao fashi* summarized methods of construction, materials usage, and hierarchies of decorations for imperial building construction in the Song dynasty, an extraordinarily inventive and enterprising period in Chinese history. Over the centuries, the manual had been copied many times and the original publication was lost. In 1918 a scholar official, Zhu Qiqian (1872–1964), discovered a nineteenth-century copy (a copy of earlier copies of the original edition), as well two individual pages believed to be from earlier twelfth-century editions. Based on these discoveries, Zhu began to reconstruct the construction manual by painstakingly correcting the text, and by mimicking twelfth-century typography, printing, and binding techniques. Zhu's amazing recreation of the *Yingzao fashi* was an exquisitely crafted publication highly praised by the scholarly world, and earned him an elevated position in the world of Chinese architectural research at the time.[18] In his mind, the 1925 edition of the *Yingzao fashi* had brought the original publication back to his time.

Memory as Text

In the process of reconstituting the *Yingzao fashi*, Zhu and his collaborators followed a well-established tradition of making 'good copies' (*shanben*), a process that improved damaged originals with edited texts and new prints that approximated the originals. In cases of the absence of the original, as with the *Yingzao fashi*, an imagined original was created. This philological endeavour is general known as 'evidential research' (*kaozheng* or *kaoju*), a tradition of scholarship that reached its height in the eighteenth century (Qing dynasty). Traditional philologists were scrupulous and thorough; they scoured vast literary fields and examined diverse physical facts to detect internal inconsistencies and factual errors of the texts, as well as errors attributable to scribes and printers, in an attempt to revise and to create a better version of the text. Evidential research was central to the Chinese scholarly tradition for many centuries and carried high cultural prestige;[19] it was regarded by Chinese reformers such as Kang Youwei and Liang Qichao as evidence of a traditional respect for historical facts. Kang Youwei, founder of the so-called New Text School, was able to use this method to pronounce Confucius a 'reformer' to justify his reform ideas. Liang Qichao, in his 'Outline of Qing Scholarship', saw in this tradition a development comparable to that of philology and textual criticism centred on the Greek and Roman antiquity in Renaissance Europe.[20] Even cultural iconoclasts of early twentieth-century China such as Hu Shi and Lu Xun had enormous respect for evidential research as one of the essential achievements of Chinese civilization.[21]

It is crucially important to recognize that, in all its ambition to establish correctness, evidential research is a tradition of 'correcting texts' instead of one of 'correcting facts'. In putting a canonical text right (*zheng*), evidential research provided an extraordinary care to the principal surrogate of the empire of figures, the Chinese writing system. What sets apart the Chinese philological tradition from that in the West is the deeply and widely held belief that the canonical texts themselves were sufficient as 'originals' when they become the 'right texts'. Instead of 'text as relic' in the archive city, we encounter 'relic as text' in the Chinese city. The concept of the 'original copy' of canonical texts seems to be an ambiguous one. Here, writing becomes both the medium of meaning and the medium of memory. In the daily functioning of the Chinese language there has always been an extensive use of 'established phrases' (*chengyu*) – units of meanings that often carry extensive memory-like information or judgement, much like in the practice of common law – which constitute a 'diachronic' character that is very different from the 'synchronic' character of many alphabetic languages.[22] With each use of *chengyu*, there appears a temporal reconstitution of an otherwise 'historical' unit of meaning. Here, meanings are not historicized. Often, many specialized areas of knowledge make use of specialized and unique square words which also serve as memory-like devices. In this understanding, memory without location as we discussed in architecture appears to be functioning in parallel to the Chinese writing system; buildings in this context of the Chinese writing system, instead of having a potential syntax, have the potential to become text. Buildings aspire to texts and their prestigious condition as 'good copies' through reconstitution in the Chinese city. There is, one is often compelled to believe, an unstoppable force, a figural imperative, to textualize and de-spatialize all cultural memories in architecture. Instead of the fetish of the ruin as in the archive city, there is the fetish of the text (calligraphy) in the Chinese city. A place becomes memorable when a poem is written, and when a painting is painted, as ways of textualizing place. Evidential research, in this sense, is China's real and intellectual equivalent to historical preservation in Western cities; it must be seen as an aspect of memory always already hybridized with preservation of monuments and sites in today's China. The figural imperative of the Chinese city was not ready to be persuaded by the implicit and explicit critiques of its memory strategies by Matteo Ricci and Liang Qichao. It seeks ever-newer 'editions' of the canonical artefacts in an attempt to ensure their continuity through reconstitutions that can indeed overcome their fragility and their inevitable status of ruin. Wuhan's Yellow Crane Tower and Hong Kong's Central Pier, among countless other examples, can indeed be seen as derivative practices of evidential research in space; with or without connoisseurship and skill, they were meant to be, I argue, good copies (*shanben*) of the ideas of Yellow Crane Tower and Central Pier. The fact that they are not good architecture as we generally judge them is perhaps irrelevant to their central purpose. They exist to enable 'urban texts' to gain full power.

There are two well-established advantages of memory without location, completeness, and durability, which have been important to the social, political, and urban realities in China. Location-based memory strategies tend to begin with authenticated fragments; narratives constructed around the fragments – histories – are written and contested in equal measure. History, as we know, is often inconvenient in the political world. Figure-based memory strategies establish completeness and incorporate fragments into this completeness. Completeness (*wanzheng*), as we have discussed in relation to the Chinese numerical schemes, the notion of abundance, and the conception of the figure, carries an essential cultural significance in the Chinese city; it is ultimately an indication of an essential vitality that is attained through the complete presence of the *yin* and the *yang*. Fragments of memory, like perspectival views in paintings, perhaps represent forms of intellectual flaws in this context, and thus are to be overcome by much more holistic conceptions. The completeness inherent in figuration is here reconceptualized as completeness of memory. The fetish of the ruin such as we find in the archive city as a primary condition for location-based memory appears often as an aberration in the Chinese city; ruins are fragments, exhibiting conditions of the lack. Figuratively, ruins are aesthetic violations; cosmically, ruins are vitalities awaiting restoration; and mnemonically, ruins are intellectual disabilities. In contemporary Chinese cities, the anxieties over the ruin appear to be quite the opposite of those found in Western cities, as they were manifested in one way in the experimental art of the late twentieth century;[23] every ruin in China is an accident, and every ruin awaits restoration to completeness.

Perhaps the more substantial advantage of memory without location is durability; when memories speak of cultural narratives with a reconstituted completeness, and without subjecting them to constant authentication, they develop a long-lasting nature. Under this condition, on the one hand, memory without location affirms a perpetual and unchanging intellectual framework as a kind of 'deep convention'; on the other hand, memory without location constantly reconstitutes itself to accommodate new conditions in their attempt to reaffirm the deep convention. The measured acceptance of new astronomical knowledge brought to China by the Jesuits in the late Ming dynasty perhaps exemplifies this complex interdependence of stability and change. In the 1630s, Xu Guanqi's major astronomical reform involved a reassessment of Chinese knowledge in astronomy, cosmological theory, instrumentation, and calendric calculations, with the observation of stars being at the centre of this reform. Xu Guangqi's tables and maps of fixed stars with the Western coordinate system of longitude and latitude, as well as additional stars observed in the West, did nothing to change the traditional naming of the constellations, which was heavily imbued with political and dynastic meanings. The Western images and constellations, originally contained in a volume entitled *Visual Figures of Fixed Stars* (*Hengxing tuxiang*), were excluded in the comprehensive record of this borrowing of Western astronomy, *Astronomical Treatises of the Chongzhen Reign* (*Chongzhen lishu*, 1629–34). Twenty-three new constellations from the southern sky invisible in China, but observed as a result of Western navigation, were acceptable by the imperial court only in the name of the completeness of a unified heaven.[24] As Max Weber and Karl Jasper contemplated and formulated the idea of defining characteristics of intellectual traditions already set in place by 200 CE (the Axial Age), they observed that the Confucian civilization was unique in sustaining an order of the past; all other independently developed civilizations – Greek, Zoroastrian, Buddhist, Hindu, Judaic – began with a deity or an impersonal principle, therefore allowing the possibility of breaking from the past. The durability of this unbroken Confucian order must be understood to be inextricably linked to memory without location.

Memory without location has enabled the extraordinary speed of change in the Chinese city in the past three decades. If a city is imagined primarily as an archaeological site, alterations to that site would require extraordinary patience and caution; this is certainly a strong feature in the works of well-respected architects such as Carlo Scarpa and Raphael Moneo. Here, new interventions are carefully distinguished from old artefacts to highlight the authenticity of the ruin. If a city is imagined primarily as a text, the cultural heritage of the city resides in the reading of the city that can indeed be replaced by newer editions without disorientation. Here, new interventions often would formally and narratively hybridize themselves with the old. With cities being at the centre of global financial speculation and capital accumulation, these two very different imaginations of the city – as an archaeological site and as a text – result in dramatically different speed of development. Money's interest is endless and demands the highest possible speed of circulation and accumulation; in this sense, there is an extraordinary alliance between the capital and memory without location, in China, to produce perhaps the fastest speed of urban expansion and renewal in the history of human settlement. Both the 1985 Yellow Crane Tower in Wuhan and the 2006 Central Pier in Hong Kong were constructed because their original sites were required for new developments, the former being the development of an enormous bridge crossing the Yangtze River, the latter being the development of a by-pass that is anticipated to increase the speed of travel along the harbour front of Hong Kong Island. Architecture as real estate is perhaps dramatically materialized in Hong Kong – the city of maximum quantities as we described in Chapter 2 – where its exceptional vibrancy is only possible through incessant rebuilding. (Hong Kong is a place where banks loan half of their capital to local property developments, and the property sector comprises about a quarter of the total Gross Domestic Product, extraordinarily high compared with other cities.) Memory without location, it may be argued, crucially enabled Hong Kong's incessant rebuilding without the inconvenience of conservation, and without the psychological disorientation of the loss of memory. The alliance between capital and memory without location must be seen to be one of the key productive forces in Chinese cities.

Memory without location is memory with mobility; this mobility of memory is fundamentally important with regard to the viability of new city developments. In the archive city analogous to an archaeological site, the centres of power – Athens and Rome – had been seen as original cities in relation to their derivative colonies. This way of conceiving the colonial city cast a long shadow in the history of cities, in which 'colonial cities' far outnumber 'original' cities. The worldwide colonial cities of successive European trading empires – Portuguese, Spanish, Dutch, French, and British – seem to have created extensive intellectual reflections on the fundamental framing of places in terms of centres and peripheries and their social, political, and aesthetic implications. On the other hand, cities imagined as a fresh start – such as Thomas More's 'no-place' (*utopia*) – seem to be critically undermined by their disconnection with location-based memory. Palmanova, Chandigarh, Brasilia, and Milton Keynes, as new cities, are all caught up in this difficult endeavour to establish a place with meanings rooted in memory. The city of Shenzhen, established in the 1980s from a population of a few thousand to 12 million today, does not seem to have experienced any forms of originality anxiety. As a city, Shenzhen played an essential economic role in China's development in the past three decades; today, it is a metropolis in every sense of the term. Beyond its obvious economic function, Shenzhen was named by UNESCO as a 'city of design', a 'culture-based city' in 2009. What can culture become in thirty years and where did it come from? There is no sense that Shenzhen is derivative, peripheral, and less desirable as a place; in fact, cities with hundreds of years of age in China emulated, at least momentarily, what Shenzhen has achieved within a relatively short period of time. It is perhaps possible to argue that memory with mobility played a crucial role in connecting a new Chinese city with centuries of tradition in China; Shenzhen, instead of being a derivative city with no authenticity or a no-place without culture, is readily considered as a new edition of the Chinese urban text, an improvement of Chinese urban imaginations, a latest 'good copy' of the Chinese city. Like the Yellow Crane Tower in Wuhan and the Central Pier in Hong Kong, Shenzhen is both a new city and a city that already embodies memories with mobility. Shenzhen's spatial and temporal frameworks are not found in ruins and archives, but in memory without location, whose popular forms may be seen in the theme parks of Splendid China, Folk Culture Village, and Window of the World as their own spatial and temporal orientations of China and the world. The mobility inherent in the memory without location transforms

Shenzhen from a *tabula rasa* to a genuinely desirable place to live for the Chinese population.

Memory without location works in the interest of the empire of figures to produce 'urban texts' in Chinese cities. The empire of figures, through its primary surrogate in the Chinese writing system, cultivates an intellectual tradition that influences all aspects of design. The sum total of this force in the production of the built environment is a complex amalgamation of figure-based linguistic strategy, a form-based classification system, a home-like psychic condition, and a text-like aesthetic quality. In the Chinese city, the newly founded institutions of the archive (museums of history, public libraries, and public record offices) serve the purpose of the figure in over-compensated forms; underneath the over-compensated forms, there seems to be a lack of care in the gathering and categorizing of authentic fragments. The Chinese city may be influenced by the archive city, but it is not an archive city; it is made of colonies of the text, of the empire of figures. Memory without location supplies an essential component that enables the empire of figures to critically shape its territories. Through objects of value, semantic distribution, and state function of architecture, these colonies make and remake their own spatial and physical realms, and harbour their own indigenous forms of creativity and criticality.

Notes

1 Liang Qichao, 'Xinshixue' (New historiography), in *Liang Qichao guanji* (The Complete Works of Liang Qichao), in 10 volumes (Beijing: Beijing chubanshe, 1999), Vol. 2, p.373.
2 Liang Qichao, 'Zhongguo wenhua shi' (History of Chinese culture), in *Liang Qichao guanji*, Vol. 9, chapter on history of Chinese cities, p.5109.
3 Liang Qichao, 'Zhongguo lishi yanjiufa' (The research method for Chinese history), in *Liang Qichao guanji*, Vol. 7, p.4108, first appeared in 1922.
4 Matteo Ricci, *Xiguo jifa* (Memory Methods of Western Countries), ed. Wu Xiangxiang (Taibei: Taiwan xuesheng shuju, 1965), pp.1–61.
5 Jonathan Spence, *The Memory Palace of Matteo Ricci* (London and Boston: Faber and Faber, 1984), p.4.
6 Ricci, *Xiguo jifa* (Memory methods), pp.20–21.
7 Frances Yates, *The Art of Memory* (London: Routledge and Kegan Paul, 1966), p.2.
8 Ibid., p.135.
9 Spence, *The Memory Palace of Matteo Ricci*, p.149. A 1603 map of eight panels of 55 cm by 200 cm is kept by Liaoning Provincial Museum.

10 Li Shiqiao, 'Writing a Modern Chinese Architectural History: Liang Sicheng and Liang Qichao', *Journal of Architectural Education* 56 (2002), pp.35–45.
11 Mike Featherstone, 'Archive', *Theory Culture & Society* 23, Problematizing Global Knowledge (2006), pp.591–96; John Phillips, 'Urban New Archiving', in Ryan Bishop, John Phillips and Wei-Wei Yeo, eds, *Beyond Description: Singapore Space Historicity* (London: Routledge, 2004).
12 Sigmund Freud, *Civilization and Its Discontents* (1930), quoted in Andrew Ballantyne, ed., *Architecture Theory: A Reader in Philosophy and Culture* (London and New York: Continuum, 2005), p.119.
13 Jacques Derrida, *Archive Fever: A Freudian Impression* (Chicago and London: University of Chicago Press, 1996), p.34.
14 Spence, *The Memory Palace of Matteo Ricci*, p.4.
15 Li Xiting, ed., *Huanghe Lou xiaozhi* (A Short History of Yellow Crane Tower) (Hong Kong: Tianma tushu, 2004), p.2.
16 Lin Zhu, *Jianzhushi Liang Sicheng* (Architect Liang Sicheng) (Tianjin: Tianjin kexue jishu chubanshe, 1997), p.64.
17 See the critique of stone rubbings by Robert E. Harrist, Jr., *The Landscape of Words: Stone Inscriptions from Early and Medieval China* (Seattle and London: University of Washington Press, 2008), pp.20–23.
18 Li Shiqiao, 'Reconstituting Chinese Building Tradition: The *Yingzao fashi* in the Early Twentieth Century', *Journal of the Society of Architectural Historians* 62:4 (2003), pp.470–89.
19 Benjamin Elman, *From Philosophy to Philology: Intellectual and Social Aspects of Change in Late Imperial China* (Los Angeles: UCLA Asian Pacific Monograph Series, 2001).
20 Liang Qichao, *Qindai xueshu gailun* (Outline of Qing Scholarship) (Beijing, 1920).
21 Wen-hsin Yeh, *The Alienated Academy: Culture and Politics in Republican China, 1919–1937* (Cambridge MA: Harvard University Press, 1990), Chapter 1, Language and Learning.
22 William Hannas, *Asia's Orthographic Dilemma* (Honolulu: University of Hawai'i Press, 1997), pp.128–29.
23 Wu Hung, *Transience: Chinese Experimental Art at the End of the Twentieth Century* (Chicago: University of Chicago Press, 2005).
24 Benjamin Elman, *On Their Own Terms: Science in China, 1550–1900* (Cambridge MA and London: Harvard University Press, 2005), Part II, Natural Studies and the Jesuits; Sun Xiaochun, 'On the Star Catalogue and Atlas of *Chongzhen Lishu*', in Catherine Jami, Peter Engelfriet and Gregory Blue, eds, *Statecraft and Intellectual Renewal in Late Ming China: The Cross-cultural Synthesis of Xu Guangqi (1562–1633)* (Leiden, Boston and Cologne: Brill, 2001), pp.311–20.

9
Colonies of Beauty and Violence

The empire of figures unleashes its plastic force – its colonization – perhaps in two stages. The first stage unfolds in the body. The body in safety in the Chinese cultural context is at the same time the body of the Chinese writing system. Memorizing thousands of square words unconnected to their phonetic properties is immensely more difficult than memorizing a few dozen alphabetic letters; the labour that is required to overcome this difficulty creates a deep emotional bond between the writing system and those who have learned to use it. More important than use, the body is also required to learn to reproduce the aesthetic dimension of the writing system: calligraphy. The purpose of calligraphy is about establishing and sustaining the crucial link between the figure and meaning, between form and content. Over centuries of its uninterrupted practice, calligraphy acquired a set of established styles – the antique *zhuanshu* style, the normative *kaishu* style, and the cursive *xingshu* and *caoshu* styles – as exemplified by past masters of calligraphy. Calligraphy is the highest form of art in the Chinese cultural context. This is figuration at its most vigorous and influential form. The combined force of memory and aesthetics is so strong that the Chinese artist Qiu Zhijie brought this emotional bond to a delightful display in his performance piece *A One-thousand-time Copy of Lantingxu*. Between 1990 and 1997, Qiu filmed himself copying perhaps the best-known and most-copied example of calligraphy, Wang Xizhi's *Lantingxu* (353 CE), one thousand times on the same piece of paper. Each copy was slightly off-set from the previous one, so that the copies looked slightly abstract after a few times; after fifty times, the entire sheet of paper became black and further copies were completed over a piece of black paper (Figure 9.1). The act of an extraordinary devotion to Wang Xizhi's calligraphic example and the strenuous labour in the execution, with a provocative sense of irony in the illegibility of the blackness, highlighted dramatically the powerful hold of the language on the intellect.

Figure 9.1 Qiu Zhijie, *A One-thousand-time Copy of Lantingxu*, 1990–1997 (courtesy of the artist)

Both Xu Bing's *Book from the Sky* (1987–91) and Qiu Zhijie's *A One-thousand-time Copy of Lantingxu* vividly demonstrate what can be described as forces of exquisite beauty and as roots of slow violence. Their stunning works, through their gratuitous labour as performances ('I very seriously labored for years on something that says nothing'[1]), speak of the fact that the primary site of these forces is the body and mind combination in the Chinese way of education; after all, one of the most important learning methods in the traditional context is 'copying books' (*chaoshu*). Memory and aesthetic sensibility are forged together through long and patient drill from a very young age. William Hannas argues that the Chinese writing system defined critically the form of education that stifles creativity in East Asian cultures – Chinese, Japanese, Korean, Vietnamese – that are influenced by the Chinese writing system. The political and social forms in these societies can be understood as resulting from the demanding task of maintaining the writing system, which incurs an unacceptable cost.[2] While it is clear, as Xu Bing and Qiu Zhijie demonstrate, that the writing system is demanding, their ingenuity and artistry also suggest that creativity takes place in unfamiliar forms in the Chinese cultural context.

The body of the Chinese writing system can perhaps be seen as the body having undergone modifications; in this sense, perhaps the most dramatic body modification in the Chinese cultural context is the binding of the foot of the female body. Body modification is common in all cultures, but several distinct features in the Chinese cultural context seem to speak of the force of figuration. In the Chinese city, body modifications tend to accentuate the differences of age rather than those of sexual characteristics. While the Victorian practice of constricting the waist highlighted the physical character of the youthful female body as the unpregnant state, the binding of the foot seems to be unconnected with features of female fertility. The deprivation of mobility of the female body probably mimicked the beginning of childhood, and subjugated the female body, like that of the child, to aesthetic manipulations. The process of modifying feet started with childhood; it prevented, slowly and violently, normal growth, and it enabled what was considered to be an exquisitely cultivated femininity by preserving a key feature of the child in its tottering movements. With the abolition of the practice of foot binding at the start of the twentieth century, the tottering movement of the child has been replaced by other child-like features in the female body in contemporary Chinese cities: the contrived small steps, the deliberate high-pitched voice, the feigned shyness, the incessant giggle, and the supposedly under-developed intelligence; these features also moved away from the accentuation of reproductive biological characteristics highly valued in many other cultural contexts. The male authoritative body, in the meantime, migrated towards the characteristics of the body in old age; the slow and deliberate deportation and speech on important occasions, the display of prudence in thoughts and actions, taps in the figure of the wisdom of old age. Through the figure of age and through the Chinese writing system, this first stage of the plastic power of the empire of figures establishes some of the most fundamental parameters of culture in Chinese cities.

The second stage of the plastic force of the empire of figures is manifested in objects of value, their semantic distributions, and the resultant state function of architecture that make up the material realm of the Chinese city. It is to these that we must now turn.

Objects of Value

Objects of value are not equal to objects of utilitarian or monetary value that we surround ourselves with today as commodities; they are valuated not by the market place, but by a cultural force. Objects of value in the Chinese city are perhaps best understood against the background of the 'priceless' things in the Western city: the relic as the object of historical value and curiosity as the object of epistemological value. The traditional cabinet of curiosities in the Western context captures this framework of evaluating things; it contains things that are neither useful nor saleable, and that possess potentials to anchor much larger systems of knowledge. Curiosities are valued by their degrees of potentiality; they possess the virtue of becoming knowledge both as substance and as systems of classification. In contrast to the cabinet of curiosities, the objects of value in the Chinese city possess the potentiality to function as figures.

We can perhaps begin our investigation with a set of objects of value in close proximity to the scene of writing, 'scenery in basin' (*penjing*), which are often placed on the study desk, or in the interior. This basin is usually made from various combinations of stones and plants; they are highly composed. Out of the elements that compose these miniature sceneries, the plants are particularly noteworthy as they are biological; they are often 'little big trees', capturing all the features of 'treeness' best exemplified in its old age – the expansiveness of the roots, the twisting of the branches, the balanced distribution of leaves – in a small form. These 'plants in basin' display clear signs of slow and forced cultivation; the miniature size is the result of restrictions over a long period of time (Figure 9.2). Different from the topiary in the French and Dutch gardens, which exhibit explicit and fast violence to achieve geometrical layouts and forms in the topiary, the restrictive forces that produce the plant in basin are internalized and subtle.

Moving beyond the study desk, another object of value is the heavily corroded limestone harvested at the bottom of Lake Taihu in Jiangsu Province (*taihu* stone) (Figure 9.3); it is highly valued for its figurative potential, seen as its capacity to present 'one thousand gestures and one hundred states' through its endless folds and numerous pores formed through millions of years of washing by waves. These folds and pores evoke associations with geographical features of land such as peaks, valleys and caves, hence the *taihu* limestones are called 'fake mountains' (*jiashan*). While visually complex in its capacity to evoke geographical characteristics of land, the *taihu* limestone contains a large amount of diverse details in a relatively small volume; it captures an epitome of 'mountainness', in miniature, in its sharpness of peaks and sheerness of cliffs. In this sense, the *taihu* stone is not a Platonic Form of mountain which would have demanded abstraction

Figure 9.2 The restricting metal wires on a *penzai* tree in Zhuozheng Yuan, Suzhou

Figure 9.3 Taihu stone in Wangshi Yuan, Suzhou

and simplification; nor is it a version of the Western grotto, which is conceived through human habitation and through becoming. The *taihu* stone is a great example of the potentiality of figure in things, an artificial construct of the mountain that surpasses, and often replaces, the original in its essential features. The *taihu* stone is one of countless kinds of stones that serve this highly popular role of figuration. The traditional Chinese literati gathered the ones that are more ambivalent for their higher potential, and the popular choices tend to be ones that resemble figures more explicitly. These plants and stones, in a garden, are placed around water and buildings to form some of the key elements in a Chinese garden.

Objects of value project their figure-based images onto the land; this is what is often experienced in geographical locations greatly appreciated in the Chinese cultural context, such as the Yellow Mountain. Located in Anhui province, this mountain range is not particularly high (around 1,800 metres in elevation) but is packed with extraordinary and unusual granite peaks, often shrouded in mist and clouds which remind one of similar features found in the *taihu* stone. Almost all 'scenic spots' are where a figure or a meaning can be identified and narrated: Buddha's hand, a rooster, an old monk, etc. A popular tour of the Yellow Mountain is almost exclusively conducted as a tour of these narrated scenic spots. This of course does not have to mean the absence of other readings of the mountain, but it does mean the primary importance of 'scenic narration', which features in almost all experiences of the Yellow Mountain. The extraordinary pine trees – stunted in growth by elevation and the lack of soil, and crooked through age – are greatly valued; some of them are named and very well known. The Pine of Welcoming Guests (*yingkesong*), an approximately 800-year-old pine tree that has a branch stretched out, is perhaps the most highly appreciated; it is narrated as a welcoming gesture. From hotel names to a painting gracing the Anhui Hall in the Great Hall of the People in Beijing, this pine tree gained extraordinary presence in twentieth-century Chinese culture. The high altitude pine trees in the Yellow Mountain are similar to the plant in basin, only here the forces of nature created their small and crooked forms. The Yellow Mountain stands at the apex of several mountain ranges in China – from the Nan Yue Mountains in the south to the Tai Shan Mountains in the north – which are also similarly filtered through this scenic narration. The scenic narration of figurative potential of land is a continuous practice that perpetuates the production of scenic spots in China; the recently developed scenic area of Zhangjiajie in Hunan Province – a place with deep valleys and sharp-rising rocks similar to those of the Yellow Mountain – is an example of the continuous cultural construction of landscape in China today. The objects of value and their projections onto the land form a web of valued landscape that functions as an essential reference of 'nature' in cultural productions in China.

One of the most persistent descriptions of places like the Yellow Mountain is 'sceneries like painting' (*fengjing ruhua*); 'like painting' is perhaps the best possible complement to, and the highest appreciation of, natural scenery. This is both an indication of nature as projections of objects of value, and the relative higher status of painting in relation to nature. The relationship never seems to be reversed. As we have discussed earlier, the training of a painter traditionally began with copying a manual of painting, rather than with painting from nature, to develop basic painting skills. The most well-known and widely used manual is called *Manual of the Mustard Seed Garden* (*Jieziyuan huazhuan*, 1679) (see p. 84), a step-by-step guide to brush stroke types and techniques highly popular since the late seventeenth century. For example, the method of painting stone is here broken down as having five steps: outline (*gou*), texture (*cun*), rub (*ca*), dot (*dian*), and render (*ran*). The methods of painting stone textures, *cunfa*, are based on brush stroke techniques analogically termed as lotus leaf *cunfa* or folded ribbon *cunfa*. Through a systematic demonstration of techniques of painting trees, stones, water, mountain, people, buildings, orchard, bamboo, plum, chrysanthemums, birds, insects as well as examples of successful techniques employed by well-known masters, the *Manual* reconstitutes all natural forms through brush strokes. The *Manual* teaches methods of framing space through three kinds of distances produced by brush strokes: the high distance (*gaoyuan*), the deep distance (*shenyuan*), and the horizontal distance (*pingyuan*). The influence of this book in Chinese painting is enormous; it is a book that summarized the past achievements and codified them into systematic rules. It projects a system of figures that approximate natural landscape through the inherent function of brush strokes, eventually replacing landscape as the primary source of nature. With this book, and many others similar to it, nature is no longer the origin of all painterly conceptions, but only a parallel system that is always already blended and reconstituted by the system of figures. If the calligraphy of *Lantingxu* is the epitome of the first order of figures in square words, the *Manual of the Mustard Seed Garden* is the leading example of the second order of figures in landscape.

It is from this set of highly cultivated objects of value that the Chinese literati garden emerged in the city, not – as one would expect in a garden of any sort – to bring nature closer to human habitation, but to lay out objects of value as projections onto nature. If the Western garden is dominated by the lawn and if 'the aesthetic purpose of the lawn is a cow pasture',[3] the aesthetic purpose of the Chinese garden is to be 'like painting' (*ruhua*), to imitate painting. Unlike those in the West, the Chinese gardens are relatively far removed from the economic function of land; the productive landscape in the Chinese tradition belongs not to gardens (*yuan*), but to fields (*tian*), while gardens and fields (*tianyuan*) indicate the totality of land under various degrees of care. The Chinese literati garden can be seen as a constructed parallel to the *Manual of the Mustard Seed Garden*. The *taihu* stones and the plants in basin serve as some of the basic elements in a Chinese garden in Suzhou, which are accompanied by a wide range of other elements such as water, light and shadows, and pavilions and corridors linking different parts of gardens. More than the Yellow Mountain, literati gardens are highly modifiable and can be made to be like paintings; the construction of Chinese literati gardens is due almost exclusively to the painterly imagination that is shown in traditional Chinese landscape paintings, a genre that dominated in the history of Chinese painting. The classical English gardens of Stowe and Stourhead in the early eighteenth century may have been modelled on late seventeenth-century landscape paintings of Claude and Poussin, but the intellectual preoccupations of the English gardens were quite the opposite from the Chinese gardens. The English gardens emulated 'nature' in the mimetic tradition against the geometrical patterns found in French and Dutch gardens, and promoted the notions of liberty and natural rights in the notions of 'natural beauty' and 'natural growth'. In the Chinese garden, the core pursuit is neither *mimesis* nor liberty, but 'mental state' (*yijing*), a poetic state of being infused with specific conditions of knowledge and emotion; it has little interest in the mimetic process. Mental state is literary in the Chinese cultural context; it is highly dependent on the reconstitution of nature through the construction of objects of value. Ultimately, mental state is rooted, via paintings, in narrations, texts, and the empire of figures.

This endeavour to make gardens like paintings not only elevated the status of painting manuals such as *Manual of the Mustard Seed Garden*, but also resulted in the curious fate of an amazing book on the craft of gardening, Ji Cheng's *The Craft of Gardens* (*Yuan ye*). Born in 1582, Ji Cheng started his literati life as an accomplished painter; as if to emphasize the painterly origins of the craft of gardening, Ji Cheng advised his readers to construct rocks by following the *cunfa* method in painting.[4] Published in 1634, *The Craft of Gardens* was largely neglected in China until the Japanese scholars discovered it in the early twentieth century as they sought canonical architectural texts in Asia comparable to those of Vitruvius, Alberti, and Palladio. The Society for Research in Chinese Architecture published a version of the text in 1933, and Tong Jun, Chen Zhi, and Chen Chongzhou, among many twentieth-century scholars in China, studied and annotated *The Craft of Gardens* with a similar urge to bring it to contemporary relevance. This twentieth-century enthusiasm about this book could not eclipse the fact that, despite its immense value, the influence of *The Craft of Gardens* on the actual development of the Chinese garden is limited, although the principles of gardening contained in *The Craft of Gardens* had been well practised for centuries. The two different fates of the two seventeenth-century publications on painting and garden – *Manual of the Mustard Seed Garden* and *The Craft of Gardens* – perhaps speak of the privilege of painting as a higher form of intellectual activity.

The systematic production of objects of value and their projection onto paintings, gardens, and the built environment, in combination, constitute what may be described as 'preferred nature' in the Chinese cultural context. This preferred nature is often mapped onto the spaces of various degrees of care; the constructed environment in China seems to be ordered through this notion of preferred nature.

Much of the scholarly attention on the traditional Chinese built environment focused on Chinese literati gardens; this is indeed a space of intensive care that resulted in tremendous cultural achievements. One must not forget the fact that the literati gardens, and their possible contemporary equivalents, make up a small part of the constructed environment in China. While objects of value, like texts, can be produced with sophistication and skill, they can also be constructed without them. Since the 1980s, there seems to be more 'illiterati gardens' than literati gardens in Chinese cities that shape land with great determination: they are monumental, expansive, influential, and in dire need of intellectual content. The rush to build development areas in Chinese cities – a trend that produced 38,600 square kilometres of 'development zones' in 2005, constituting one-and-a-half times the entire existing urban area of China[5] – tremendously accelerated the development of illiterati gardens in China. In many Chinese cities large stretches of land are altered almost to the complete destruction of existing architectural, urban, ecological, and geological conditions, in the interest of new constructions that reconstitute preferred nature. The preferred nature here is often made of undifferentiated collections of well-known literary references, mythical narratives of locations, and references of political significance. Ji Cheng's advice on the twin principles of gardening in the propensity

Figure 9.4 Tangerine Island, Changsha, Hunan Province

of the site (*shi*) and in the borrowing of the surrounding geographical features (*jie*) seem to have been largely lost here. The unruly offspring of the empire of figures is exemplified by the case of the 5-kilometre long, narrow Tangerine Island in the Xiang River in the central Chinese city of Changsha (Figure 9.4). Saturated with narratives based on ancient historical events, early twentieth-century villas of Chinese politicians and foreign traders, and the many visits of Mao Zedong since his youth, this long island has recently been totally re-landscaped to invent what should have been there: extensive plantation of tangerine trees which gave it its name, and a huge sculpture of the youthful Mao who gave it its fame. Sculpted in 2009 by a team of sculptors from Guangzhou Academy of Fine Arts, led by Li Ming, the 32-metre tall sculpture of the youthful Mao is pregnant with narratives, such as the number of measurements of the stones being the same as the numbers of Mao's birthday. The newly constructed Tangerine Island totally transformed the existing site beyond recognition; in the process, it reconstituted the central narratives of the island through a range of features that seem to have been demanded by a popular cultural memory shaped in the empire of figures.

Semantic Distributions

Syntactical orders – derived from the Platonic universal bond – seem to be a powerful imagination in the Western city; semantic distributions are fundamental as a major substance of any experience of a Chinese city. Semantic distributions of objects of value in Chinese cities populate the city with 'micro narratives'; this is achieved through placing texts in strategic positions in order to turn objects of value, finally, into texts. Perhaps the most direct form of this practice is inscription of texts onto the land form that closely resemble objects of value (Figure 9.5). The key text for Tangerine Island in Changsha is Mao's *Changsha*, written in 1932 following a Song-dynasty poetic template; the poem is carved on a piece of rock specially brought in as the poetic centrepiece of the entire island (Figure 9.6). Inscriptions in Greek and Roman cities tend to appear on buildings;[6] anything beyond buildings would have been seen to be 'graffiti'. In the Chinese context, inscribing and carving of text on land are not graffiti; they are essential assistance towards readings of land as text, which is at the heart of any experience of land.[7] Inscribing texts on natural sceneries parallels the practice of inscribing texts on landscape paintings; in both cases, landscape cannot be read fully without texts. In Wen Zhengming's (1531) depictions of the Humble Administrator's

Colonies of Beauty and Violence

Figure 9.5 Text carved on rocks, Fuzhou, Fujian Province

Figure 9.6 Mao's poem 'Changsha' carved on stone, Tangerine Island, Changsha, Hunan Province

Garden (Zhuozheng Yuan) in Suzhou, text and painting were paired, creating a format that has had a lasting influence. It is perhaps worth noting that Wen Zhengming is largely portrayed as a painter in

191

contemporary scholarship in English, while he was chiefly remembered as a writer and calligrapher in Ming dynasty Chinese writings; Wen's paintings are frequently illustrated, but his writings seem to be rarely shown in Western publications.[8] As if to emphasize the lasting importance of the parallel between writing and painting, Emperor Qianlong, in 1736, produced similar image/text pairs to depict forty scenes of the imperial pleasure garden Yuan Ming Yuan, painted by court artists.[9] Perhaps as a dramatic display of the occupation of paintings by text, the seals – stamps made of highly stylized text in red – are printed at prominent locations on painting scrolls at their 'beginnings' and 'ends', as if to introduce and conclude paintings as texts. The poems that occupy important locations on landscape paintings and in literati gardens, providing essential meanings to paintings and gardens, perhaps subtly but firmly legitimize the practice in China of reciting or composing poems at scenic spots. The fames of the Yellow Crane Tower in Wuhan and Tangerine Island in Changsha are deeply rooted in the well-known poems that are associated with these places. The invocation of texts while viewing the land – through carvings, poetic recitations, and compositions – transforms landscape into elements of semantic distributions. In all places of commonly acknowledged beauty, texts seem to have been permanently fused with the land and architecture to construct a blended meaning of the landscape and architecture. In the case of the Yellow Mountain this textual heritage is so extensive and deep-rooted that it is almost impossible to attain a fresh reading of the land form.

It is perhaps not a coincidence that the act of 'painting' is often described in Chinese as an act of writing (*xie*); painting the mental

Figure 9.7 Xu Bing, *Landscript*, 2004 (courtesy of Xu Bing Studio)

state (*yijing*) literally means 'writing the mental state' (*xieyi*). This is the state of things that Xu Bing attempted to illustrate in his *Landscript* series (from 1999, Figure 9.7), in which the brush strokes in the traditional Chinese landscape paintings do not paint the landscape but write it with square words; 'I learned that *cun fa* is a kind of writing'.[10] The Chinese landscape painting is a function of the brush, and the brush is the primary instrument in the materialization of the Chinese square words. If Monet's landscape dissolves objects into the indistinct continuum of light, Xu Bing's *Landscript* crystallizes them into the Chinese square words. Xu Bing materialized in this work what normally takes place in the mind as a fluid process of blending land and text in a search for narratives.

It is perhaps possible to argue that one of the most important ways to experience architecture in the Chinese city is to recognize their literary and poetic meanings as text. This is architecture as semantic distributions, enabled by texts. There is a textualization of architecture, just as there is a textualization of land. In the Western architectural tradition, textual inscriptions on buildings play a relatively minor role; they are often integrated into the building materially and remain highly abstracted as if they aspired to the status of the image. Reliefs and fresco paintings have self-assured presence with their dazzling display of techniques inherent to the art form; they often participate in

Figure 9.8   Entrance to Yuelu College, Changsha, Hunan Province

architecture and contribute to it through perspectival illusions. It is crucial to understand that text plays a different role in Chinese architecture, through a double process of conventionalization of buildings and intellectualization of texts. The main entrance is dominated by a set of texts: on top of the entrance a panel indicates the naming of the building, and often on the sides of the entrance scrolls present a poetic reading of the building. The entrance to one of the most venerable educational institutions in China, the Yuelu College in Changsha, established in 976, demonstrates the domination of text in architecture (Figure 9.8). While the top panel announces the name of the college, the couplets on the side speak, with cultivated literary elegance in its mixture of humour and entitlement, of its conceptual place in China as perhaps the most venerable educational institution (right scroll: 'only in Chu one finds talent'; left scroll: 'only in this place one finds the best'). Chu is the ancient name for the area of China that is now mostly occupied by Hunan Province, with Changsha as its provincial capital. Like in most traditional buildings, texts continue to appear layer by layer as one proceeds into the interior spaces. Text demands its own materiality and space, as separate panels that command the buildings and courtyards. While buildings are intellectually mute in their conventionality, texts are often semantically unique, vibrant, evocative, and innovative; they can be highly stimulating and inspiring, full of poetic content in great contrast with the rather repetitive architecture. This textual dimension of Chinese architecture, both as text panels and as a way to understand the Chinese built environment, perhaps suffers the most in the twentieth-century attempt to retrofit a Western framework of architecture onto the Chinese building tradition.

Semantic distributions are perhaps most clearly manifested in literati gardens; through these gardens we can perhaps gain insights into how, in more subtle and hybridized forms, they operate in contemporary Chinese cities. The Humble Administrator's Garden in Suzhou, despite the changes over many centuries, exemplifies semantic distributions through the integration of text and architecture. If a map of semantic distributions of the garden is drawn (Figure 9.9), the garden seems to acquire a very different dimension in its ability to enable experiences. Intertwined with the names of buildings are additional sets of textual inscriptions on scrolls and tablets which require separate documentations. The intellectual content brought in by texts is extraordinary; it cuts across all types of textual allusions to object, scenery, intangible reference, metaphor, emotion, indication, history, and literature; the spatial experience is inextricably linked with the intellectual content embedded in these texts. The semantic distributions here are not organized to produce a grand narrative – the garden is not an essay;

Colonies of Beauty and Violence

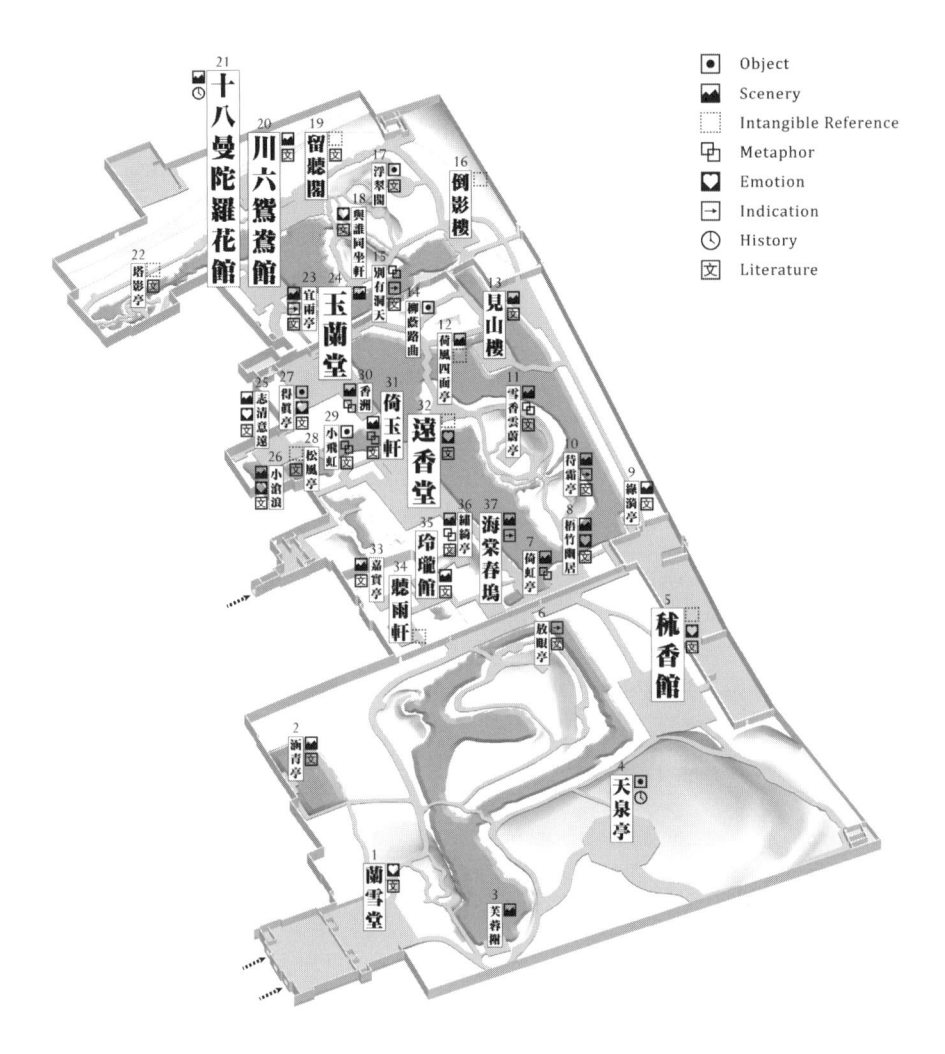

The Humble Administrator's Garden (Zhuozheng Yuan)

1. Orchid-Snow Hall
2. Green-Embracing Pavilion*
3. Lotus Waterside Pavilion
4. Heavenly-Springs Pavilion
5. Sorghum-Fragrance House
6. Looking-Far-Away Pavilion*
7. Leaning-on-the-Rainbow Pavilion
8. Pavilion amid-Secluded-Wutong-and-Bamboo
9. Green-Ripple Pavilion
10. Frost-Awaiting Pavilion*
11. Pavilion of Fragrant-Snow-and-Colorful-Clouds
12. Pavilion in Lotus Breezes*
13. Seeing-the-Hill Two-Storied Building
14. Winding-Path-under-Willow-Shade Corridor
15. Unique-Beauty Half-Pavilion
16. Inverted-Image Two-Storied Building
17. Floating-Jade Two-Storied Building
18. With-Whom-to-Sit Lounge
19. Lingering-to-Listen Pavilion
20. 36-Mandarin-Duck Hall
21. 18-Datura Hall
22. Pagoda-Shadow Pavilion
23. Two-View Pavilion*
24. Magnolia Hall
25. Pure-Will-and-Far-Reaching-Mind Study
26. Little-Surging-Wave Watercourt
27. Truth-Obtaining Pavilion*
28. Wind-from-the-Pine Pavilion
29. Little-Flying-Rainbow Corridor-Bridge
30. Fragrant-Isle Landboat
31. Leaning-on-Jade Hall
32. Distant-Fragrance Hall
33. Fine-Fruit Pavilion
34. Listening-to-the-Rain Hall
35. Exquisite House
36. Embroidered-Silk Pavilion
37. Spring-Begonia-Cove House

Figure 9.9 A textual representation of the Humble Administrator's Garden (Zhuozheng Yuan), Suzhou

195

they are strategically placed open references that engage with the mind. There is a placement strategy – a 'garden design method' – that takes advantage of literature-inspired qualities: the duration-based narrative quality found in the use of suspense, foreshadowing, and contrast of spaces as one moves meanderingly through the twists and turns of the garden path; the parallelism-based spatial and temporal juxtapositions in allusions, allegories, and flashbacks as one mines the knowledge of past literary achievements.[11] The ability to manipulate within this complex web of meanings seems to be endless, and endlessly pleasurable. The parallelism is particularly characteristic and effective through literary devices; the small fan-shaped pavilion in the western part of the Humble Administrator's Garden (number 18 in Figure 9.9), oddly named 'With Whom to Sit Pavilion', makes a reference to the self-mocking sociality in a poem by the eleventh-century poet Su Shi: 'With whom to sit? Bright moon, breezes, and myself.' This link to the past is made possible by the prominent display of the name of the pavilion, through the calligraphy of Yao Mengqi in the nineteenth century, reproduced on a wooden plate. The richness, innovation, cultivation, and the pleasure of space enabled by these texts alter the spatial experiences of the garden crucially. Semantic distributions play a primary role in the success and failure of literati gardens as spaces and

Figure 9.10 Entrance to Administrative Centre, Dongyang, Zhejiang Province

Figure 9.11 Nanmenkou shopping street, Changsha, Hunan Province

as intellectual pleasure grounds. Here, architecture without text is unimaginable; removing the text from architecture would have removed its intellectual content. In the world of semantic distributions, poetry reigns supreme in the empire of figures, forging its sensibilities in the productions of paintings, gardens, and reconstituted land.

Architecture as text has a bewildering range of forms in the contemporary Chinese city. The desire to frame all spatial thresholds with texts surfaces at the time of the Chinese New Year, when every family places red scrolls to mask their doorways. Text scrolls on government buildings certainly tap into the valence of this traditional architectural feature for status of authority (Figure 9.10). But the most exaggerated form of architecture as text occurs in the context of commercial buildings; here, the ancient sensibility to the beauty of texts is transformed into an outburst of undifferentiated abundance, as in the example of the main pedestrian shopping street in Changsha (Figure 9.11), forming a high contrast with those found in the Yuelu College in the same city. The Yuelu College and the pedestrian shopping street in Changsha are two ends of a spectrum of architecture as text. Their delicate and careless displays of elegant and functional texts, in crucial ways, define the Chinese city visually. They are physical manifestations of the primacy of text, its occupation of land and architecture; they turn land and architecture into colonies of its own visual and semantic distributions.

It is in this context that we examine contemporary discourses of architectural theory and practice in China that parallel those in the West. In the context of international exchange of architectural design services, the tendency of semantic distributions in the Chinese city is more subtle than their traditional form, but nevertheless unmistakable. The major buildings of the 2008 Beijing Olympics, as we have previously discussed, are highly influenced by figurative qualities as distinct and self-centred forms, paralleling the characteristics of objects of value discussed earlier in this chapter. The 'bird's nest' stadium and the 'water cube' swimming complex – in red and blue, perhaps invoking fire and water – work together with the Great Hall of the People, the Museum of Revolutionary History, the Monument of People's Heroes, and the Mausoleum of Chairman Mao in Tiananmen Square, as well as the imperial palaces and ritual grounds of the Ming and Qing dynasties. These reconstitutions of the centre of the city of Beijing make it one of the longest-lasting political capitals in the world, a present that is continuously constructed from an order of the past.[12] Behind the Beaux-Arts planning and architectural principles in these twentieth-century additions to Tiananmen Square, there is a much deeper text-based readability rooted in the Forbidden City. Semantic distributions, in this case political rather than poetic, maintain a firm presence.[13] It is perhaps possible and necessary to see almost all new and important architecture in Chinese cities in this light; semantic distributions in Chinese architecture determine the formal characters of Chinese cities; this is quite different from forces of function and typology.

Instead of forming a critical link in the chain of materiality of the empire of figures, semantic distributions in the Western city seem to have a dialectical relationship with syntactical orders, which continuously moderate the impact of semantic distributions on the city. If meanings are signified by, rather than inhered in, the production of architecture, semantic distributions through architecture in the Western architectural tradition tend to be short-lived; a recent attempt to see architecture as semantic distributions, in the works of Charles Moore, Charles Jencks, and Paolo Portoghesi in the 1980s, reflected its intellectual vulnerability in the Western architectural tradition. The third Earl of Shaftesbury used the notion of the emblematic 'second character' to describe the capacity of constructing meanings in graphic forms, but he made a clear distinction between the graphic and literary arts.[14] This second character is reframed by Erwin Panofsky as 'iconography' and 'iconology'.[15] The fact that this 'system of meaning' in Western arts has to be defended in these treatises is perhaps a reflection of its intellectual status; if

Shaftesbury and Panofsky were to formulate a defence of art in the Chinese writing system, they would probably have to defend 'visuography' and a 'visualogy' in Chinese art.[16] In making the visual art independent of language, the Western tradition reinforces the visual art with the notion of *techné*, a crucial knowledge outside semantic distributions that is most appropriate to specific art forms. Through *techné*, art stands in defiance of language. *Techné* both defines the art and grounds it in innovation. This is perhaps one of the most fascinating aspects of the visual arts in the Western tradition, its propensity to reinvent forms of art. In the West, architecture's most energetic engagement with language is not in semantics, but in syntax; productive architectural theories stemming from the studies of the rules of meaning, such as those of Bill Hillier, Christopher Alexander, George Steiner, and Peter Eisenman, situate architecture and the city in an engaging context. Texts, in this Western context, aspire to be architecture.[17] The Chinese semantic distributions do not appeal to syntax; art and architecture never leave systems of meaning, always already conceived as inherent components of these systems of meaning. Architecture and the city, here, aspire to be texts. In the Chinese city there is nothing outside semantics, just as there is nothing outside the empire of figures. The separation of literature from architecture, as the current model of architectural education in China, leaves the traditional forces of figuration often without sufficient guidance, running amok to produce travesties of design. Hypothetically, schools of architecture in China, if they were to aspire to some form of traditional excellence in the constructed environment, would have to be merged with departments of literature in contemporary academia.

The State Function of Architecture

One of the most important features of Chinese cities is that the production of architecture has always been imagined as a state function. The normative functions of the Chinese state throughout history have a very detailed materiality, as objects of value and semantic distribution. Compared with the Western traditions of architecture, this Chinese state function of architecture is clearly more determined and thorough; it is state determination rather than state regulation. State function is different from state use; when Wren stated that architecture has its political use, it is probably the latter that inspired and guided him. Perhaps this feature of the Chinese state function of architecture was a result of a different concept of property ownership; in the Western tradition, property ownership has been for a long time one of the most important foundations of society. The notion of the constitutional monarchy and the balance of power, as framed by John Locke, would hardly be possible without a cherished right to the ownership of property. This principle still stands firmly today as one of the most respected fundamental values in Western cities. In this context, landowners – from courtiers to capitalists – manifest their rights through architecture, defined in some ways as an anti-state act that kept the state use of architecture in check. In the Chinese tradition, however, ownership of land was never a distinct concept; imperial bestowment – in the form of the courtyards and gardens of princes and courtiers dotted around the best parts of imperial cities – carried in the traditional sense more legitimacy than any kind of property rights. The Western cities – from Washington to London – were a complete surprise to the Chinese as they first encountered them; the well-known early reformer Liang Qichao, when travelling in America and Europe in the early twentieth-century, was amazed by the obvious links between architecture and society; they seemed to be so differently constructed to reflect precisely the 'character of a nation', a feature that was obviously lacking in the grading systems of buildings in China.

State function, in contrast, works with the absence of large private landowners in imperial China. In this sense, despite their cultural prestige, literati gardens in China were relatively marginal in terms of space production; it was the imperial system of distribution of buildings that populated and regulated the Chinese city. In imperial China, the built environment belonged to a material order of things that was, in the most important cities, within the controls of the Ministry of Rites; construction manuals, in the Chinese classification of knowledge, fell under categories of political administration rather than that of history or literature. Architecture did not have its own discipline. As we have discussed in Chapter 1, a city like Beijing had been deeply influenced by a complex set of numerical schemes in its realization; it would be difficult to separate the design of the Forbidden City from this complex set of numerical dictations. Integrated into this complex set of numerical schemes are the strict orders of quantities that correspond to a social hierarchy as it may have been formulated by a specific dynasty; in the Tang dynasty (618–907) capital Chang'an, urban spaces were warded into units and imperial officials were divided into nine grades, leading to, when combined with sub-grading within the rank, thirty different grading categories. In the Qing dynasty (1644–1912), imperial officials were divided into two categories as either literary or military, each encompassing nine grades and nine sub-grades. Unlike the caste and aristocratic systems based on bloodline, grading had no particular restriction on social mobility; the civil examinations, together with recommendations, served as an important infrastructure to offer social mobility. Grading is different from the economically grounded social class; while class often produces common moral and aesthetic standards specifically associated with that class, grading is grounded in the idea of privilege. Developed from a universal need for bureaucracy, the Chinese organization of grades seems to be particularly material, strictly enforced, and long lasting; it is a system of people grading rather than job grading.[18] Within this personal privilege-based order of grades, buildings, together with many other artefacts such as dress and possessions, were strictly regulated to be a parallel material order. The Song-dynasty manual of construction *Yingzao fashi* (1103), while offering an extraordinary window to understand ancient timber constructions, documents this imperial practice of buildings as material grades. At the heart of the manual is the idea of eight grades of timber size called *cai*, measured by the section of the arm of the bracket set. Each size leads to corresponding changes in the sizes in all other building components in the building of the same grade; it also measures quantities of materials and labour.[19] The Qing dynasty construction manual, *Gongcheng zuofa zeli* (1734), adopted a system of eleven grades.[20] Liang Sicheng (1901–72) eagerly read *cai* as close to both the diameters of the Western classical orders which were used as the basic measuring unit for other parts of the orders and the modern modular system in Western architecture,[21] but this dislocated the meaning of *cai*. *Cai* is different from the module in the classical order and in the modern modular system; while the Western classical module indicates a different order that can be delicate in the Corinthian and strong in the Doric, *cai* is a measurement of size of an identical order. The eight grades of *cai* did not measure eight different kinds of buildings, but the same building in eight different sizes which corresponded to grades. Functioning in tandem with *cai*, the number of intercolumniations used for a building, *jian*, was also graded. In certain periods in history, commoners were allowed to have only three, while imperial buildings could be constructed with up to nine or eleven. The absence of typological and structural differentiations in traditional Chinese architecture is crucial to this size-based grading system; *cai* and *jian* became the core components in the building grading system. The *Yingzao fashi*, unlike Western architecture treatises, is a demonstration of the state occupation of architecture in imperial China. The official records in China were filled with descriptions of the graded distributions of buildings; very little attention was paid to the function and structure of these buildings.[22]

This ancient bureaucratic structure that occupied architecture has a range of important manifestations in contemporary Chinese cities, despite the fact that twentieth-century Chinese architecture had undergone tremendous transformations under the Western influence. Today, the state function of Chinese architecture is a complex system of status and privileges which is interwoven with the normative state functions from central to local. This is manifested, in one important way, through the institutions of architectural design as work units (*danwei*). As much as private sector functions are dressed up to appear as state functions, state functions have taken up some features of the private sector functions without losing its central characteristics. This contemporary hybrid – state function taking up some appearances of private corporations – is highly effective and influential as a model for Chinese architecture. Both as a *danwei* and as a production unit of architectural design, the state-owned Design Institute (*shejiyuan*) plays a uniquely important role in Chinese architecture. Established in the 1950s to take up the task of designing the reconstruction of China after decades of wars, these Design Institutes reinvented themselves to become some of the most productive and influential architectural design institutions in China. They combine state legitimacy with cost-effectiveness as well as professional and technical competence, becoming increasingly competitive in the context of international competitions. Among the design giants in today's China, Shanghai Xiandai Architectural Design (SXDA), China Architecture Design & Research Group (CAG), Beijing Institute of Architectural Design (BIAD), Shenzhen General Institute of Architectural Design and Research (SADI), Architectural Design and Research Institute of Tongji University (TJAD), all came from this background, and all are outstanding as effective design institutions; they overshadow private design firms. From Tiananmen Square (1950s) to the Olympic Games (2008) and Shanghai Expo (2010), these design institutes combined their state legitimacy with an ancient tradition and contemporary demand. The BIAD, for instance, employs about 1,500 professionals (as of 2009); it has twenty-nine 'ateliers', each led by a talented and recognized architect or engineer. From its establishment to today, BIAD has designed an astonishing 15 billion square metres of floor space all over China.

Architectural design firms and architects are graded in contemporary Chinese cities: grade one (*jiaji*), grade two (*yiji*), or grade three (*bingji*) for design firms, and class one (*yiji*) or class two (*erji*) for registered architects. These parallel the grading system of the vast array of bureaucratic positions standardized throughout China. Perhaps unique in the world, Chinese cities also have a strict system of grades, which is accompanied by distinct levels of resource distribution. In orders of importance, Chinese cities belong to one of five categories: capital, provincial capital, provincial city, prefecture city, and towns. In order of administrative differentiation, at the top of the ranking order of cities are Special Administrative Regions (Hong Kong, Macau), Special Economic Zones (Shenzhen, Zhuhai), followed by Direct Administrative Cities (Beijing, Tianjin, Shanghai, Chongqing), Provincial Capitals, Sub-Provincial Cities, Prefecture Cities, County Cities, and a bottom layer of a large number of towns.[23] None of these are typological differentiations; they are state functional categories. The state determination of the grades of cities in China has an immense impact on the ways in which these cities develop in the context of emulations and competition for prestige, status, and resources. This impact is particularly strong in the design of new administrative centres. In the late 1990s when the city of Shenzhen planned its new administrative centre, it followed Beijing's axial plan – a combined spatial arrangement of the Imperial Palace and Tiananmen Square – against the backdrop of a hill. Although it was designed by the New York-based architectural firm Lee/Timchula Architects, this new administrative centre revisits an ancient diagram of order in Beijing that had been reconstituted in the 1950s. The Shenzhen administrative centre is dominated by the roof the City

Figure 9.12 City centre of Dongyang, Zhejiang Province

Hall; its gigantic size and disconnection with the function of the roof highlight the nature of this roof as a figure, perhaps a contemporary reconstitution of the imperial rooflines of Beijing. Kisho Kurokawa's landscape master plan for the Shenzhen city centre in 1997 adds a layer of richly narrated artificial landscape called 'urban score'; certainly more literary than musical, the urban score invents semantic distributions that work together with the ordered administrative centre. Arata Isozaki's Cultural Centre – a concert hall and a library – stands as an object of value; while typologically different, the concert hall and the library have identical exterior forms, perhaps recalling the absence of typological differentiation in the Chinese architectural tradition.

Between Tiananmen Square and the new administrative centre of Shenzhen – two temporal and geographical ends of state occupation of architecture – there lies a vast landscape of similar-looking administrative centres in Chinese cities. In the complex rankings of cities, the city of Dongyang in Zhejiang Province is a lowly Prefecture City with a population of 820,000. Traditionally known for its woodcarving and talent (as seen in the number of successful candidates in the imperial examinations), today it is known for its production of modern building materials and its provision of filming sites (the film studio city of Hengdian falls within its administration). The new city centre is built across the Dongyang River from the traditional city centre, laid out as a grand diagram, dominated by the massive Administrative Centre (Figure 9.12) which is larger than those in many larger cities. Spread along a grid next to the main building are a series of buildings indicating other government functions, such as the procuratorate, the public security bureau, the trade and commerce building, and a court house. While the Administrative Centre is designed in a contemporary style, the Dongyang People's Court House and Administrative Building is modelled loosely on Western classical designs with Corinthian porticoes and a dome. Constructed by a local construction firm Guanghong Construction in 2004 and winning several provincial construction awards, the Administrative Centre and the People's Court House are rather generic in designs; they are certainly far removed from the high-profile public building projects in Beijing and Shenzhen. However, their unremarkable designs are more than compensated for by their bulk; the expansive square in front of the Administrative Centre shares the same diagrammatic quality as those of Beijing and Shenzhen, and the contrived Western classicism sits uncomfortably in the context of a traditional Zhejiang prefecture. The absurdly large, empty, and spatially daunting Administrative Centre of Dongyang gives us another side of state occupation of architecture that expresses a political aspiration grounded in its extraordinary economic success; here, architecture is used as a strategy for municipal advancement in the strict system of grading cities, constructing and distributing architecture as semantically distributed objects of value.

From the body to land, from gardens to cities, the plastic power of figuration produces an aesthetic and moral order in the form of an endless variety of colonies of beauty and violence, in the interest of the empire of figures. It grounds all cultural productions in the text as their archetype, blending form and meaning, demanding memorization and practice, distributing semantic contents, and enforcing material grades. Through its colonies, figuration gives a distinct formal character to the countless numerical schemes and the circles of spatial care that permeate in every Chinese city.

Notes

1 Xu Bing, 'An Artist's View', in Jerome Silbergeld and Dora C. Y. Ching, eds, *Persistence/Transformation* (Princeton: Princeton University Press, 2006), p.99.
2 William Hannas, *The Writing on the Wall: How Asian Orthography Curbs Creativity* (Philadelphia: University of Pennsylvania Press, 2003).
3 Thorstein Veblen, *The Theory of the Leisure Class*, ed. Martha Banta (Oxford: Oxford University Press, 2007; first published in 1899), p.90.
4 Zhang Jiaji, *Yuan Ye quanshi* (The Complete Annotation of Yuan Ye) (Taiyuan: Shanxi guji chubanshe, 1993), p.288, p.308.
5 Qiu Baoxing, *Duiying jiyu yu tiaozhan* (Response, Opportunity and Challenge) (Beijing: Zhongguo jiangong chubanshe, 2009), p.54.
6 Lawrence Keppie, *Understanding Roman Inscriptions* (Baltimore: Johns Hopkins University Press, 1991).
7 This practice is described in Robert E. Harrist, Jr., 'Reading Chinese Mountains: Landscape and Calligraphy in China', *Orientations* 31 (Hong Kong, December 2000), pp.64–69; *The Landscape of Words: Stone Inscriptions from Early and Medieval China* (Seattle and London: University of Washington Press, 2008). Craig Clunas, *Empire of Great Brightness: Visual and Material Cultures of Ming China, 1368–1644* (Honolulu: University of Hawai'i Press, 2007), p.109.
8 Craig Clunas, *Fruitful Sites: Garden Culture in Ming Dynasty China* (Durham: Duke University Press, 1996), p.105. In the same book, out of about ten paintings by Wen depicting the Zhuozheng Yuan, only one accompanying calligraphy was reproduced and discussed as 'research data'. See ibid., pp.25–37.
9 Shen Yuan and Tang Dai, *Yuanmingyuan sishijing tuyong* (Paintings and Poems of Forty Scenes of Yuan Ming Yuan), ed. Jiyi (Beijing: Shijie tushu chubanshe, 2005).

10 Xu Bing, 'An Artist's View', p.109.
11 Fung describes this feature as 'remembered text' and 'immediate scene', in Stanislaus Fung, 'The Language of Cultural Memory in Chinese Gardens', in Tony Atkins and Joseph Rykwert, eds, *Structure and Meaning in Human Settlements* (Philadelphia: University of Pennsylvania Museum of Archaeology and Anthropology, 2005), pp.123–34. Contemporary textbooks on gardens history, such as Zhou Weiquan, *Zhongguo gudian yuanlin shi* (History of Classical Chinese Gardens) (Beijing: Qinghua daxue chubanshe, 1990), pp.14–15, routinely liken gardens to texts and paintings.
12 Beijing's history 'is difficult to separate from that of the empire or nation', Lillian M. Li, Alison Dray-Novey and Haili Kong, *Beijing: From Imperial Capital to Olympic City* (New York: Palgrave Macmillan, 2008), p.3.
13 For readings of Beijing as a political space, see Zhu Jianfei, *Chinese Spatial Strategies: Imperial Beijing, 1420–1911* (London and New York: Routledge, 2003); Wu Hung, *Remaking Beijing: Tiananmen Square and the Creation of a Political Space* (Chicago: University of Chicago Press, 2005).
14 Shaftesbury, *Second Characters, or the Language of Forms*, ed. Benjamin Rand (Cambridge: Cambridge University Press, 1914).
15 Erwin Panofsky, *Meaning in the Visual Arts* (London: Peregrine Books, 1970).
16 My reading of the argument for a 'visual culture' in the Ming dynasty – an unviable enterprise at first glance – in Clunas, *Empire of Great Brightness*, would be precisely this defence: rescuing Chinese art from its literary dependency.
17 Jane Rendall, *Site-Writing: The Architecture of Art Criticism* (London, I. B. Tauris, 2010), can be seen to be an example of 'text aspiring to architecture', in contrast with 'architecture aspiring to text'.
18 Yan Buke, *Pinwei yu zhwei, Qin Han Wei Jin Nanbeichao guanjie zhidu yanjiu* (Grades and Positions: A Study of the Bureaucratic Systems from Qin to North and South Dynasties) (Beijing: Zhonghua shuju, 2002).
19 Li Shiqiao, 'Reconstituting Chinese Building Tradition: The *Yingzao fashi* in the Early Twentieth Century', *Journal of the Society of Architectural Historians* 62:4 (2003), pp.470–89.
20 Liang Sicheng, *Qingshi yingzao zeli* (Construction Methods of Qing Dynasty) (Beijing: Society for Research in Chinese Architecture, 1934).
21 Liang Sicheng, *Zhongguo jianzhushi* (History of Chinese Architecture) (Hong Kong: Joint Publishing, 2000; first published 1943), p.5.
22 Liang Sicheng, *Zhongguo jianzhushi*, p.10.
23 Gu Chaolin, *Zhongguo chengshi tixi, lishi, xianzhuang, zhanwang* (The System of Chinese Cities and Towns, History, Current Conditions and Prospects) (Beijing: Shangwu yinshuguan, 1992).

Conclusion

Trade overlays a surface of common urban practices and spaces on all cities; exchange requires standardization of labour, value, currency, measurements, time, and this has always been a feature of cities since the long and complex history of cultural exchanges along the Silk Road. This common layer of urban practices and spaces has had an amazing impact on cities since the late twentieth century. The combined influences of the collapse of the Soviet bloc, neoliberalism, and digitally enabled international finance since the late twentieth century amplified this surface of common urban practices and spaces, and distracted efforts to describe cities of different kinds. We seem to live in a world of similar transportation systems, media exposure, talk and talent shows, branded goods and services, culture and fashion trends, digital platforms, and holiday experiences; on this basis, we seem to construct similar conceptions of worth, love, value in relation to life. There is a world of contemporary architecture that parallels various other financially driven 'world developments' through standardization (normative designs) and market visibility (iconic designs). All these constitute a form of 'geoculture' that primes human activities to serve large and speedy financial operations.[1] This contemporary condition certainly places the very discipline of architecture under enormous stress, as architecture today often plays a role in international finance that is far removed from those of traditional concerns for structure, function, tectonics, and intellectualization. However, beneath this common surface – the seemingly 'One World, One Dream' condition – there lie radically different ideals for the city. These ideals are both ancient and contemporary; 'the Chinese city, despite all analogies differed decisively from that of the Occident', Max Weber states without ambiguity in *The Religion of China* in which the Chinese city features prominently in his attempt to explain the absence of capitalism in China;[2] the Chinese city, Weber concluded, lacked the oath-bound political associations, armed citizenry, craft and merchant guilds, city leagues, and above all, political autonomy to be capitalist.[3] In China, the city seems to have fewer freedoms than the village and the county, and this is certainly a consequence of the strict grading systems of the state that imposed severe limits on the freedom of cities. In the tradition of the state function of architecture, the Chinese city never seems to have declared its freedom from slavery and from kingship; the Chinese city internalized labour and hierarchy, and integrated itself into the material mechanisms of the state.

Perhaps China had always had access to a different economic life that is not capitalist and that is now constructing capitalism in a new way;[4] this book attempts to put substance to this claim. Chinese cities in the Song dynasty and late Ming dynasty participated actively in creating and sustaining economies that were the largest in the world. This extraordinary history of Chinese economic life supplies a useful context for the urban realities in China today. By the end of the first decade in the twenty-first century, Chinese cities take the form of about 655 concentrated areas of buildings and people, covering about 24,000 square kilometres of urban area with an addition of 38,600 square kilometres of 'development zones', accommodating about 600 million people. Each year, about 15 million people move to cities in China, resulting in about 2 billion square metres of floor area to be constructed and perhaps an unquantifiable amount of land and space altered. About 57 per cent of the economic production takes place on the east coast, where about 10 per cent of the people gather around three large areas: the Beijing–Tianjin–Tangshan axis, the Yangtze River Delta, and the Pearl River Delta.[5] All of these, both achievements and problems, are far from incidental or practical consequences; throughout a continuous cultural development for over two millennia, the Chinese city had both adhered to an ancient idea of the city encapsulated by the Zhou diagram of a walled compound with three gates on each side, and transformed to respond to a viable economic life exemplified by Song dynasty and late Ming dynasty cities. The formulation of Chinese cities has been grounded in a civilization that, in Granet's words, 'recorded a large proportion of the sum of human experience. No other has, for so many years, served as a bond between so many of the human race.'[6] The 300 million or so people who are projected to move to cities in the next decades would probably not reverse this powerful and long-lasting cultural force, although they may challenge it to formulate new strategies. The rise of the Chinese city in the past three decades is not a story about China alone, but one about the current world system of finance, labour, and consumption; the growing prominence of Chinese cities in the world system forces us to consider them in the intellectual context of urban/rural ideals that have resulted in both unimaginable gains and unfathomable environmental problems today.

The discourse of the Western city – its public spaces and architecture – has been rooted in the cultural traditions of the West; this has been a foundational assumption in urban theory. This cultural assumption of the city often results in misconceived frameworks for studies on the Chinese city and in misguided reports of empirical data from China. This Western 'city of civic virtue', with all its concerns with the cultivation of the combatant body, divisions of labour, differentiations of class, and establishment of manners and tastes, elevates the status of the community outside the family. It creates a psychic disturbance towards homeliness, and sustains a scientific distrust of figurative thoughts. It is, in this sense, both a cause and an effect of the abstract alphabetic languages that position speech before writing, meaning before image; the Western intellectual enterprise of structuralism is simultaneously concerned with structures of language, intellect, society, and architecture. In China, we encounter the 'city of corporeal defence', where endless reproductions of physical and intellectual protection against all possible real and imagined dangers flourish. It is a social and spatial form that is grounded in personalized connections (*guanxi*) – derivatives of the family archetype – that create networks of safety both in space and in business opportunities. The Chinese writing system imposes a perpetual homelike condition onto the intellect, reconstituting a complete realm of moral values of differentiated care, and an aesthetic pleasure in figuration. For more than a century, Chinese intellectuals considered these features as having been the obstacles of change, which was urgently needed at the end of the nineteenth century as China struggled against Western powers on the geopolitical stage at the time. However, the aspirations of China's new century as imagined by the renowned reformer Liang Qichao at the start of the twentieth century – a new constitution, legal system, knowledge structure, historical framework, and city – did not constitute a break with the past; he upheld Confucianism as the central tenet of Chinese culture, very unlike radical revolutionaries in China who wished for nothing short of an eradication of tradition. In this sense, Liang Qichao maintained the ancient preference for Confucianism over legalism, except in his case, he worked towards a new balance of the two, with late nineteenth-century Western constitutional frameworks replacing indigenous Chinese thoughts in legalism. At the same time, the Chinese revolutionaries did not manage to turn the Chinese city into the Western city; nationalist reconstruction of the 'indigenous Chinese culture', Mao's distrust of the city and remake of it in the image of the productive village, and Deng's harvest of the productive potentials of the family all seem to have reformulated the Chinese city in line with some aspects of its most ancient archetype. Throughout this book, we have seen this ancient archetype of the Chinese city in several guises: in its hoarding function as the city of numerical schemes, maximum quantities, and their associated conditions of labour; in its protective function as the city of safety, degrees of care, and antiseptic barriers; in its aesthetic function as empire of figures, figurative memories without location, and colonies of figurative beauty and violence. After 100 years of ceaseless reforms, it appears that it is not the features of the traditional Chinese city that were the obstacles of change; it takes time for them to reformulate themselves into effective strategies under radically different geopolitical conditions.

The Chinese city, in its insistence on its intellectual conceptions despite dramatic changes, offers not an alternative future, but a thinking space for new strategies of urban renovation. The city of civic virtue, the city of corporeal defence, and their distinct ways of engaging with finance, make available a triangulated area where future cities can perhaps be reformulated. As the greatest artefacts constructed in the interest of human life, cities also harbour neurotic and destructive behaviours; it is as if all the little rational and smart decisions made in daily life and in political strategizing come together to form giant amalgamations of irrationality. The Western city turns the peasant world upside down and cultivates a denigration of labour; it creates 'quarantines of life and matter'[7] of the human and the nonhuman and transforms every desire for humans to a desire for things. The Chinese city maintains a closer intellectual link with labour and things, but does not legislate numerical limits, and creates a world of *jianghu* instead of public space through spatial degrees of care that can be, and often has been, highly destructive to the environment. These would not have really mattered had it not been for our increasing capacity to pursue 'good life' – made up almost entirely of components of a system of objects whose production and consumption exhaust resources and pollute the environment beyond repair – and our determination to expand and perpetuate this way of life, often described as a 'dream' as if to highlight its enormous distance from fundamental biological and intellectual needs. The city has been at the centre of both the cultivation of desire and the consumption of goods, as Max Weber and Fernand Braudel detailed in their analyses of the relationship between the rise of the city and capitalism in the West.[8] The city has perverted the goodness of 'natural forms of life' to produce endless delights in 'unnatural pleasures', as Adam Smith and Lewis

Mumford observed critically.[9] At the end of the fourteenth century, Florence represented the start of an urban age for Europe when the European Renaissance began to take its first steps; it was the city and its financial innovations that promoted the rise of Renaissance culture. At the same time, the Hongwu Emperor in China imposed a strict regime of control to guarantee an empire of contented peasant families who were all to be ideally self-sufficient; Hongwu's China turned its back on the city and forcefully pursued a form of life much closer to its biological rhythm. These are perhaps two iconic moments in history; two dramatically different ideals of life that influenced almost all subsequent developments of human settlements as trade between Europe and China flourished in the era of navigation and colonization. These are also two useful polarities of thought which contribute towards a renovation of much larger conceptions of the city; in an age of climate change and permanent environmental modification, a deep and far-reaching renovation of the city is crucial. The combined forces of our cities – in concocting absurd dreams of good life and in fulfilling them – are enormous, and enormously destructive if they remain anthropocentric; in Chinese cities, the dream of good life has often been undermined by dirty streets, polluted air and water, never-ending traffic jams, poisonous food, endless greed, and indifference to the environment. In the world system of international finance and the single world division of labour, any notion of good life is intertwined with those in the Chinese city. It is unfortunate that such powerful forces accumulate with great effectiveness at the moment when we know the least what to do with them: we have lost our fear of the supernatural, gained confidence in science and technology, and seen our endeavour to moderate the power of capital fail. Between the city of civic virtue, the city of corporeal defence, and international finance, there is a thinking space for cities to legislate beyond the protection of interests of nations and rights of humans; all cities must legislate not only with all other cities, but with all things. It will not only be transnational oil pipelines, global shipping lanes and airspaces, and the polar icecaps that make up the materiality of world politics; it will also be the knowledge of the city – with its amalgamations of quantities, defences of territories, and schemes of beauty – that supplies the materiality of world politics. The intellectual foundations of the Chinese city will have an important role to play in the reformulation of the conception of good life in the context of a renewed understanding of the freedoms and the rights of humans and things.

Notes

1. Immanuel Wallerstein, *The Modern World-system I: Capitalist Agriculture and the Origins of the European World-economy in the Sixteenth Century* (Los Angeles: University of California Press, 2011).
2. Max Weber, *The Religion of China: Confucianism and Taoism* (New York: The Free Press, 1951), p.13.
3. Ibid., pp.14–15.
4. Giovanni Arrighi, *Adam Smith in Beijing: Lineages of the Twenty-first Century* (London and New York: Verso, 2007); Michael Keith, Scott Lash, Jakob Arnoldi and Tyler Rooker, *China Constructing Capitalism: Economic Life and Urban Change* (London and New York: Routledge, 2013).
5. Niu Wenyuan, ed., *China's New Urbanization Report 2009, 2010, 2011* (Beijing: Science Press), pp.6–7; Qiu Baoxing, *Duiying jiyu yu tiaozhan* (Response, Opportunity and Challenge) (Beijing: Zhongguo jiangong chubanshe, 2009); Gu Chaolin, *Zhongguo chengshi tixi, lishi, xianzhuang, zhanwang* (The System of Chinese Cities and Towns, History, Current Conditions and Prospects) (Beijing: Shangwu yinshuguan, 1992).
6. Marcel Granet, *Chinese Civilization* (New York: Alfred A. Knopf, 1930), p.1.
7. Jane Bennett, *Vibrant Matter: A Political Ecology of Things* (Durham and London: Duke University Press, 2010), p.vii.
8. Weber, *The Religion of China*; Fernand Braudel, *Civilization and Capitalism, 15th to 18th Centuries*, in 3 volumes (New York: Harper & Row, 1984).
9. Adam Smith, *An Enquiry into the Nature and Causes of the Wealth of Nations*, in 2 volumes (London: Methuen, 1961); Lewis Mumford, *The City in History: Its Origins, Its Transformations, and Its Prospects* (San Diego, New York and London: Harvest Books, 1961).

Bibliography

Leon Battista Alberti, *On the Art of Building in Ten Books*, trans. Joseph Rykwert, Neil Leach and Robert Tavernor (Cambridge MA: The MIT Press, 1988).
American Institute of Architects Academy of Architecture for Health, *Guidelines for Design and Construction of Hospital and Health Care Facilities* (Washington DC: The American Institute of Architects Press, 1998).
Hannah Arendt, *The Human Condition* (Chicago and London: University of Chicago Press, 1958).
Aristotle, *The Basic Works of Aristotle*, ed. Richard McKeon (New York: The Modern Library, 2001).
Giovanni Arrighi, *Adam Smith in Beijing: Lineages of the Twenty-first Century* (London and New York: Verso, 2007).
Erich Auerbach, *Mimesis: The Representation of Reality in Western Literature*, trans. Willard R. Trask (Princeton: Princeton University Press, 1953).
Francis Bacon, *The Philosophical Works of Francis Bacon*, ed. John M. Robertson (London: George Routledge, 1905).
Francis Bacon, *The Advancement of Learning* (London: J. M. Dent & Sons Ltd, 1973).
Andrew Ballantyne, ed., *Architecture Theory: A Reader in Philosophy and Culture* (London and New York: Continuum, 2005).
Jean Baudrillard, *Selected Writings*, ed. Mark Poster (Stanford: Stanford University Press, 1988).
Jean Baudrillard, *Simulacra and Simulation* (Ann Arbor: University of Michigan Press, 1994).
Ulrich Beck, *Risk Society: Towards a New Modernity* (London: SAGE, 1992).
Carol Benedict, *Bubonic Plague in Nineteenth-century China* (Stanford: Stanford University Press, 1996).
Walter Benjamin, 'The Work of Art in the Age of Mechanical Reproduction', in Hannah Arendt, ed., *Illuminations* (New York: Harcourt, Brace & World, 1968), pp.217–52.
Jane Bennett, *Vibrant Matter: A Political Ecology of Things* (Durham and London: Duke University Press, 2010).
Cécile and Michel Beurdeley, *Giuseppe Castiglione: A Jesuit Painter at the Court of the Chinese Emperors* (London: Lund Humphries, 1971).
Ryan Bishop, John Phillips and Wei-Wei Yeo, eds, *Beyond Description: Singapore Space Historicity* (London: Routledge, 2004).
David Bray, *Social Space and Governance in Urban China: The Danwei System from Origins to Reform* (Stanford: Stanford University Press, 2005).
Timothy Brook, *The Confusions of Pleasure: Commerce and Culture in Ming China* (Los Angeles and London: University of California Press, 1998).
Peter Brown, *The Body and Society: Men, Women, and Sexual Renunciation in Early Christianity* (New York: Columbia University Press, 1988).

Ricky Burdett and Deyan Sudjic, eds, *The Endless City* (London: Phaidon, 2007).
Thomas J. Campanella, *The Concrete Dragon: China's Urban Revolution and What It Means for the World* (New York: Princeton Architectural Press, 2008).
Centers for Disease Control and Prevention, *Guideline for Disinfection and Sterilization in Healthcare Facilities* (Atlanta: CDC, 2008).
Cheng Xiangge and Sun Shiyan, *Shichangxing gongyouzhi* (Market Collective Ownership) (Shanghai: Shanghai sanlian shudian, 1998).
Kenneth Clark, *The Nude: A Study in Ideal Form* (Princeton: Princeton University Press, 1972).
Craig Clunas, *Fruitful Sites: Garden Culture in Ming Dynasty China* (Durham: Duke University Press, 1996).
Craig Clunas, *Elegant Debts: The Social Art of Wen Zhengming (1470–1559)* (Honolulu: University of Hawai'i Press, 2003).
Craig Clunas, *Superfluous Things: Material Culture and Social Status in Early Modern China* (Honolulu: University of Washington Press, 2004).
Craig Clunas, *Empire of Great Brightness: Visual and Material Cultures of Ming China, 1368–1644* (Honolulu: University of Hawai'i Press, 2007).
Jeffrey W. Cody, *Building in China: Henry K. Murphy's 'Adaptive Architecture', 1914–1935* (Hong Kong: The Chinese University Press, 2001).
Beatrice Colomina, ed., *Sexuality and Space* (New York: Princeton Architectural Press, 1992).
Alan Colquhoun, 'The Superblock', *Essays in Architectural Criticism, Modern Architecture and Historical Change* (Cambridge MA: The MIT Press, 1985).
Confucius, *Lunyu*, trans. James Legge, *The Chinese Classics*, in 7 volumes (Oxford: The Clarendon Press, 1893).
Herrlee Glessner Creel, 'On the Nature of Chinese Ideography', *T'oung Pao* (second series) 32:2/3 (1936), pp.85–161.
Herrlee Glessner Creel, 'The Role of the Horse in Chinese History', *The American Historical Review* 70 (1965), pp.647–72.
Lincoln Cushing, 'Revolutionary Chinese Posters and Their Impact Abroad', in Lincoln Cushing and Ann Tompkins, *Chinese Posters: Art from the Great Proletarian Cultural Revolution* (San Francisco: Chronicle Books, 2007).
Guy Debord, *The Society of the Spectacle* (New York: Zone Books, 1995).
John DeFrancis, *The Chinese Language: Fact and Fantasy* (Honolulu: University of Hawai'i Press, 1984).
Demographia, 'World Urban Population Density by Country & Area', retrieved from www.demographia.com/db-intlua-area2000.htm (13 July 2011).
Harry den Hartog, *Shanghai New Towns: Searching for Community and Identity in a Sprawling Metropolis* (Rotterdam: 010 Publishers, 2010).
Jacques Derrida, *Archive Fever: A Freudian Impression* (Chicago and London: University of Chicago Press, 1996).
Mary Douglas, *Purity and Danger: An Analysis of Concepts of Pollution and Taboo* (Harmondsworth: Penguin Books, 1970).
Mary Douglas, *Natural Symbols: Explorations in Cosmology* (Harmondsworth: Penguin Books, 1973).
Shawn Eichman, 'The Art of Taoist Scriptures', *Orientations* 31 (Hong Kong: December 2000), pp.36–44.
Benjamin Elman, *From Philosophy to Philology: Intellectual and Social Aspects of Change in Late Imperial China* (Los Angeles: UCLA Asian Pacific Monograph Series, 2001).

Bibliography

Benjamin Elman, *On Their Own Terms: Science in China, 1550–1900* (Cambridge MA and London: Harvard University Press, 2005).
John King Fairbank and Merle Goldman, *China: A New History* (Cambridge MA: Harvard University Press, 1998).
Mike Featherstone, 'Archive', *Theory Culture & Society* 23, Problematizing Global Knowledge (2006), pp.591–96.
Mike Featherstone, Mike Hepworth and Bryan S. Turner, eds, *The Body, Social Process and Cultural Theory* (London: SAGE, 1991).
Hsiao-tung Fei (Fei Xiaotong), *Peasant Life in China: A Field Study of Country Life in the Yangtze Valley* (London: Routledge & Kegan Paul, 1939).
Hugh Ferriss, *The Metropolis of Tomorrow* (New York: Ives Washburn, 1929).
James A. Flath, *The Cult of Happiness: Nianhua, Art, and History in Rural North China* (Vancouver: UBC Press, 2004).
Michela Fontana, *Matteo Ricci* (Lanham: Rowman & Littlefield, 2011).
Kenneth Frampton, *Labour, Work and Architecture* (London: Phaidon, 2002).
Maurice Freedman, *Chinese Lineage and Society: Fukien and Kwangtung* (London: The Athlone Press, 1966).
Maurice Freedman, Editorial notes on his translation of Marcel Granet, *The Religion of the Chinese People* (New York: Harper & Row, 1975).
Milton Friedman, 'Asian Values: Right ...', *National Review* 49 (1997), pp.36–37.
John Friedmann, *China's Urban Transition* (Minneapolis: University of Minnesota Press, 2005).
Fu Xinian, 'Mingdai gongdian tanmiao deng da jianzhuqun zongti guihua shoufa de tedian' (The characteristics of the planning of large building groups in the Ming dynasty), *Jianzhu lilun lishi wenku* (Compendium of Essays in History and Theory of Architecture) (Beijing: Zhongguo jianzhu gongye chubanshe, 2010), pp.85–106.
Stanislaus Fung, 'The Language of Cultural Memory in Chinese Gardens', in Tony Atkins and Joseph Rykwert, eds, *Structure and Meaning in Human Settlements* (Philadelphia: University of Pennsylvania Museum of Archaeology and Anthropology, 2005), pp.123–34.
Jacques Gernet, *Daily Life in China on the Eve of the Mongol Invasion, 1250–1276*, trans. H. M. Wright (London: George Allen & Unwin, 1962).
Jacques Gernet, *A History of Chinese Civilization*, trans. J. R. Foster (Cambridge: Cambridge University Press, 1982).
Edward Glaeser, *Triumph of the City: How Our Greatest Invention Makes Us Richer, Smarter, Greener, Healthier, and Happier* (Harmondsworth: Penguin Books, 2012).
Ernst H. Gombrich, *The Story of Art* (London: Phaidon, 1995).
Marcel Granet, *Chinese Civilization* (New York: Alfred A. Knopf, 1930).
Marcel Granet, *La Pensée chinoise* (Paris: La Renaissance du livre, 1934).
Gu Chaolin, *Zhongguo chengshi tixi, lishi, xianzhuang, zhanwang* (The System of Chinese Cities and Towns, History, Current Conditions and Prospects) (Beijing: Shangwu yinshuguan, 1992).
Guo Daiheng, ed., *Zhongguo gudai jianzhu shi* (History of Ancient Chinese Architecture), Vol. 3 (Beijing: Zhongguo jianzhu gongye chubanshe, 2003).
Laurent Gutierez, Valérie Portefaix and Ezio Manzini, eds, *HK Lab* (Hong Kong: Map Book Publishers, 2002).
David L. Hall and Roger T. Ames, *Thinking Through Confucius* (Albany, NY: State University of New York Press, 1987).

David L. Hall and Roger T. Ames, *Anticipating China: Thinking Through the Narratives of Chinese and Western Culture* (New York: State University of New York Press, 1995).

William Hannas, *Asia's Orthographic Dilemma* (Honolulu: University of Hawai'i Press, 1997).

William Hannas, *The Writing on the Wall: How Asian Orthography Curbs Creativity* (Philadelphia: University of Pennsylvania Press, 2003).

Marta E. Hanson, *Speaking of Epidemics in Chinese Medicine* (London and New York: Routledge, 2011).

Robert E. Harrist, Jr., *The Landscape of Words: Stone Inscriptions from Early and Medieval China* (Seattle and London: University of Washington Press, 2008).

Heng Chye Kiang, *Cities of Aristocrats and Bureaucrats: The Development of Medieval Chinese Cityscapes* (Singapore: Singapore University Press, 1999).

Heritage Foundation, 2013 Index of Economic Freedom, retrieved from www.heritage.org/index/ranking (2 September 2013).

Herodotus, *The Histories*, trans. Aubrey de Sélincourt (London: Penguin Books, 1954/2003).

HKCSS, Statistics on Poverty in 2010, retrieved from www.hkcss.org.hk/cm/cc/press/documents/2010poverty.doc (29 June 2011).

Ho Peng Yoke, *Li, Qi and Shu: An Introduction to Science and Civilization in China* (Hong Kong: Hong Kong University Press, 1985).

Robert Hooke, *Micrographia* (London, 1665).

Max Horkheimer and Theodor W. Adorno, *Dialectics of Enlightenment* (Stanford: Stanford University Press, 2002).

Huangdi neijing (The Inner Cannon of Huangdi), ed. Yao Chunpeng (Beijing: Zhonghua shuju, 2009).

Martin Jay, *Downcast Eyes: The Denigration of Vision in Twentieth-Century French Thought* (Berkeley and London: University of California Press, 1993).

Jiren Feng, *Chinese Architecture and Metaphor: Song Culture in the Yingzao Fashi Building Manual* (Honolulu and Hong Kong: University of Hawai'i Press, 2012).

François Jullien, *The Propensity of Things: Towards a History of Efficacy in China* (New York: Zone Books, 1995).

François Jullien, *Detour and Access: Strategies of Meaning in China and Greece* (New York: Zone Books, 2004).

Carl Jung, 'Foreword', *I Ching*, trans. Richard Wilhelm (Princeton: Princeton University Press, 1967).

Michael Keith, Scott Lash, Jakob Arnoldi and Tyler Rooker, *China Constructing Capitalism: Economic Life and Urban Change* (London and New York: Routledge, 2013).

Lawrence Keppie, *Understanding Roman Inscriptions* (Baltimore: Johns Hopkins University Press, 1991).

Friedrich A. Kittler, *Gramophone, Film, Typewriter* (Stanford: Stanford University Press, 1999).

Richard Curt Klaus, *Brushes with Power: Modern Politics and the Chinese Art of Calligraphy* (Berkeley: University of California Press, 1991).

Lawrence E. Klein, *Shaftesbury and the Culture of Politeness: Moral Discourse and Cultural Politics in Early Eighteenth-Century England* (Cambridge: Cambridge University Press, 1994).

Rem Koolhaas, Bruce Mau, Hans Werlemann, Office for Metropolitan Architecture, *S,M,L,XL* (New York: Monacelli Press, 1995).

Rem Koolhaas, et al. *The Great Leap Forward* (Cologne: Taschen, 2002).
Joel Kotkin, *The City: A Global History* (New York: The Modern Library, 2005).
Philippe Lacoue-Labarthe, 'Oedipus as Figure', *Radical Philosophy* 118 (March/April 2003), pp.7–17.
Nadir Lahiji and D. S. Friedman, eds, 'At the Sink: Architecture in Abjection', *Plumbing: Sounding Modern Architecture* (New York: Princeton University Press, 1997).
Lai Delin, *Jindai Zhejiang Lu* (Who's Who in Modern Chinese Architecture) (Beijing: Zhongguo shuidian chubanshe, 2006).
Scott Lash, *Another Modernity, A Different Rationality* (Oxford: Blackwell, 1999).
Scott Lash, *Critique of Information* (London: SAGE, 2002).
Bruno Latour, *We Have Never Been Modern* (Cambridge MA: Harvard University Press, 1993).
Le Corbusier, 'A Coat of Whitewash, the Law of Ripolin', *The Decorative Art of Today*, trans. James I. Dunnett (Cambridge MA: The MIT Press, 1987).
David Leatherbarrow, *Architecture Orientated Otherwise* (New York: Princeton Architectural Press, 2009).
David Leatherbarrow and Mohsen Mostafavi, *Surface Architecture* (Cambridge MA: The MIT Press, 2005).
Angela Ki Che Leung and Charlotte Furth, eds, *Health and Hygiene in Chinese East Asia: Policies and Publics in the Long Twentieth Century* (Durham and London: Duke University Press, 2010).
Anthony Ley, *A History of Building Control in England and Wales, 1840–1990* (Coventry: RICS Books, 2000).
Lillian M. Li, Alison Dray-Novey and Haili Kong, *Beijing: From Imperial Capital to Olympic City* (New York: Palgrave Macmillan, 2008).
Li Shiqiao, 'Writing a Modern Chinese Architectural History: Liang Sicheng and Liang Qichao', *Journal of Architectural Education* 56 (2002), pp.35–45.
Li Shiqiao, 'Reconstituting Chinese Building Tradition: The *Yingzao fashi* in the Early Twentieth Century', *Journal of the Society of Architectural Historians* 62:4 (2003), pp.470–89.
Li Shiqiao, *Power and Virtue: Architecture and Intellectual Change in England, 1660–1730* (London and New York: Routledge, 2006).
Li Shiqiao, 'Concealment and Exposure: Imagining London after the Great Fire', in Ryan Bishop, Gregory Glancey and John Phillips, eds, *The City as Target* (London and New York: Routledge, 2012), pp.180–99.
Li Xiting, ed., *Huanghe Lou xiaozhi* (A Short History of Yellow Crane Tower) (Hong Kong: Tianma tushu, 2004).
Liang Qichao, *Qindai xueshu gailun* (Outline of Qing Scholarship) (Beijing, 1920).
Liang Qichao, *Liang Qichao guanji* (The Complete Works of Liang Qichao), in 10 volumes (Beijing: Beijing chubanshe, 1999).
Liang Sicheng, *Qingshi yingzao zeli* (Construction Methods of Qing Dynasty) (Beijing: Society for Research in Chinese Architecture, 1934).
Liang Sicheng, *Zhongguo jianzhushi* (History of Chinese Architecture) (Hong Kong: Joint Publishing, 2000; first published 1943).
Lin Zhu, *Jianzhushi Liang Sicheng* (Architect Liang Sicheng) (Tianjin: Tianjin kexue jishu chubanshe, 1997).
John Locke, *Some Thoughts Concerning Education* (London, 1693).
Adolf Loos, 'Plumbers', *Spoken into the Void*, trans. Jane O. Newman and John H. Smith (Cambridge MA: The MIT Press, 1987).

Esther Lorenz, 'Real Image, Fake Estate', *The International Journal of Design in Society* 6:2 (2013), pp.11–26.

Lu Duanfang, *Remaking Chinese Urban Form: Modernity, Scarcity and Space, 1949–2005* (London and New York: Routledge, 2006).

Karrie MacPherson, *A Wilderness of Marshes: The Origins of Public Health in Shanghai, 1843–1893* (Maryland: Lexington Press, 2001).

Mao Zedong, *Maozedong xuanji* (Selected writings of Mao Zedong) (Beijing: Remin chubanshe, 1991).

Gina Marchetti, Esther M. K. Cheung and Tan See-kam, eds, *Hong Kong Screenscapes: From the New Wave to the Digital Frontier* (Hong Kong: Hong Kong University Press, 2010).

William McNeill, *Plagues and Peoples* (New York: Anchor Press, 1976).

Meng Fanren, *Mingdai gongting jianzhu shi* (History of Palace Architecture of the Ming Dynasty) (Beijing: Zijincheng chubanshe, 2010).

The Ming Code, trans. Jiang Yonglin (Seattle and London: University of Washington Press, 2005).

Mohsen Mostafavi and David Leatherbarrow, *On Weathering: The Life of Buildings in Time* (Cambridge MA: The MIT Press, 1993).

Lewis Mumford, *The City in History: Its Origins, Its Transformations, and Its Prospects* (San Diego, New York and London: Harvest Books, 1961).

Susan Naquin, *Peking: Temples and City Life, 1400–1900* (Berkeley, Los Angeles, London: University of California Press, 2000).

Barry Naughton, *The Chinese Economy: Transition and Growth* (Cambridge MA: The MIT Press, 2007).

Joseph Needham, *Science and Civilization in China*, Vol. 2 (Cambridge: Cambridge University Press, 1956).

Ni Pengfei, ed., *Annual Report of Urban Competitiveness* (Beijing: Social Sciences Academic Press, since 2003).

Florence Nightingale, *Notes on Hospitals* (London: Longman, 1863).

Niu Wenyuan, ed., *China's New Urbanization Report 2009, 2010, 2011* (Beijing: Science Press, 2009, 2010, 2011).

Omega Centre, Bartlett School of Planning, and Hong Kong University of Hong Kong, *Hong Kong Airport Railway* (n.d.), retrieved from: www.omegacentre.bartlett.ucl.ac.uk/studies/cases/pdf/HK_AIRTRAIN_PROFILE_180511 (26 April 2013).

Richard Padovan, *Proportion: Science, Philosophy, Architecture* (London and New York: E & FN Spon, 1999).

Erwin Panofsky, *Gothic Architecture and Scholasticism* (Latrobe: Archabbey Press, 1951).

Erwin Panofsky, *Meaning in the Visual Arts* (London: Peregrine Books, 1970).

Harold Peake and Herbert John Fleure, *The Steppe and the Sown* (New Haven: Yale University Press, 1928).

Plato, *Timaeus and Critias*, trans. Desmond Lee (London: Penguin Books, 1977).

Alice Poon, *Land and the Ruling Class in Hong Kong*, second edition (Hong Kong: Enrich Professional Publishing, 2011).

Karl Popper, *The Logic of Scientific Discovery* (London: Hutchinson, 1968).

Roy Porter, *The Greatest Benefit to Mankind: A Medical History of Humanity from Antiquity to the Present* (London: HarperCollins, 1997).

Qiu Baoxing, *Zhongguo chengshihua jincheng zhongde chengshi guihua biange* (Urban Planning and Reform in the Process of China's Urbanization) (Shanghai: Tongji daxue chubanshe, 2005).

Qiu Baoxing, *Duiying jiyu yu tiaozhan* (Response, Opportunity and Challenge) (Beijing: Zhongguo jianzhu gongye chubanshe, 2009).

B. Renaud, F. Pretorius and B. Pasadilla, *Markets at Work: Dynamics of the Residential Real Estate Market in Hong Kong* (Hong Kong: Hong Kong University Press, 1997).

Jane Rendall, *Site-Writing: The Architecture of Art Criticism* (London: I. B. Tauris, 2010).

Matteo Ricci, *Xiguo jifa* (Memory Methods of Western Countries), ed. Wu Xiangxiang (Taibei, Taiwan xuesheng shuju, 1965).

Ruth Rogaski, *Hygienic Modernity: Meanings of Health and Disease in Treaty-Port China* (Berkeley: University of California Press, 2004).

Colin Rowe, 'The Mathematics of the Ideal Villa: Palladio and Le Corbusier Compared', *Architectural Review* (March, 1947), pp.101–104.

Stephen M. Rowlinson and Anthony Walker, *The Construction Industry in Hong Kong* (Hong Kong: Longman, 1995).

Ilka and Andreas Ruby, eds, *Urban Transformation* (Berlin: Ruby Press, 2008).

Klaas Ruitenbeek, *Carpentry and Building in Late Imperial China: A Study of the Fifteenth-century Carpenter's Manual Lu Ban Jing* (Leiden: Brill, 1996).

Bertrand Russell, *History of Western Philosophy* (London: Routledge, 2000; originally published 1946).

Richard Sennett, *Flesh and Stone: The Body and the City in Western Civilization* (New York: W. W. Norton & Company, 1994).

Shaftesbury, *Characteristicks of Men, Manners, Opinions, Times*, in 3 volumes (London, 1714).

Shaftesbury, *Second Characters, or the Language of Forms*, ed. Benjamin Rand (Cambridge: Cambridge University Press, 1914).

Shao Yong, *Huangji Jingshi Shu* (Book of Supreme Ordering Principles), annotated by Wei Shaosheng (Zhengzhou: Zhongzhou guji chubanshe, 2007).

Shen Yuan and Tang Dai, *Yuanmingyuan sishijing tuyong* (Paintings and Poems of Forty Scenes of Yuan Ming Yuan), ed. Jiyi (Beijing: Shijie tushu chubanshe, 2005).

Shi Gexin, *Zhongguo hongguanshi, luanshijuan* (The Macro-history of China: The Volume of Chaotic Eras) (Zhengzhou: Daxiang chubanshe, 2003).

Jerome Silbergeld and Dora C. Y. Ching, eds, *Persistence/Transformation: Text as Image in the Art of Xu Bing* (Princeton: Princeton University Press, 2006).

Adam Smith, *An Enquiry into the Nature and Causes of the Wealth of Nations*, in 2 volumes (London: Methuen, 1961).

Song Geng, *The Fragile Scholar: Power and Masculinity in Chinese Culture* (Hong Kong: Hong Kong University Press, 2004).

Jonathan Spence, *The Memory Palace of Matteo Ricci* (London and Boston: Faber and Faber, 1984).

Nancy Steinhardt, ed., *Chinese Architecture* (Beijing, New Haven and London: Yale University Press, 2002).

Bernard Stiegler, *Technics and Time 1: The Fault of Epimetheus* (Stanford: Stanford University Press, 1998).

Michael Sullivan, *The Meeting of Eastern and Western Art* (Berkeley and London: University of California Press, 1989).

Sun Dazhang, ed., *Zhongguo gudai jianzhu shi* (History of Ancient Chinese Architecture), Vol. 5 (Beijing: Zhongguo jianzhu gongye chubanshe, 2002).

Sun Xiaochun, 'On the Star Catalogue and Atlas of *Chongzhen Lishu*', in Catherine Jami, Peter Engelfriet and Gregory Blue, eds, *Statecraft and Intellectual Renewal in*

Late Ming China: the Cross-cultural Synthesis of Xu Guangqi (1562–1633) (Leiden, Boston and Cologne: Brill, 2001), pp.311–20.
Jeremy Taylor, *Hospital and Asylum Architecture in England, 1840–1914* (London and New York: Mansell, 1991).
John D. Thompson and Grace Goldin, *The Hospital: A Social and Architectural History* (New Haven and London: Yale University Press, 1975).
Thucydides, *History of the Peloponnesian War*, trans. Rex Warner (New York and London: Penguin Books, 1972).
Tong Jun, *Jiangnan yuanlin zhi* (Record of Gardens in Jiangnan) (Beijing: Zhongguo gongye chubanshe, 1963).
James D. Tracy, ed., *City Walls: The Urban Enceinte in Global Perspective* (Cambridge: Cambridge University Press, 2000).
Bryan S. Turner, *The Body and Society* (London: SAGE, 1996).
Urban Renewal Authority, *Urban Renewal: New Horizons, Annual Report 2011–2012* (Hong Kong: Urban Renewal Authority, 2012).
Leon Van Schaik, *Spatial Intelligence, New Futures for Architecture* (Chichester: John Wiley & Sons Ltd, 2008).
Thorstein Veblen, *The Theory of the Leisure Class*, ed. Martha Banta (Oxford: Oxford University Press, 2007, first published in 1899).
Vitruvius, *Ten Books on Architecture*, trans. Ingrid D. Rowland and Thomas Noble Howe (Cambridge: Cambridge University Press, 1999).
Immanuel Wallerstein, *The Modern World-system I: Capitalist Agriculture and the Origins of the European World-economy in the Sixteenth Century* (Los Angeles: University of California Press, 2011).
Wang Hui, *Xiandai Zhongguo sixiang de xingqi* (The Rise of Modern Chinese Thought), second edition (Beijing: SDX Joint Publishing Company, 2008).
Wang Hui, *The End of the Revolution: China the Limits of Modernity* (London and New York: Verso, 2009).
Wang Min'an, 'On Rubbish', trans. Li Shiqiao, *Theory, Culture & Society* 28 (2011), pp.340–53.
Wang Xuetai, *Shuihu, Jianghu* (Xian: Sha'anxi renmin chubanshe, 2011).
Max Weber, *The Religion of China: Confucianism and Taoism* (New York: The Free Press, 1951).
Chris Webster, Georg Glasze and Klaus Frantz, 'The Global Spread of Gated Communities', Special Issue, *Environment and Planning B* 29:3 (2002), pp.315–20.
Weiping Wu and Piper Gaubatz, *The Chinese City* (London and New York: Routledge, 2013).
Wen-hsin Yeh, *The Alienated Academy: Culture and Politics in Republican China, 1919–1937* (Cambridge MA: Harvard University Press, 1990).
Mark Wigley, *White Walls, Designer Dresses* (Cambridge MA: The MIT Press, 1995).
Julia Wilkinson, 'A Chinese Magistrate's Fort', in Greg Girard and Ian Lambot, *City of Darkness: Life in Kowloon Walled City* (Surrey: Watermark Publications: 1993).
Rudolf Wittkower, *Architectural Principles in the Age of Humanism* (London: The Warburg Institute, 1949).
Rudolf Wittkower, 'The Changing Concept of Proportion', *Idea and Image: Studies in the Italian Renaissance* (New York: Thames and Hudson, 1978).
Christopher Wren III, *Parentalia* (London, 1750).
Wu Fulong, 'Rediscovering the "Gate" Under Market Transition: From Work-unit Compounds to Commodity Housing Enclaves', *Housing Studies* 20 (2005), pp.235–54.

Wu Fulong, ed., *Globalization and the Chinese City* (London and New York: Routledge, 2006).
Wu Hung, *Transience: Chinese Experimental Art at the End of the Twentieth Century* (Chicago: University of Chicago Press, 2005).
Wu Hung, *Remaking Beijing: Tiananmen Square and the Creation of a Political Space* (Chicago: University of Chicago Press, 2005).
Don J. Wyatt, *The Recluse of Loyang: Shao Yung and the Moral Evolution of Early Sung Thought* (Honolulu: University of Hawai'i Press, 1996).
Xiao Tangbiao, *Zongzu zhengzhi, cunzhi quanli wangluo de fenxi* (Clan Politics: An Analysis of the Web of Power in the Village Rule) (Beijing: Shangwu yinshuguan, 2010).
Xu Shubin, *Jindai Zhongguo jinazhuxue de dansheng* (The Beginning of Chinese Modern Architecture) (Tianjin: Tianjin daxue chubanshe, 2010).
Xu Wenrong, *Puojie shiji nanti* (Solving the Difficult Problem of the Century) (private printing, 2003).
Xu Yinong, *The Chinese City in Space and Time: The Development of Urban Form in Suzhou* (Honolulu: University of Hawai'i Press, 2000).
Yan Buke, *Pinwei yu zhwei, Qin Han Wei Jin Nanbeichao guanjie zhidu yanjiu* (Grades and Positions: A Study of the Bureaucratic Systems from Qin to North and South Dynasties) (Beijing: Zhonghua shuju, 2002).
Yang Weisheng, *Liang Song wenhua shi* (History of Northern and Southern Song Dynasties) (Hangzhou: Zhejiang daxue chubanshe, 2008).
Yang Yongsheng, ed., *Zhejiang Lu* (Record of Philosophical Craftsmen) (Beijing: Zhongguo jianzhu gongye chubanshe, 2004).
Frances Yates, *The Art of Memory* (London: Routledge and Kegan Paul, 1966).
Rikkie Yeung, *Moving Millions: The Commercial Success and Political Controversies of Hong Kong's Railways* (Hong Kong: Hong Kong University Press, 2008).
Ying Xiaoli, *Caogen zhengzhi, nongmin zizhu xingwei yu zhidu bianqian* (Grass Root Politics, the Autonomous Actions of Peasants and Systems Change) (Beijing: Zhongguo shehui kexue chubanshe, 2009).
You-tien Hsing, *The Great Urban Transformation: Politics of Land and Property in China* (Oxford: Oxford University Press, 2010).
Yu Xinzhong, 'Night Soil and Waste in Modern China', in Angela Ki Che Leung and Charlotte Furth, eds, *Health and Hygiene in Chinese East Asia: Policies and Publics in the Long Twentieth Century* (Durham and London: Duke University Press, 2010).
Zhang Jiaji, *Yuan Ye quanshi* (The Complete Annotation of Yuan Ye) (Taiyuan: Shanxi guji chubanshe, 1993).
Zhou Weiquan, *Zhongguo gudian yuanlin shi* (History of Classical Chinese Gardens) (Beijing: Qinghua daxue chubanshe, 1990).
Zhu Jianfei, *Chinese Spatial Strategies: Imperial Beijing, 1420–1911* (London and New York: Routledge, 2003).

Index

Illustrations are indicated by page numbers in bold, and end-of-chapter notes are indicated by the page number followed by "n" and the note number.

abundance xiv–xv, 139
   and agriculture 7
   in Chinese language 7, 10–11
   fertility 7
   Hong Kong 28, 29, 32
   and 'just right' 19–20
   market places 14
   in modern China 14–15
   in paintings 9
   and quantity control 6–7, 9
   and scarcity 20
   uniformity in 69–73
   universal desire for 6–7
   see also just right
Achilles and Ajax Playing Draughts (vase) 150
Ad Herennium 164
age-based hierarchy 85
agriculture
   prudence in 81
   and quantity control 20
   stable social conditions for 79–80
Airport Express Rail 39
Alberti, Leon Battista 18, 19, 20, 26n21, 134n9
Alexander, Christopher xvi, 199
Andreu, Paul 71
architects, biographies of xx
Architectural Design and Research Institute of Tongji University (TJAD) 202
architecture
   anti-bacterial surfaces 128
   appropriateness 19
   and capital 45
   and Chinese writing system 143, 144–5
   as commodity 35
   design by quantity management 44–5
   design firms, grades of 202
   design as work units 202
   disinfection 118, 128
   disposable 131, 132
   function 22–3

architecture *cont.*
   group design 69–71
   historiography 165–6
   homogenous surfaces 118
   intercolumniations 201
   life-span of buildings 131–2, 133
   linguistic metaphor in design 23
   proportion 17, 20, 21–2, 23, 29
   as real estate 176
   roughness and age 128
   standardization 44–5, 69
   as state function 199–205
   with text **193**, 194–7
   thin surfaces 118
   use of glass 92–3
   whiteness 118, 121–2, **121–3**, 124–5
'architecture of finance' 39
archive cities 166–7, 170, 177, 178
Arendt, Hannah xxiii, 57
   Human Condition, The 57–8, 59
Aristotle 89, 99
   Nichomachean Ethics 80
   Politics 103, 156
Arnoldi, Jacob xxiii
Arrighi, Giovanni xxiii, xxviin31
Asian Games 2010 48
Atkins Design Studio 65
Auerbach, Erich 150, 161n17
authenticity 167, 170
axial spreading 13, 15, 203

Ba Jin, *Family* 157
Bacon, Francis 21, 26n26, 26nn28, 139–40
   Advancement of Learning 152
bacteriology 126–7
Baroque 20, 118
Baudrillard, Jean 54n22, 142, 154, 160n10
Baumgarten, Alexander, *Aesthetica* 19
beaches 113
beauty
   love of 21
   and proportion 21

Index

Beck, Ulrich, *Risk Society* 90
Beijing
   Chang'an Avenue 114
   Forbidden City **13**, 104
      concubine quarters 12–13
      form and function 145–6
      Hall of Supreme Harmony 145–6, **147**
      and numerical schemes 12–13
      sons of the emperor 13
      spacing regulation 13
   Great Hall of the People 15, 70, 198
   International Airport 144
   Jinmao Tower 144
   Mausoleum of Chairman Mao 198
   Museum of Revolutionary History 15, 70, 198
   National Aquatic Centre 15, 145
   National Grand Theatre 144
   Olympic Stadium 15, 145, 198, 202
   Olympic Village **15**, 71
   themed development 64
   Tiananmen Square 5, 15, 70, 114, 198, 202
      protest xxiii
Beijing Institute of Architectural Design (BIAD) 70–1, 202
Beijing-Tianjin Axis 53
Benjamin, Walter 154, 161n22, 167, 179n19
Bianliang 14
Bible 150
big character posters 145
Board of Health 117
body
   in art 81–2, 88, 90
   and combat 87, 88, 95
   concept of corporeal defence 100, 101, 102, 130, 209
   in contemplation 81
   in danger 86–90
   and debating mind 89–90
   exercise 95–6
   in gardens 84
   health 95, 98–9, 100
   of literati 81, 82
   modification 182–3
   nakedness 90–1
   preservation 83
   and *qi* 18
   reform from safety of combatant 93
   in safety 81–6, 93–6, 98, 100
   transformation of the female body 94, 182–3
   yin and *yang* 8
Boerschmann, Ernst xxi

Book of Changes xv, 7, 8, 12, 18, 66, 67, 83
   colours 121
books 11, 86
Boxer Rebellion 93
Braudel, Fernand 210
Brook, Timothy xxiii, xxvin2
Brunelleschi 146
bubonic plague 115n1, 118
Buddhism 121, 143

Cai Yuanpei 158
calendar reform 165
calligraphy 180, **181**, 182
   copying books 182
   creativity 182
   styles 180
Camillo, Guilio 164
Cao Xueqing
   Dream of the Red Chamber 157
capitalism 59–60, 207, 208
carelessness 111–15
casinos 67–8
Castiglione, Baldassare
   Book of the Courtier 19, 60
Castiglione, Giuseppe 11–12, 148
cathedrals 28
Centre for Disease Control and Prevention 127
Chadwick, Edwin 117
chance narratives 66–8
   gambling 67–8
Chang'an 200
Changsha
   balconies behind metal cages **106**
   entrance to Yuelu College **193**, 197
   Nanmenkou shopping street **197**
   Tangerine Island **189**, 190, 192
Chen Chongzhou 188
Chen Zhi 188
Chengdu-Chongqing Basin 53
chiaroscuro 91, 92
China Architecture Design and Research Group (CAG) 202
Chinese Academy of Sciences, *China's New Urbanization Reports* xxii
Chinese Academy of Social Sciences, *Annual Report on Urban Competitiveness* xxii
Chinese Constitution: amendment 1988 46
Chinese language, established phrases 173
Chinese New Year 159, 197
   peasant paintings 9
Chinese writing system xvi–xvii, 139
   aesthetic qualities 143–4
   and alphabet-based language xvi
   calligraphy 180, **181**, 182

Chinese writing system *cont.*
  completeness 148
  components of characters 140
  and dialects 140–1
  form and meaning blend 139–40
  Kangxi zidian 140
  and memory 163, 180
  number of characters 140
  and painting 192–3
  phonetic or character-based? 141
  priority over speech 141–2
  proposed adoption of alphabetic writing 158
  punctuation and grammatical symbols 141
  standardization 142
  text as image 150, 154
chinoiserie 20–1
chora 17, 18, 20, 24
Christianity
  and body 88
  images 154
  view of labour 57, 58
Chuta, Ito xxi
Cicero, *De oratore* 164
city of a billion things 24, 28
city of industrialization 80
Clunas, Craig xxiii, xxviiin35, 74n19,22, 205n8, 206n16
colonial cities 177
colours 18, 121, 126
Colquhoun, Alan 45, 54n23
combat 87, 95
  and competition 88, 94–5
Commune by the Great Wall 69–70
communes 105
competition 88, 94–5
Complete Library in Four Branches of Literature 11, 86
completeness 148, 174–5
Confucianism xvii–xviii, xix–xx, 18, 209
  family structure 56, 103
  freedom/restraint formulation 72
  scholars 88
Confucius xv, xviii, 56, 61, 73n2, 102, 173
  Analects 89
  Spring and Autumn Annals 162
connoisseurship 2, 61, 62
consumerism 58
  and identity 63
convergence of behaviour 69
convergence of goals 69, 71
corporeal defence 100, 101, 102, 130, 209
cosplay **63**–4
courage 80

courtyard houses 103–4
Creel, Herrlee Glessner 74n27, 142, 160n8
Crimean War 123
Crystal Palace 92
Cui Hao 168
Cultural Revolution xviii, 95, 145

Dafen 49
danger 86–93
  aesthetics of 90–3
  and carelessness 80
  in the city 88
  and combat 87, 88–90
  and dangerous knowledge 80
  in the environment 83–4
  and mind 89
  and prudence 86–7
  and risk 90
Daoism 9, 143
Darmaratus 87
data indexing 23
Datang 50
Debord, Guy 154, 161n21
defence (*weisheng*) 100
DeFrancis, John 141, 160n3
degrees of care 98–1000
  care of strangers 98
  carelessness 111–15
  jianghu 111–15
  protected homes 102–7
  units of economic interest 107–11
  walls 99–102
density 130
Derrida, Jacques 167, 179n13
dialectics 89
dialogues 89
diet 83
Dionysus 86
'doctrine of the mean' 18
Dong Qichang 156
Dongyang
  city centre **203**, 204
  entrance to Adminsitrative Centre **196**
  Lu House 103, **104**
  People's Court House and Administrative Building 204–5
Douglas, Mary 88, 97n17
Dream of the Red Chamber 84

Earth God 66
Edison, Thomas 155
Eisenman, Peter 199
elements 8, 17
elevator, invention of 28
Enlightenment 22

Index

environment 83
evidential research 172–4
 'correcting texts' 173
exercises in open spaces 95
Exposition des Arts Décoratif (1925) 126

Fachwerk 146
Fairbank, John King and Goldman, Merle xxvin10, 8, 25n4
families 85, 102–3
 foundation components of families 102
 hierarchy 102, 109
 and state 103
Farnsworth House 93
Farrell, Terry 41
Fei Xiaotong 49, 54n31, 102
fengshui 18, 67
Ferriss, Hugh, *Metropolis of Tomorrow, The* 28, 29
fertility 7, 9
figuration xvii, 139
 and Chinese writing system 139, 142–3
 completeness 148
 figurelessness 148, 149–50
 function following figure 145–6
 and home 156–60
 and largeness 145
 mimesis 150, 152
 mimicking reality 148
 principles 144–8
filial piety 85
Florence 211
Fontana, Dominico 13
footbinding 182
Foster, Norman 71
Foucault, Michel 124, 166
Four Monks 155, 156
Four Wangs 155
France: Academie Royale des Sciences 124
Frankfurt School 55
Freud, Sigmund xiv, 157
 Civilization and its Discontents 166
 'Uncanny, The' 103, 156
Friedman, Milton 30, 53n6
Fujian Province, Round House 103
function in design 22–3

gambling 67–8
gardens and gardening 84–5, 187–8
 elements of nature 85
 garden histories xxi–xxii
 interiorized 104
 and text 194–5
gift giving rituals 108
Glaeser, Edward xix

glass 92–3
gods 66–7
Gombrich, Ernst H. 91, 150, 151, 160n16
Gong Jianchuan 70
Gongcheng zuofa zeli 201
grades of cities 203, 207–8
Grand View Garden 84
Granet, Marcel xxiii, xxviiin32, 25n8, 139, 143, 208, 212n6
 Pensée chinoise, La 9
Grantham, Sir Alexander 34
Great Canon of the Yongle Era 11, 86
Great Leap Forward 94
Great Wall of China 107
Greek architecture 21–2
Greek sculpture 81
Greeks 57, 60, 86–7, 89, 99
 mimesis 150
 nudity 90–1
 polis 91, 100, 156–7
group activities 69
Guan Yonghe 168
Guangzhou 15, 101
 Opera House 144
Guideline for Disinfection and Sterilization in Healthcare 127
gymnasia 95–6, 98

Hall, David and Ames, Roger xviii, xxiii, xxvin6
Hall, Peter xiv
Han dynasty 102
Hangzhou 64
Hannas, William 141, 154, 160n2, 179n22, 182
Hanson, Julienne xvi
Hardouin-Mansart, Jules 13
health 14, 83, 95, 98–9
 discovery of bacteria 126–7
 miasma theory of disease 123–4
 population density and infection 130
 see also hygiene
Hegel, G.W.F. 89
Hengdian 50, **51**
 film and television production 50, 51
 planning 52
Herodotus, *Histories* 87
hierarchy 59–60, 60–1, 112
 age-based 85
 in families 102
 social advancement 61–2
hieroglyphic 158
high rise appartments 105–6
 grouped in micro-districts 106–7

high speed railways 107
Hillier, Bill xvi, 199
histories of architecture xxi, 165–6
history and historiography 165
 Confucian order 175–6
 evidential research 172–3
 'historical fact' 162
 and philology 172–3
 and temporal relocation 172
Hobbes, Thomas 23
Hollywood Reporter 50
home 156–60
 and homecoming 159
 and the uncanny 156–7
Homer 87
 Odyssey 150
homes *see* high rise appartments; protected homes
Hong Kong 28–46
 abundance 16
 Airport Core Programme (ACP) 42
 anti-bacterial surfaces 128
 architectural profession 38–9
 architecture and health risks 32
 architecture and standardization 44–5, 69
 archtectural design 44–5
 Arts Centre **120**
 Bank of China building 67
 British rule 29–30
 bubonic plague 127
 building density 5
 Central Pier 169–**70**, 171, 174, 176
 Centre for Health Protection 127
 ceramic tiles 128
 compared with New York 28–9
 compared with Venice 28–9
 complexity 24–5
 comprehensive development 44
 cosplay **63**
 demolition and renewal 128, 131–2, 176
 design 38–9
 disinfection 131
 economy 29–31
  land speculation 30–2
  real estate prices 31
 foreign workers 56
 Furama Hotel 131
 gambling 67
 Hang Seng Bank 67
 Hilton Hotel 131
 history 29–30
 HSBC 67
 hygiene 119, 120, 131
 infection control 127–8
 International Commerce Centre (ICC) 44

Hong Kong *cont.*
 International Finance Centre 124
 Jubilee Gardens 35
 Kowloon Station 39, 40, **40**, 42, 44–5
 Kowloon Walled City 32–5, **33**, 48, 125
  crime and filth 34
  demolition 33
  density 33–4
 labour market 55–6
 land-use rights 46, 47
 life-span of buildings 131–2
 loss of heritage 169
 Mass Transit Railway Corporation 39, 41, 42–3
 migration from China 42, 124
 minimum dimensions 29
 off-white shine 125–6, 126–9
 open grid 29
 Outline Zoning Plan (OZP) 44
 property developers 47
 proportional and functional quantities 29
 public spaces 113–14
 quantity management 44–5
 railway development 42–3
 Sai Yeung Choi Street **120**
 SARS (Severe Acute Respiratory Syndrome) 119, 124, 130
 Shatin
  Grand Century Plaza 126
  New Town Plaza 124, **125**, 125–6, 132, **132**
  Palazzo 35, 36, **37**, 64
  Palazzo, Jubilee Gardens and Royal Ascot **36**, **38**
  Royal Ascot 35, 36
 tall buildings 29
 terminal developments 39, 41–6
 themed development 64
 Tin Shui Wai 34–5, **34**
 as treaty-port city 118
 urban renewal 128
 urbanization 124
 walls and handrails 100–1, **102**
 whiteness 122–3, 124–5
Hong Ren 156
Hongwu, Emperor xv, 59–60, 80, 211
Hooke, Robert 28, 152, 154
 Micrographia 152, **153**
Horkheimer, Max and Adorno, Theodor W. 154, 161n20
horse racing 67
hospitals 123, 124, 127
houses *see* courtyard houses; protected homes; villas
Hu Shi 173

Index

Hua Tuo 58
Huang Qiaoling 64
hygiene 117–19, 121
   and building materials 127–8
   disinfection 133
   'front door' areas 119
   hospitals 124
   infection barriers 130–2, 133
   and patriotism 119
   and treaty-port cities 118–19

Ibsen, Henrik
   Doll's House, A 104, 158
identity 63–6
idling centres 95, 98
images
   and authenticity 155
   in Christianity 154
   as falsehood 154–5
   'image' in Chinese writing 155
imperial administration xix
imperial book collections 11
imperial examinations 61, 62
Imperial Inspected Encyclopedia of the Taiping Era 11, 86
Industrial Revolution 88
infectious diseases 118–19
Inner Canon of Huangdi 83
inside and outside 101, 111
International Council on Monuments and Sites (ICOMOS) 167
Italy 101

Jasper, Karl 175
Jencks, Charles 198
Ji Cheng, *Craft of Gardens, The* 188
Jianchuan Museum Cluster 70
jianghu 111–15
Jiangsu 49
Johnson, Philip 93
Jullien, François xxiii, xxviiin32, 25n9, 82
Jülu City 162
Jung, Carl 8, 25n1
Junius, Francisco, *Painting of the Ancients, The* 19
Jurchens 14
just right 16–22
   in architecture 19
   in conduct 19
   less and more 20
   see also abundance

Kang Youwei 173
Kant, Immanuel 89, 126
   Critique of Judgment 19

Keith, Michael et al xxiii, xxviiin34
Khitans 14
Kittler, Friedrich 155, 161n26
knowledge 11, 18, 86
   transparency 91
Koch, Robert 127
Kohn Pedersen Fox 41
Koolhaas, Rem et al xxii, xxviin25, 27n36
Koolhaas, Rem, *S,M,L,XL* 23, 155
Kotkin, Joel xix, xxvin7
Kun Can 156
Kurokawa, Kisho 204
Kwu Tung 64

labour 55–68
   agricultural labour 58, 59
   Chinese conceptions 55, 56, 58–9
   in Chinese language 58
   Christian view 57, 58
   and consumerism 58
   cultural context 55
   in Cultural Revolution 59
   dependencies 62–8
      chance dependency 66–7
      identity 63–6
   freedom 56, 57
   and hierarchy 56
   and leisure 55, 57, 58
   Marxist view 55, 57, 60
   physical and mental 58
   transformative power 59
   Western context 57
   and work 57–8, 60
Lacoue-Labarthe, Philippe xvii, xxvin5, 142
Lake Taihu 184
land banks 47
land-use rights 46
landscape 185–6
   in painting 83–4, 186–7
   see also gardens and gardening
Lash, Scott xxiii, 92, 97n32, 161
Le Corbusier 20, 27n32, 117–18, 122, 126, 134n11
   Towards a New Architecture 17
leaving home 103
Lee Kwan Yew 51
Lei family xx
Leonardo da Vinci 88, 99
Lévi-Strauss, Claude xvi
Li Bai 168
Li Dazhao 94
Li Hongzhang 93
Li Jie xix, xx
Li Ming 190

227

Li Qinfu 64
Liang Qichao xx, xxviin18, 93, 165–6, 173, 174, 179n20, 200, 209
  Compendium for the Research Method of Chinese History 165
  history of Chinese cities 162–3, 171
  New Historiography 165
  Research Method for Chinese History 165
Liang Sicheng xxi, 146, 165–6, 201, 206n20
  'Architecture and the Restoration Plan for the Temple of Confucius' 171
  history of architecture 165–6
life-span of buildings 131–2, 133
Lin Huiyin xxi
literati 62, 81, 82, 187–8
Liu Changchun 95
Liu Dunzhen xxi
Locke, John 96n14, 121, 200
  Some Thoughts Concering Education 87
London 28
  Golders Green 41–2
London School of Economics xxii
Loos, Adolf 117–18, 121, 133n1
Louis XIV 13
Lu Ban xx
Lu Wan'gai 163
Lu Xun 104–5, 158, 173
Lynch, Kevin xvi

Ma Yuehan 93–4
Macau
  gambling 67–8
  Grand Lisboa **68**
McNeill, William, *Plagues and Peoples* xvi
Manchus 80
manners 62
  in China and the West 60–1
Manual of the Mustard Seed Garden 83, **84**, 186–8
Mao Yuanyi
  Treatise on Military Preparations 165
Mao Zedong xxiv–xxv, 73n12, 209
  calligraphy 143
  Changsha 190, **191**
  and Chinese writing 158
  communes 105
  'Huaghe Lou' 168
  hygiene 119
  promotion of sport 94–5
  transformative power of labour 59
  visits to Changsha 190
  Yangtze River swim 94
map making 164–5
market economy 60
market places 14

marriage 63
  group marriages 69
martial art 82
Marx, Karl 89
Marxism 55, 154
material and ideal 154
May Fourth Movement xviii, 104, 157, 158
media theories 154–5
memory
  and Chinese writing system 167–8
  and durability 175
  with mobility 177
  places of memory 164–5, 166–70
  as text 172–8
  without location 176–8
merchants 14
miasma theory of disease 123–4
Michael Wilford & Partners 92
Michelangelo 88, 89
micro-districts 106–7, 110
migration to cities 208
mimesis 150, 152, 154
mind, debating 89–90
Ming dynasty xxiii, xxv, 58, 62, 103, 111, 208
  astronomical knowledge 175
  hierarchy 112
  imperial regulations 12
  social order 14
  wall building 99
miniaturised trees 183–**4**
minimalism 20
Ministry of Rites xix, 200
modernization xvii
Moneo, Raphael 176
money, use of xxiii
Mongols 14, 80, 100
Moore, Charles 198
moral propriety 19
moral uprightness 146
More, Thomas, *Utopia* 177
movies 112
Mumford, Lewis, *City in History, The* xiv, xix, xxv, 20, 29, 57, 211
museums 15, 70, 157, 166–7, 170, 178
music 72

Nanjing 70
Netherlands 101
new cities 48, 177
'new urbanization' xxii
New York 28–9
  Flatiron Building 28
  Woolworth Building 28
Ni Pengfei xxvii

Index

Nietzsche, Friedrich 88
  Gay Science, The 80
Nightingale, Florence xvi
  Notes on Hospitals 118, 123–4, 127–8, 133
numbers
  in Chinese cities 24
  in Chinese language 10–11
  and Forbidden City 12–13, 24
  from *yin* and *yang* binary 7–8
  meanings of 12
  in modern cities 14–15
  numerical schemes 5–6, 7–9, 144
  and *qi* 18
  significance of xiv, xv
  stopping at a billion 24

objects of value 183–90
  gardens 187–8
  'preferred nature' 188
  'scenery in basin' 182–3
  taihu limestone 184–5
  Yellow Mountain 185–6
Olympic Games
  ancient 88
  Chinese, 2008 76, 95
Olympic Stadium 15, 145, 198, 202
One Hundred Days Reform 162
Opium War 29, 93
orders of things (*wanwu*) 24
Otis, Elisha 28

Padovan, Richard, *Proportion* 23
painting
  body in safety 81–2
  Chinese and Western 91–2
  depictions of war 82
  foreshortening 148
  gardens 84
  landscape 83–4
  and language 199
  market places 14
  one hundred horses 11–12
  perspective 91, 92, 93, 148
  proportion 19
  shadows 91, 92, 93
  violence 82
  whiteness 121
  and writing 192–3
Palladio, Andrea 28
  Four Books of Architecture 17, 29
Pan Shiyi 69
Panofsky, Erwin 97n19, 198, 199, 206n15
Parthenon 91

Pasteur, Louis 126
Paxton, Joseph 92
Peacham, Henry 60, 62
Pearl River Delta 53
Pei, I.M. 67
Pericles 90
Perrault, Charles 21–2
philology 172–3
physical education 93–4
Picasso, Pablo xvii, 93
piety 85
Pine of Welcoming Guests 186
planning, rule-based 6
Plato 22, 23–4, 89, 105, 126, 154, 190
  Timaeus xiv–xv, 17–19, 18, 20, 91
plumbing 117
pollution
  beaches 113
  rivers and lakes 112–13
  streets 113
  see also hygiene
Poplar and Stepney Workhouse Infirmary 124
Popper, Karl 80, 96n5
Portoghesi, Paolo 198
prestige projects 107
private housing 47
productive binary 7
  in painting 9
  and Western duality 7
property ownership 199–200
proportion 17–18, 20, 21–2, 23
  decline of 22–3
  mathematical roots 22
  and morality 19
  and prudence 80
  and rise of science 21, 22–3
protected homes 102–7
  balconies 106
  courtyard houses 103–4
  enclosed rooms 108–9
  in imperial China 103, 104
  and importance of family 102–3
  marketization 106
  metal cages 105
  villas 105
prudence xv–xvi, 139
  in agriculture 81
  and body 80
  Chinese conception 80–1
  as destructive 86
  economic 86
  Greek conception 86–7
  and security of home 159
  virtue of age 85

229

Public Health Act (1848) 117
public spaces xxiv, 11–12, 98, 101
　care 113–15
　exercises 95
　and hygiene 113–14

qi 18
Qian Xuantong 158
Qianlong, Emperor 11, 91, 146, 148, 192
Qing dynasty 59, 84, 119, 168, 201
　grades of officials 200–1
Qingshi yingzao zeli **147**
Qiu Anxiong 154
　New Book of Mountains and Seas 152, **153**, 159
Qiu Baoxing 54n33, 132, 135n40
Qiu Zhijie, *One-thousand-time Copy of Lantingxu, A* 180, **181**, 182
Qu Qiubai 158
quantitative characters of cities 5
quantity regulation
　and abundance 6–7
　in Chinese cities 24
　concept of just right 16–20
　defining role 5
　and density 6
　Hong Kong 28
　and knowledge 11
　out of regulation 5
　and spacing regulation 11–12
　wealth and poverty 5
Quintilian, *Institutio Oratoria* 164

Raphael 19, 89
red (colour) 121
relational circles 108
　dining rooms 109
　karaoke room 109
　serving food 109
Renaissance 21, 22, 88, 89, 211
research in 20th century xx–xxiii
　and Western understanding xxiii
resident registration 5
Ricci, Matteo 91, 163–5, 167–8, 174
　Memory Methods of Western Countries 163–4, 167, 171
　world map 164–5
rise of city xix
rise of science 21
risk 90
rivers and lakes 111, 112–13
　pollution 112–13
Romans 81, 100
Rome 13, 126
Ronald Lu and Partners 35

Rooker, Tyler xxiii
Rowe, Colin, 'Mathematics of the Ideal Villa, The' 22
rubbish 113
Rufer House 117, 133
ruins 175
Russell, Bertrand xvi, xxvin3, 86, 87, 151

safety xvi, 79–86, 93–6, 98
　'conspicuous safety' 111
　and micro-districts 107
sanitation 98–9, 117
Saussure, Ferdinand de xvi, 141
saving 86
Scarpa, Carlo 176
scenic spots 185–6
Schall, Adam 165
scholarship 61
schools: disinfection 131
seasons 8
security *see* degrees of care
sedentary life 79, 80
Sensai, Nagayo 117
sewage 117
Shaftesbury, Earl of 22, 126, 198–9
　Characteristicks of Men, Manners, Opinions, Times 19, 62
Shanghai 47, 101
　Expo Best Urban Practices Pavilion 49, 202
　model of Songjiang **48**
　One City, Nine Towns Development Plan 64–5
　Songjiang, Thames Town **65**
　Television Tower 144
　themed development 64–6
　treaty-port cities 118
Shanghai Xiandai Architectural Design (SXDA) 202
Shao Yong xv, xxvin1, 8, 24
Shek Kip Mei 124
Shenzhen 15, 48, 177–8, 203
　administrative centre 203–4
　city centre **16**
　Dafan Village 49
Shenzhen General Institute of Architectural Design and Research (SADI) 202
Shi Tao 156
Shibasaburo, Kitasato 127
shine 125–30
Siku quanshu xix
silence 72
Simonides 163–4

Index

Singapore 47, 51, 126
  Esplanade, Marina Bay 92–3
  Fullerton Hotel 35
Sino Land 35
Sirén, Osvald xxi
Sistine Chapel 89
Sixtus V 13
sixty-four hexagrams 7–8
Smith, Adam xxv, 210
  Wealth of Nations, The 59, 60
Soane, John 167
social security 85
social welfare 98
  by work units 109–10
Socialist Realism 95
SOHO 70
Song Confucianism xxv
Song dynasty xix–xx, xxv, 102–3, 146, 162, 201, 208
  market places 14
Song Yingxing, *The Exploitation of the Works of Nature* xx
Songjiang 47–8
  Thames Town 47
sound and silence 72–3
Soviet Socialist Realism 15
spacing regulation 11–12
Sparta 87, 90, 99
sports 94, 95
  see also Olympic Games
state family 103, 107
state ownership of urban areas 47
Steiner, George 199
Steinhardt, Nancy xxi, 115n5
strangers 85, 108
  care of 98
  migrant workers 114
streets, rubbish in 113
study of Chinese cities xx
Sun Hung Hai Properties 64
Sunzi, *Art of War* 82
superblocks 45
Suzhou
  Humble Administrator's Garden **10**, 190, 191, **195**
  Taihu stone in Wangshi Yuan **185**
  Zhouzheng Yuan, restricting wires on tree **184**

Tai Chi 95
tall buildings 28, 105–7
  in villages 48
Tang dynasty 146, 200
tangible/intangible heritage 170–1
taste 19, 20, 56, 62

texts 190–7
  carved on rocks **191**
  in gardens 194, **195**, 196
  parallelism 196
textualization 142
theme parks 66, 177
themed development 64–6
thirds 17
three forces (Plato) 17
Three Gorges Dam 107
Thucydides 90, 97n22
Tianjin 101
  treaty-port cities 118
Tianjin, Peasant painting from Yangliuqing **10**
timber size grades (*cai*) 201
Tin Shui Wai 34–5
  Kingswood Villa 35
To, Johnnie 112
Tokyo 42
Tong Jun, *Record of Gardens in Jiangnan* xxi–xxii, 188
Tongji University 52
trade 59–60
treaty-port cities 118
Tsinghua College 93–4

UNESCO 170–1
urban planning 52–3
urban villages 49, 52
urbanization xxii, xxiii–xxiv, xxv, 46–53, 189, 208
  on city fringes 47–8
  cluster type organization 50, 52
  eastern rural China 49
  market type organization 51–2
  paternal type organization 50–1, 52

van der Rohe, Mies 93
Vasari, Giorgio 19
Veblen, Thorstein, *Theory of the Leisure Class, The* 57, 60
Venice 28–9
Venice Charter 167, 171
Versaille 13
Villa Savoy 133
villages and property development 48–9
villas 105
violence
  in art 82
  and combat 87
  moralization 87
Vitruvius, *Ten Books of Architecture* 17, 20, 22, 88, 91, 188

231

walls 99–102
    and care of ground and buildings 101
    of courtyards 103–4
    of European cities 99
    forming spaces 101
    frontier and corporeal defence 100–1
    inside and outside 101
    quantity in China 99
    within the cities 99–100
Wang Hui xxiii, xxv, xxviiin33, 74n16, 155
Wang Jian 155
Wang Shimin 155
Wang Xizhi, *Lantingxu* 180
Wang Yuanqi 155
Wanli, Emperor 165
Warrior's Leave-Taking, The 150, **151**
water, love of 117
Water Margin 111, 111–12, 112
Weber, Max 116n20, 175, 210, 212n2
    Religion of China 207
Wei Yan 11
weight of matter 21
Weissenhofsiedlung 122
Wells, H.G., *Outline of History* 165
Wen Zhengming 9, 62, 81
    Leaning Jade Pavilion **82**
    Terrace of Mental Distance, Humble Administrator's Garden **10**, 190, 191
Wen Zhenheng, *Treatise on Superfluous Things, A* 62
Wenzhou 50, 51
Western capitalism 60
Western cities xix
whiteness 118, 121–3, 124–5, 130
Wittgenstein, Ludwig xvi
Wittkower, Rudolf 27n34
    Architectural Principles in the Age of Humanism 22
women
    in sport 94
    transformation of body 94, 182–3
Wong & Ouyang 41
Woo, John 112
work units 109–11
    design 110
    security teams 111
    social facilities 110
World Exposition 48
Wren, Christopher 22, 99, 132, 135n41, 199
Wu Li 91–2

Wudi, Emperor 80
Wuhan, Yellow Crane Tower 168, **169**, 171, 174, 176, 192

Xerxes, Emperor 87
Xianbeis 80
Xiannongtan Temple 59
Xu Bing xvii
    Book from the Sky 148, **149**–50, 159, 182
    Landscript **192**, 193
Xu Guanqi
    Astronomical Treatises of the Chongzhen Reign 165, 175
    Visual Figures of Fixed Stars 175
Xu Wenrong 50, 52, 54n36

Yale University Press xxi
Yangtze River Delta 53
Yao Mengqi 196
Yersin, Alexandre 127
yin and *yang* 7–8
    in the Forbidden City 12
Yingzao fashi xix, 172, 201–2
Yiwu 51
    Muslim traders 52
    planning 52–3
    shops **52**
Yuan dynasty 100
Yuan Ming Yuan 192

Zhan Wang 129–30
    Clean Ruins 129
    Urban Landscape **129**
Zhang Tao xv
Zhang Xin 69
Zhang Yuchen 64
Zhang Zeduan 14, 16
Zhejiang 49, 51
Zhejiang Planning Institute 52–3
Zheng He 165
Zhou Weiquan xxviin23
    History of Classical Chinese Gardens xxi
Zhu Da 156
Zhu Qiqian xx, 172
Zhuji 50
Zhuozheng Yuan 9
    Terrace of Mental Distance, The Humble Administrator's Garden **10**
Zoning Law 28
Zuo Qiuming 58